*Weight Watchers*

# Entertains

*with the chefs from The Culinary Institute of America*

## WEIGHT WATCHERS PUBLISHING GROUP

*Creative and Editorial Director*
Nancy Gagliardi

*Art Director*
Ed Melnitsky

*Food Editor*
Eileen Runyan

*Editorial Assistant*
Jenny Laboy-Brace

*Production Manager*
Alan Biederman

*Photographer*
Rita Maas

*Food Styling*
William Smith

*Prop Styling*
Cathy Cook

## THE CULINARY INSTITUTE OF AMERICA

*President*
Tim Ryan

*Vice President and Dean of Culinary, Baking, and Pastry Studies*
Victor Gielisse

*Director, Food and Beverage Institute*
Mary Cowell

*Editor/Writer*
Mary Donovan

*Photo Editor*
Sarah Bales

*Photo Studio Manager*
Elizabeth Corbett Johnson

*Photographer (how-to)*
Lorna Smith

## ACKNOWLEDGMENTS

Weight Watchers and The Culinary Institute of America would like to acknowledge the following individuals for their assistance in preparing this book: Frana Baruch, David Bonom, Sophia Cowell, Kathleen Delehanty, Cynthia DePersio, Aaron Herman, Morey Kanner, Wendy Karn, Jean Kressy, Lisa Lahey, Maureen Luchejko, Lynn Messina, David Middendorf, Margaret Otterstrom, Carol Prager, Elana Raider, John Reilly, Lynne Tonnelli, Barbara Turvett, Betty Van Nostrand, Rosemarie Visbeck.

## A WORD ABOUT WEIGHT WATCHERS

Since 1963, Weight Watchers has grown from a handful of people to millions of enrollments annually. Today, Weight Watchers is recognized as the leading name in safe and sensible weight control. Weight Watchers members form a diverse group, from youths to senior citizens, attending meetings virtually around the globe. Weight-loss and weight-management results vary by individual, but we recommend that you attend Weight Watchers meetings, follow the Weight Watchers food plan, and participate in regular physical activity. For the Weight Watcher meeting nearest you, call 800-651-6000. Also, visit us at our Web site: WeightWatchers.com.

# TABLE OF CONTENTS

## *spring*

## *summer*

## *fall*

## *winter*

# INTRODUCTION

Holidays. Graduations. Birthdays. Weddings. For most of us these deeply felt occasions, which serve to mark the milestones of our lives, are truly the best of times. They may only last for a few hours, but we plan them for days (sometimes weeks!), making sure that everything is just so and just right. We dust from top to bottom, unearth our best china, polish the silver, smooth out the good Irish linen, and wash the crystal. We think, plan, reposition, think some more, organize, arrange, and carefully attempt to orchestrate every last detail. In this way we ensure that an important celebration is memorable and magical for all who attend.

And then there's the food, the entertaining glue that holds all our hard work together. While some contend it's the people who make the party, we all know that more hours are spent fine-tuning the menu than the list of invitees. The menu, in fact, is what separates the real entertaining players from the mere party-givers. A great menu transforms a very good party into a special, singularly memorable event, undoubtedly one that people will talk about long after you've bid farewell to the last of the revelers.

At Weight Watchers, our love of entertaining and creating great food (that also happens to be good for you) is what prompted us to team up, once again, with The Culinary Institute of America (CIA). And so we bring you *Weight Watchers Entertains with the Chefs from The Culinary Institute of America.* Being the premier cooking school in America, the CIA knows a thing or two about entertaining: Each year, their experts turn out thousands of graduates—young chefs who will teach, cook, and/or manage the finest restaurants, resorts, and hotels around the globe. In addition, the CIA campus is an entertaining destination. There, charity and other special events are held on a grand scale, hosting everyone from dignitaries to scholars to celebrities (culinary and otherwise).

To create *Weight Watchers Entertains with the Chefs from The Culinary Institute of America,* we worked with the CIA's masters to compile more than 30 special menus that are dazzlingly delicious and surprisingly easy to prepare. We've also added bonus "Chef's Tips" to help make your culinary ventures run as smoothly as a professional's. In addition, we've included complete nutritional analysis and *POINTS* values based on Weight Watchers **Winning Points** Plan for all recipes.

A word about watching your weight when entertaining: We know it's a challenge, but it's not impossible. With these menus we've tried to keep recipes as low in *POINTS* as possible without sacrificing great flavor. Our best advice is to plan ahead for days you know you'll be having a special meal, as well as compensating the day after. This way you can enjoy the food and festivities, trying a little of everything, without the guilt.

Whether you're presenting your first family Thanksgiving, hosting a small wedding, or tackling dinner for a dozen of your closest friends, *Weight Watchers Entertains with the Chefs from The Culinary Institute of America* will make all your special occasions spectacular.

Happy entertaining!

Nancy Gagliardi
Creative Editorial Director

# *spring*

# AN EVENING AT THE OSCARS

*Bellini*

—

*Cajun-Spiced Shrimp Cocktail with Mango Salsa*

—

*Chicken with Chipotle Cream on Tortilla Chips*

—

*Caviar on New Potatoes with Chive Cream*

—

*Red Snapper Seviche*

—

*Roast Beef Crostini with Apple-Horseradish Cream*

—

*Pancetta and Shiitake–Stuffed Mushrooms*

—

*Petite Phyllo Cups with Yogurt and Rose Petal Jam*

## *Bellini*

**MAKES 12 SERVINGS**

Kick off Oscar Night with this peach and champagne cocktail, which was created at the legendary Venice landmark, Harry's Bar, in the 1930s. Substitute two (750-ml) bottles of nonalcoholic sparkling apple cider for the champagne, if you like.

2  **(750-ml) bottles champagne or sparkling white wine, chilled**

1  **(750-ml) bottle nonalcoholic sparkling apple cider, chilled**

3  **cups peach nectar, chilled**

2  **tablespoons fresh lemon juice**

24  **fresh raspberries**

Pour ½ cup of the champagne and ¼ cup of the apple cider into each of 12 champagne flutes. To each add ¼ cup of the peach nectar, ½ teaspoon of the lemon juice, and 2 raspberries. Serve at once.

Per serving (1 cup): 131 Cal, 0 g Fat, 0 g Sat Fat, 0 mg Chol, 13 mg Sod, 13 g Carb, 1 g Fib, 0 g Prot, 18 mg Calc. *POINTS: 2.*

# Cajun-Spiced Shrimp Cocktail
## with Mango Salsa

**MAKES 12 SERVINGS**

Wow your guests with this surprising shrimp cocktail. If you prefer, substitute any other packaged seasoning mix, such as Jamaican-jerk or other spicy mix, in place of the Cajun seasoning. To make ahead, cook the shrimp the day before, wrap, and refrigerate. You can also store the mango salsa in the refrigerator for up to three days.

1 **large ripe mango, peeled, seeded, and finely chopped**
½ **cup finely chopped red bell pepper**
¼ **cup finely chopped red onion**
3 **tablespoons chopped fresh cilantro**
1 **tablespoon fresh lime juice**
¼ **teaspoon salt**
⅛ **teaspoon freshly ground pepper**
4 **teaspoons Cajun seasoning**
36 **extra-large shrimp (about 1½ pounds), peeled and deveined**
3 **teaspoons olive oil**

*1.* To prepare the salsa, combine the mango, bell pepper, onion, cilantro, lime juice, salt, and pepper in a bowl; set aside.

*2.* Place the Cajun seasoning in a small bowl. Dip both sides of each shrimp in the seasoning to coat. Heat a large nonstick skillet over medium-high heat. Swirl in 1½ teaspoons of the oil, then add half of the shrimp, without overcrowding the skillet. Cook until the shrimp are just opaque in the center, 2–3 minutes on each side. Repeat with the remaining shrimp and oil. Let the shrimp cool to room temperature.

*3.* Place the mango salsa in a serving bowl. Hang the shrimp around the rim of the bowl. Serve at once.

Per serving (3 shrimp with 2 ½ tablespoons salsa): 50 Cal, 1 g Fat, 0 g Sat Fat, 51 mg Chol, 284 mg Sod, 4 g Carb, 0 g Fib, 6 g Prot, 14 mg Calc. ***POINTS: 1.***

*Chef's Tip:* Use two or three pretty bowls (preferably pedestaled) or a few elegant martini glasses to serve the shrimp and salsa, placing them at various locations around the room.

*Bellini, Cajun-Spiced Shrimp Cocktail with Mango Salsa, and
Chicken with Chipotle Cream on Tortilla Chips*

# Chicken with Chipotle Cream on Tortilla Chips

**MAKES 12 SERVINGS**

You can prepare all the parts to this tasty Mexican snack up to a day ahead, then assemble just before the party: Prepare the chicken, and make the chipotle cream and the onion relish; refrigerate in separate containers. To save even more time, use sliced, precooked, seasoned chicken breasts, available in your supermarket's meat section. Chipotle peppers are dried, smoked jalapeños. They are available dry or canned in adobo sauce. Look for cans of chipotle in adobo in Latin-American markets and some well-stocked supermarkets.

| | |
|---|---|
| 3 | skinless boneless chicken breast halves, about 1¼ pounds |
| 2 | teaspoons canola oil |
| ¾ | teaspoon salt |
| ¾ | teaspoon ground cumin |
| ¾ | teaspoon paprika |
| ⅓ | cup light sour cream |
| 1 | chipotle pepper in adobo sauce, finely chopped |
| ½ | teaspoon adobo sauce |
| 2 | small onions, finely chopped |
| 2 | garlic cloves, minced |
| 4 | teaspoons sugar |
| 2 | teaspoons cider vinegar |
| 36 | baked or other low-fat tortilla chips, about 6 ounces |
| 8 | fresh basil leaves, thinly sliced |

*1.* Combine the chicken, 1 teaspoon of the canola oil, ¼ teaspoon of the salt, the cumin, and paprika in a bowl; cover and refrigerate 30 minutes. Spray a ridged grill pan or nonstick skillet with nonstick spray and set over medium-high heat. Add the chicken and cook until browned on the outside and cooked through, 6–8 minutes on each side. Cool 5 minutes, then thinly slice on a diagonal into 36 slices; set aside.

*2.* Combine the sour cream, chipotle pepper, adobo sauce, and ¼ teaspoon of the salt in a small bowl; set aside.

*3.* Heat a medium nonstick skillet over medium heat. Swirl in the remaining 1 teaspoon oil, then add the onions, garlic, and sugar. Cook, stirring occasionally, until golden, 7–10 minutes. Add the vinegar and the remaining ¼ teaspoon salt; cook until the vinegar evaporates, about 2 minutes.

*4.* Spread each tortilla chip with ½ teaspoon of the onion mixture; top with 1 slice of chicken, ½ teaspoon chipotle cream, and 3 basil slices, making a total of 36 hors d'oeuvres.

Per serving (3 pieces): 136 Cal, 3 g Fat, 1 g Sat Fat, 28 mg Chol, 253 mg Sod, 15 g Carb, 1 g Fib, 12 g Prot, 21 mg Calc. ***POINTS: 3.***

# Caviar on New Potatoes with Chive Cream

**MAKES 12 SERVINGS**

This elegant European classic can be costly but, if time is money, you'll be saving in spades. The best and most expensive caviar is from beluga sturgeon; the next best are the osetra and sevruga caviars. Lumpfish and whitefish caviars are also popular and much less expensive alternatives.

16  **small new or red potatoes (about 1 pound), scrubbed**
4  **tablespoons crème fraîche**
2  **ounces caviar**
**Finely chopped fresh chives**

*1.* Bring the potatoes, with enough water to cover, to a boil in a large saucepan. Reduce the heat and simmer, covered, until the potatoes are easily pierced with the tip of a sharp knife, 15–18 minutes. Drain the potatoes, then let cool. Slice off the ends of the potatoes, then cut each crosswise into 3 slices, making a total of 48 slices.

*2.* Top each potato slice with ¼ teaspoon crème fraîche and ⅛ teaspoon caviar. Garnish with chopped chives.

Per serving (4 pieces): 59 Cal, 2 g Fat, 1 g Sat Fat, 33 mg Chol, 75 mg Sod, 8 g Carb, 1 g Fib, 2 g Prot, 20 mg Calc. *POINTS: 1.*

———◆———

*Chef's Tip:* A fun way to serve this appetizer is to place the potato slices in overlapping rows on one half of a large platter. Place a small bowl of crème fraîche, a small bowl of chopped chives, and a small bowl of caviar (set in a larger bowl of ice) on the other half of the platter. Place demitasse spoons in the caviar, crème fraîche, and chive bowls. Allow guests to assemble their own appetizers.

# Red Snapper Seviche

**MAKES 12 SERVINGS**

This hugely popular appetizer—all the rage of Nuevo Latino restaurants—has its roots in Latin America. The dish consists of raw fish marinated in lime juice or other citrus juice. (The acidity of the juice "cooks" the fish and firms the flesh, turning it opaque.) It is essential to purchase the freshest fish possible. Be sure to buy from a reputable fishmonger and check that the fish smells like the sea and looks shiny. The tortilla chips can be baked, then stored in an airtight container for up to three days.

1 teaspoon ground cumin

1 teaspoon salt

½ teaspoon paprika

6 (6-inch) fat-free flour tortillas, each cut into 8 wedges

1 ½ pounds skinless boneless red snapper fillet, cut into ¼-inch pieces

1 small red onion, finely chopped

1 jalapeño pepper, seeded and finely chopped (wear gloves to prevent irritation)

¾ cup fresh lime juice

¼ cup fresh orange juice

2 tablespoons chopped fresh cilantro

*1.* Preheat the oven to 350°F.

*2.* Combine the cumin, ½ teaspoon of the salt, and the paprika in a small bowl. Arrange the tortilla wedges in a single layer on 2 baking sheets. Spray lightly with nonstick spray; sprinkle with the cumin mixture. Bake until crisp, 9–11 minutes.

*3.* Combine the red snapper, onion, jalapeño, lime juice, orange juice, cilantro, and the remaining ½ teaspoon salt in a bowl. Refrigerate, covered, 1 hour, stirring every 15 minutes. Spoon the seviche into a serving bowl and serve with the tortilla chips in a basket on the side.

Per serving (¼ cup seviche with 4 chips): 98 Cal, 1 g Fat, 0 g Sat Fat, 30 mg Chol, 301 mg Sod, 9 g Carb, 1 g Fib, 12 g Prot, 29 mg Calc. ***POINTS: 2.***

———◆———

*Chef's Tip:* Using a slotted spoon, divide the seviche among 12 small bowls or stemmed glasses. Present them to your guests on a beautiful tray.

# Roast Beef Crostini with Apple-Horseradish Cream

**MAKES 12 SERVINGS**

Buy the roast beef fresh the day of the party. If you like, try thinly sliced roast pork tenderloin instead of the beef, and pear instead of apple in the horseradish cream. The horseradish cream can be made the day before and stored in the refrigerator, and the bread can be baked and stored in an airtight container for up to two days.

1 (8-ounce) French baguette, cut into 48 slices

1 garlic clove, peeled and cut in half

3 ounces light cream cheese or Neufchâtel, softened

⅓ cup low-fat mayonnaise

4 teaspoons prepared horseradish, squeezed dry

1 small Granny Smith apple, finely chopped

6 ounces deli-sliced roast beef, cut into strips

Chopped fresh parsley

*1.* Preheat the oven to 400°F. Arrange the bread slices in a single layer on 2 baking sheets. Bake until crisp and lightly golden, 6–7 minutes. Cool 2 minutes, then rub each slice with the garlic; set aside.

*2.* Combine the cream cheese, mayonnaise, and horseradish in a bowl. Stir in the apple.

*3.* Arrange the bread slices on a work surface. Top each with a few roast beef strips and a scant ½ teaspoon apple-horseradish cream. Sprinkle with the parsley.

Per serving (4 crostini): 119 Cal, 5 g Fat, 2 g Sat Fat, 14 mg Chol, 223 mg Sod, 13 g Carb, 1 g Fib, 6 g Prot, 28 mg Calc. ***POINTS: 3.***

*Chef's Tip:* Arrange the crostini on a large platter, lined with curly green or red leaf lettuce.

# Pancetta and Shiitake–Stuffed Mushrooms

**MAKES 12 SERVINGS**

Rich, earthy flavors from shiitake and white mushrooms meld with flavorful pancetta and sherry, making a tasty appetizer. To make this recipe ahead, stuff the mushrooms (but don't bake them), then cover and refrigerate for up to two days. When ready to serve, bake in a 375°F oven until heated through, 12 to 15 minutes. Pancetta is Italian bacon that is spiced and cured, but not smoked. It is available at most specialty markets and some large supermarkets.

36 fresh white mushrooms, about 1½ pounds (stems removed and finely chopped)
2 ounces pancetta, chopped
1 large shallot, chopped
3 garlic cloves, minced
½ pound fresh shiitake mushrooms, stems discarded and caps finely chopped
½ teaspoon salt
⅛ teaspoon freshly ground pepper
¼ cup dry sherry
¼ cup chopped fresh parsley
3 tablespoons grated Parmesan cheese

*1.* Preheat the oven to 375°F. Line a jelly-roll pan or baking sheet with foil. Stand a rack inside the pan. Place the white mushroom caps, stem-side down, on the rack and bake until almost softened, about 15 minutes. Remove from the oven and set aside.

*2.* Spray a large nonstick skillet with nonstick spray and set over medium-high heat. Add the pancetta and cook, stirring occasionally, until crisp. Transfer to a paper towel-lined plate and set aside.

*3.* Add the shallot and garlic to the same skillet and cook, stirring often, until softened, 2–3 minutes. Stir in the chopped white mushroom stems, chopped shiitake mushrooms, salt, and pepper. Cook, stirring occasionally, until the mushrooms give off their liquid and it evaporates, 10–12 minutes. Add the sherry and cook until it evaporates, 1–2 minutes. Remove from the heat and stir in the pancetta, parsley, and Parmesan cheese.

*4.* Spray the foil-lined jelly-roll pan with nonstick spray. Fill the mushroom caps with the shiitake mixture, mounding slightly. Stand the mushroom caps in the jelly-roll pan and bake until heated through, 10–12 minutes.

Per serving (3 stuffed mushrooms): 69 Cal, 5 g Fat, 2 g Sat Fat, 6 mg Chol, 152 mg Sod, 5 g Carb, 1 g Fib, 3 g Prot, 31 mg Calc. **POINTS: 2.**

◆

*Chef's Tip:* Serve on a doily-lined platter to prevent the mushrooms from slipping around.

# Petite Phyllo Cups with Yogurt and Rose Petal Jam

**MAKES 12 SERVINGS**

Rose petal jam—made from rose petals, lemon, and sugar—gives a distinctive and delicious Middle-Eastern flavor to this dessert. You can find rose petal jam in well-stocked supermarkets and Middle-Eastern markets. For a spectacular presentation, arrange the cups on a rose petal–lined platter and, if you like, garnish each cup with a sliver of a rose petal.

2 cups plain fat-free yogurt

6 teaspoons sugar

6 (12 x 17-inch) sheets phyllo dough, at room temperature

½ cup rose petal jam or preserves

¼ cup pistachio nuts, finely chopped

*1.* Place the yogurt in a wire sieve, lined with a damp paper towel, over a bowl. Let stand in the refrigerator 2 hours or overnight.

*2.* Preheat the oven to 375°F. Spray 2 (12-cup) mini-muffin pans with nonstick spray. Using a total of 1½ teaspoons of the sugar, lightly sprinkle each cup with sugar; set aside.

*3.* As you work, keep the sheets of phyllo covered with plastic wrap to keep them from drying out. Place 1 phyllo sheet on a clean, dry work surface; lightly spray with nonstick spray and sprinkle with ¾ teaspoon sugar. Repeat with 2 more sheets and 1½ teaspoons sugar. With a pizza wheel or sharp knife cut the phyllo into 24 squares. Gently press each square into a muffin cup, flattening the dough against the bottom. Bake until lightly golden and crisp, 7–8 minutes. Immediately remove the phyllo cups from the pan and cool on a rack. Repeat once more with the remaining 3 sheets of phyllo and 2¼ teaspoons sugar, making a total of 48 cups.

*4.* Fill each cup with 1 teaspoon strained yogurt, then top with ½ teaspoon rose petal jam. Sprinkle each cup with ¼ teaspoon of the chopped pistachios.

Per serving (4 pieces): 122 Cal, 4 g Fat, 1 g Sat Fat, 1 mg Chol, 64 mg Sod, 19 g Carb, 1 g Fib, 4 g Prot, 89 mg Calc. *POINTS: 3.*

———◆———

*Chef's Tip:* The empty phyllo cups can be made up to a week ahead, carefully packed in an airtight container, and kept at room temperature. If they get a little soft, simply place them back into the muffin tins and bake at 375°F for 3 to 4 minutes.

# PASSOVER DINNER

*Matzo Ball Soup*

—

*Steamed Green Beans with Roasted Tomatoes*

—

*Wine-Braised Brisket*

—

*Potato and Onion Kugel*

—

*Kale Sautéed with Garlic*

—

*Tzimmes*

—

*Almond Macaroons*

—

*Chocolate Soufflé Cake*

## Matzo Ball Soup

### MAKES 8 SERVINGS

Matzo balls are typically made with matzo meal, eggs, schmaltz (rendered chicken fat), and seasonings. Our matzo balls are equally moist and tender using vegetable oil instead of the schmaltz.

- **1 cup low-sodium matzo meal**
- **3 egg whites, lightly beaten**
- **1 large egg, lightly beaten**
- **½ cup club soda**
- **½ teaspoon salt**
- **¼ teaspoon freshly ground pepper**
- **1 tablespoon vegetable oil**
- **6 cups low-sodium chicken broth**
- **1 cup fresh or thawed frozen green peas**
- **½ cup thinly sliced carrot**
- **½ cup thinly sliced parsnip**
- **¼ cup chopped fresh parsley**

*1.* To make the matzo balls, combine the matzo meal, egg whites, egg, club soda, salt, and pepper in a food processor. Process 15–20 seconds to blend. Add the oil and pulse just until incorporated. Transfer to a bowl; cover and refrigerate 30 minutes.

*2.* Bring 8 cups of lightly salted water to a simmer in a soup pot. With wet hands, shape the matzo mixture into 16 (1-inch) balls. Carefully drop the balls into the pot one at a time and simmer, covered, until cooked through, about 40 minutes.

*3.* Meanwhile, simmer the chicken broth, peas, carrot, and parsnip in a large saucepan until the vegetables are tender, 15–20 minutes.

*4.* Drain the cooked matzo balls; drop into the broth mixture and simmer until heated through. Stir in the parsley just before serving.

Per serving (¾ cup soup with 2 matzo balls): 135 Cal, 3 g Fat, 1 g Sat Fat, 30 mg Chol, 286 mg Sod, 18 g Carb, 2 g Fib, 7 g Prot, 24 mg Calc. ***POINTS: 3.***

# Steamed Green Beans with Roasted Tomatoes

### MAKES 8 SERVINGS

Roasting intensifies the flavor of fresh fruits and vegetables—without adding a single **POINT.** Roasting tomatoes is particularly beneficial if they're off-season or less than fully ripe. Roast as many tomatoes as you have on hand, with or without the herbs and garlic. You can refrigerate roasted tomatoes in zip-close plastic bags for up to a week and add to salads, pasta dishes, sandwiches, soups, or stews.

3  **plum tomatoes, cut into ¼-inch slices**
2  **tablespoons chopped fresh chives or dill**
1  **garlic clove, minced**
½  **teaspoon salt**
**Freshly ground pepper, to taste**
2  **pounds fresh green beans, trimmed**
2  **tablespoons olive oil**
1  **tablespoon balsamic vinegar (or more to taste)**

*1.* Preheat the oven to 375°F. Spray a rack with olive-oil nonstick spray and place on a foil-lined baking sheet.

*2.* Place the tomatoes on the rack; spray with olive-oil nonstick spray and sprinkle with the chives, garlic, salt, and pepper. Roast until the tomatoes are browned and have an intense, sweet aroma, 30–40 minutes.

*3.* Meanwhile, put the green beans in a steamer basket; set in a saucepan over 1 inch of boiling water. Cover tightly and steam until very tender, about 8 minutes.

*4.* Heat a large nonstick skillet over high heat. Swirl in the oil, then add the green beans and roasted tomatoes. Cook, stirring occasionally, until very hot, about 2 minutes. Transfer to a platter and drizzle with the vinegar. Serve warm or at room temperature.

Per serving (⅓ cup): 37 Cal, 2 g Fat, 1 g Sat Fat, 0 mg Chol, 98 mg Sod, 5 g Carb, 1 g Fiber, 1 g Prot, 17 mg Calc. **POINTS: 1.**

*Chef's Tip:* To save time, you can substitute ¼ cup sun-dried tomatoes, packed in oil, for the roasted tomatoes. Be sure to thoroughly drain the tomatoes of oil, then pat them dry with paper towels before using.

# Wine-Braised Brisket

**MAKES 8 SERVINGS**

Although this holiday favorite may take a few days to complete, the results are well worth it. The first day the meat marinates in a mixture of red wine, vegetables, and herbs, then the next day it slowly simmers until moist and fork-tender. Better yet, the rich, hearty flavor of the dish actually improves when refrigerated overnight, so it pays to plan ahead.

**1 cup dry red wine**
**2 carrots, chopped**
**2 celery stalks, chopped**
**1 small onion, chopped**
**4 garlic cloves, minced**
**1 teaspoon whole black peppercorns**
**1 teaspoon fresh thyme leaves, or ¼ teaspoon dried**
**1 (2-pound) beef brisket, trimmed of all visible fat**
**1 teaspoon salt**
**Freshly ground pepper, to taste**
**1 tablespoon vegetable oil**
**¼ cup tomato paste**
**3 cups low-sodium beef broth**
**1 tablespoon cornstarch**
**1 tablespoon cold water**

*1.* Combine the wine, carrots, celery, onion, garlic, peppercorns, and thyme in a large zip-close plastic bag; add the brisket. Squeeze out the air and seal the bag; turn to coat the brisket. Refrigerate, turning the bag occasionally, at least 8 hours or up to 24 hours.

*2.* Preheat the oven to 350°F. Remove the brisket from the marinade; set the marinade aside. Pat the brisket dry. Season with the salt and pepper. Heat a large Dutch oven over medium-high heat. Swirl in the oil, then add the brisket. Cook until well-browned, about 4 minutes on each side.

*3.* Transfer the brisket to a plate. Discard any fat from the pot. Add the tomato paste and cook over low-medium heat until it darkens to a rust color, 3–4 minutes. Add the reserved marinade. Bring to a boil, scraping up any browned bits from the bottom of the Dutch oven. Return the brisket to the Dutch oven; add the broth and bring to a simmer. Cover, transfer to the oven, and bake until the brisket is very tender when pierced with a fork, 3½–4 hours.

*4.* Transfer the brisket to a cutting board; cover loosely with foil and keep warm. Skim off any excess fat from the cooking liquid with a spoon. Process the liquid in a food processor or blender, in batches, until smooth. Return the sauce to the pot and bring to a simmer. Combine the cornstarch and water in a cup; drizzle into the sauce. Cook, stirring constantly, until the mixture boils and thickens, about 2 minutes. Slice the brisket and serve with the sauce.

Per serving (⅛ of brisket with ¼ cup sauce): 267 Cal, 7 g Fat, 3 g Sat Fat, 110 mg Chol, 370 mg Sod, 11 g Carb, 1 g Fib, 35 g Prot, 30 mg Calc. ***POINTS: 6.***

# Potato and Onion Kugel

**MAKES 8 SERVINGS**

Kugel is a potato or noodle pudding that's most often served as a side dish. We've lightened the classic potato version, without sacrificing a bit of flavor, by mashing buttery-tasting Yukon Gold potatoes with sweet caramelized onions and fresh herbs.

4 medium Yukon Gold or russet
  potatoes, peeled and
  quartered
¾ teaspoon salt
2 tablespoons olive oil
2 medium onions, thinly sliced
2 teaspoons minced garlic
Freshly ground pepper, to taste
½ cup low-sodium chicken broth
  or water
2 large eggs, lightly beaten
2 egg whites, lightly beaten
½ cup low-sodium matzo meal
1 teaspoon baking powder
1 teaspoon minced fresh chives
1 teaspoon finely chopped
  flat-leaf parsley
1 teaspoon finely chopped
  fresh thyme

1. Preheat the oven to 350°F. Spray a nonstick 8-inch square baking pan with nonstick spray.
2. Bring the potatoes, ½ teaspoon of the salt, and enough water to cover to a boil in a large saucepan. Reduce the heat and simmer, covered, until the potatoes are tender, 15–20 minutes. Drain and mash; transfer to a large bowl.
3. Meanwhile, heat a large nonstick skillet over low-medium heat. Swirl in the oil, then add the onions, garlic, the remaining ¼ teaspoon salt, and the pepper. Cook, stirring frequently, until the onion mixture is softened and golden, about 15 minutes.
4. Add the onion mixture, broth, eggs, egg whites, matzo meal, baking powder, chives, parsley, and thyme to the potatoes; stir until blended. Spread the mixture in the baking pan. Bake until the kugel puffs and browns, 30–35 minutes.

Per serving (½ cup): 180 Cal, 1 g Fat, 1 g Sat Fat, 53 mg Chol, 180 mg Sod, 32 g Carb, 4 g Fib, 4 g Prot, 24 mg Calc. **POINTS: 3.**

---

*Chef's Tip:* For the best texture and flavor, drain the potatoes as directed in Step 2 except, before mashing, return the potatoes to the pot. Heat over low heat, shaking the pot occasionally, until the potatoes dry and are no longer steamy, 2 to 3 minutes. To make the kugel ahead, bake, let cool, then cover and refrigerate overnight. Reheat in a 300°F oven until hot, about 15 minutes.

# Kale Sautéed with Garlic

**MAKES 8 SERVINGS**

Nutrient-rich kale cooks more quickly than you think. It's especially tasty when paired with gently sautéed garlic and a squeeze of fresh lemon juice.

**1 tablespoon vegetable oil**
**4 garlic cloves, thinly sliced**
**1½ pounds fresh kale, cleaned
and coarsely chopped**
**2 teaspoons fresh lemon juice**
**¼ teaspoon salt**
**Freshly ground pepper, to taste**

*1.* Heat a large nonstick skillet over low heat. Swirl in the oil, then add the garlic. Cook until fragrant, 2–3 minutes.

*2.* Increase the heat to high. Stir in the kale, a few handfuls at a time, allowing it to wilt before each addition. (If necessary, add 1 or 2 tablespoons of water to help cook the kale.)

*3.* Reduce the heat to medium-high. Cook, stirring frequently, until the kale is tender, 5–8 minutes longer. Drizzle with the lemon juice, then season with the salt and pepper.

Per serving (⅓ cup): 70 Cal, 4 g Fat, 1 g Sat Fat, 0 mg Chol, 110 mg Sod, 9 g Carb, 2 g Fib, 3 g Prot, 117 mg Calc. ***POINTS: 1.***

*Chef's Tip:* To avoid any last minute scrambling, clean and chop the kale ahead of time, dry thoroughly, and refrigerate in a large zip-close plastic bag for up to two days.

# Tzimmes

*Tzimmes* (or *tsimmes*) is a sweet-tasting stew with vegetables (most often carrots), dried fruit, and sometimes meat. The sweetness of this dish, the type of dried fruit, and even the size and shape of the carrots can be matters of great debate. Our preference is to bump up the vegetables, reduce the sugar by using a variety of dried fruits, and skip the meat.

2 cups water

2 tablespoons packed
  brown sugar

1 tablespoon pearl barley

½ cinnamon stick

Pinch freshly grated nutmeg

½ pound fresh pumpkin or
  winter squash, peeled and cut
  into chunks (2 cups)

4 dried apricot halves, chopped

2 dried black mission figs,
  chopped

2 pitted prunes, chopped

2 tablespoons golden raisins

¼ teaspoon salt

*1.* Bring the water, sugar, barley, cinnamon, and nutmeg to a boil in a large saucepan. Reduce the heat and simmer, covered, until the barley is almost tender, 15–20 minutes.

*2.* Add the pumpkin, apricots, figs, prunes, raisins, and salt. Cover and simmer, stirring occasionally, until the pumpkin and barley are tender, 15–20 minutes. If necessary, add more water to prevent scorching.

Per serving (⅓ cup): 90 Cal, 0 g Fat, 0 g Sat Fat, 0 mg Chol, 200 mg Sod, 23 g Carb, 3 g Fib, 1 g Prot, 34 mg Calc. ***POINTS: 1.***

*Chef's Tip:* This dish can be prepared and refrigerated in an airtight container up to two days ahead. Reheat over medium heat in a saucepan, or serve at room temperature.

# Almond Macaroons

**MAKES 8 SERVINGS**

Almond paste gives these traditional Passover cookies rich flavor. This cookie dough has a tendency to stick to the baking sheets, so it's worth taking the extra step of lining the sheets with parchment or wax paper. Look for parchment in the baking aisle at the supermarket. Store the macaroons in an airtight container at room temperature for up to two days or freeze for up to three weeks.

½ **cup sugar**

2 **egg whites**

4 **ounces almond paste,**
  **cut into pieces**

*1.* Preheat the oven to 350°F. Line 2 insulated baking sheets (or 4 standard baking sheets arranged in 2 stacks) with parchment paper.

*2.* With an electric mixer at low speed, beat the sugar and 1 egg white until frothy. Add the almond paste and beat until smooth. Add the remaining egg white and beat until smooth, scraping the bowl occasionally with a rubber spatula. The mixture should spread easily without running.

*3.* Spoon the dough into a pastry bag fitted with a ½-inch round tip. Pipe the dough onto the baking sheets, 1-inch apart making 24 round cookies. (Or drop the dough by teaspoons onto the baking sheets.)

*4.* Bake until the tops are cracked and light golden brown, 18–20 minutes. Cool completely on the parchment paper on a rack. When the macaroons are cool they will lift away from the paper easily.

Per serving (3 cookies): 48 Cal, 1 g Fat, 0 g Sat Fat, 0 mg Chol, 8 mg Sod, 6 g Carb, 0 g Fib, 1 g Prot, 0 mg Calc. ***POINTS: 1.***

# Chocolate Soufflé Cake

**MAKES 16 SERVINGS**

Beaten eggs are an acceptable leavening for Passover, and many traditional cakes, such as delicate sponge and soufflé cakes, include a good number of them. Semisweet chocolate is also commonly used because it contains no dairy solids. Fresh berries make a great topping for this cake.

6 **ounces semisweet chocolate, chopped**
4 **tablespoons margarine**
4 **egg yolks**
½ **cup sugar**
¼ **cup Grand Marnier liqueur**
7 **egg whites**

*1.* Preheat the oven to 350°F. Spray an 8-inch round cake pan with nonstick spray.

*2.* Melt the chocolate and the margarine in a double boiler set over barely simmering water. Stir until smooth; set aside.

*3.* With an electric mixer at high speed, beat the egg yolks and ¼ cup of the sugar in a large bowl until tripled in volume and soft peaks form. Gently stir in the Grand Marnier. Set aside.

*4.* With clean beaters, with an electric mixer at medium speed, beat the egg whites in another large bowl until thickened and foamy. Beat in the remaining ¼ cup sugar, 1 tablespoon at a time, until shiny, soft peaks form.

*5.* Using a large rubber spatula, gently fold the chocolate mixture into the beaten yolks until almost blended. Gently fold in the beaten whites, one-third at a time, until just blended. Pour the batter into the cake pan. Bake until a toothpick inserted in the center comes out clean, about 50 minutes. Cool completely in the pan on a rack. Loosen the edges of the cake with a knife; unmold onto a serving plate. Refrigerate at least 1 hour before serving.

Per serving (⅟₁₆ of cake): 115 Cal, 5 g Fat, 3 g Sat Fat, 57 mg Chol, 30 mg Sod, 14 Carb, 0 g Fib, 3 g Prot, 10 Calc. ***POINTS: 3.***

*Chef's Tip:* It's best to use a long, thin sharp knife to cut this cake. Before each cut, dip the blade into hot water then wipe dry with a clean towel. This is easier to do in the kitchen before bringing the cake to the table.

*Chocolate Soufflé Cake*

## Ham and Artichoke Nibbles

**MAKES 8 SERVINGS**

Fresh chives, one of the first herbs in the spring garden, make a lovely garnish for these simple hors d'oeuvres. If chives are not available, substitute finely chopped flat-leaf parsley. These nibbles can be made a couple of hours ahead, covered loosely with plastic wrap, and refrigerated.

2 tablespoons low-fat mayonnaise

½ teaspoon grated lemon rind

4 (1-ounce) slices lean ham

4 canned artichoke hearts, quartered lengthwise and well drained

2 teaspoons finely chopped fresh chives

*1.* Combine the mayonnaise and lemon rind in a small bowl.

*2.* Spread the mayonnaise mixture over the ham, and cut each slice of ham lengthwise into 4 strips. Roll each strip of ham around an artichoke quarter and fasten with a toothpick. Arrange the hors d'oeuvres on a plate and sprinkle with the chives.

Per serving (2 hors d'oeuvres): 42 Cal, 2 g Fat, 0 g Sat Fat, 8 mg Chol, 308 mg Sod, 3 g Carb, 1 g Fib, 4 g Prot, 11 mg Calc. ***POINTS: 1.***

*Chef's Tip:* For a sophisticated presentation, use long, slender, whole chives to fasten the ham around the artichokes.

# Mushroom Bisque

Hot, light, and soothing, this soup makes a lovely starter for a traditional sit-down Easter dinner. For a more exotic mushroom flavor, use half cremini (a full-flavored brown button mushroom) and half white mushrooms.

2 teaspoons extra-virgin olive oil

1 onion, chopped

2 celery stalks, chopped

1 carrot, chopped

2 pounds fresh white mushrooms, halved if large

7 cups low-sodium vegetable or chicken broth

¾ teaspoon dried rubbed sage

¾ teaspoon dried thyme

½ teaspoon salt

¼ teaspoon freshly ground pepper

4 teaspoons finely chopped fresh cilantro

*1.* Heat a nonstick Dutch oven over medium-high heat. Swirl in the oil, then add the onion, celery, and carrot. Cook, stirring occasionally, until the onion is softened, about 5 minutes.

*2.* Add the mushrooms and cook, stirring occasionally, until softened, about 10 minutes. Add the broth, sage, thyme, salt, and pepper; bring to a boil. Reduce the heat and simmer, covered, until the vegetables are tender, about 30 minutes. Remove from the heat, uncover, and let stand until the soup is cool enough to handle, about 30 minutes.

*3.* Pour the soup in batches into a blender or food processor; puree. Return the soup to the Dutch oven and heat thoroughly. If necessary, thin with additional broth. Sprinkle with the cilantro and serve.

Per serving (generous 1 cup): 70 Cal, 2 g Fat, 0 g Sat Fat, 0 mg Chol, 211 mg Sod, 9 g Carb, 2 g Fib, 5 g Prot, 26 mg Calc. ***POINTS: 1.***

---

*Chef's Tip:* To save time on Easter morning, prepare the bisque, without the cilantro, up to three days ahead and refrigerate in an airtight container. Reheat in a large saucepan until completely heated through, thinning with more broth, if necessary. Sprinkle with the cilantro before serving.

# Whole-Wheat Crescent Rolls

**MAKES 12 SERVINGS**

These hearty, honey-tinged rolls complement the earthy flavors in the Mushroom Bisque and the snappy freshness of the Field Salad. To make ahead, wrap the cooled rolls in heavy-duty foil, then freeze for up to a month. To serve, heat the unwrapped rolls on a baking sheet in a 450°F oven, 3 to 4 minutes.

- 1 cup warm (105–115°F) water
- 2 tablespoons honey
- 1 package active dry yeast
- 1½ cups all-purpose flour
- 1 cup whole-wheat flour
- 1½ teaspoons salt

*1.* Combine the water and honey in a 2-cup measuring cup; sprinkle in the yeast and let stand until foamy, about 5 minutes.

*2.* Combine the all-purpose flour, whole-wheat flour, and salt in a food processor. With the machine running, pour the yeast mixture through the feed tube; pulse about 1 minute until the dough forms a ball. Turn the dough out onto a lightly floured surface and knead a few times until smooth.

*3.* Spray a large bowl with nonstick spray; put the dough in the bowl. Cover lightly with plastic wrap and let the dough rise in a warm spot until it doubles in size, about 35 minutes.

*4.* Spray a baking sheet with nonstick spray. Punch down the dough. Sprinkle a work surface lightly with flour. Turn the dough onto the surface; cut in half. Roll each half into a 10-inch circle. Cut each circle into 6 wedges. Roll each wedge, from the wide side, and form into a crescent. Place, pointed-end down, on the baking sheet. Repeat with the remaining dough, arranging the rolls 1 inch apart. Cover lightly with plastic wrap and let rise in a warm spot until they double in size, about 35 minutes.

*5.* Preheat the oven to 375°F. Bake the rolls until they are golden brown and sound hollow when lightly tapped, about 15 minutes. Remove the rolls from the baking sheet and cool on a rack. Serve warm or at room temperature.

Per serving (1 roll): 103 Cal, 0 g Fat, 0 g Sat Fat, 0 mg Chol, 292 mg Sod, 22 g Carb, 2 g Fib, 3 g Prot, 7 mg Calc. **POINTS: 2.**

———◆———

*Chef's Tip:* To mix the rolls by hand, combine the water, honey, and yeast in a large bowl; set aside until foamy. Stir in the all-purpose flour, whole-wheat flour, and salt until the dough starts to gather around the spoon. Turn out the dough on a lightly floured surface; knead until the dough is smooth and elastic, about 10 minutes.

*Field Salad with Asparagus and Whole-Wheat Crescent Rolls*

# Field Salad with Asparagus

**MAKES 8 SERVINGS**

This fresh spring salad is easy because it uses prewashed mesclun greens and a simple dressing. Choose loose mesclun or the bagged variety, whichever looks freshest. Thin asparagus spears work well here. If the stalks are thick, cut lengthwise in half before cutting into pieces. The asparagus can be prepared up to a day ahead and stored in the refrigerator.

¾  pound fresh asparagus, trimmed and cut diagonally into 1½-inch pieces

12  cups mesclun

2  tablespoons balsamic vinegar

2  tablespoons tomato juice

1½  teaspoons extra-virgin olive oil

1  garlic clove, minced

¼  teaspoon salt

¼  teaspoon coarsely ground pepper

*1.* Put the asparagus in a steamer basket; set in a saucepan over 1 inch of boiling water. Cover tightly and steam until bright green and crisp-tender, 1½–2 minutes. Rinse under cold water to stop the cooking, drain well, and pat dry with paper towels.

*2.* Combine the mesclun and asparagus in a large bowl. Whisk together the vinegar, juice, oil, garlic, salt, and pepper in a small bowl. Pour the dressing over the salad; toss to coat. Serve at once.

Per serving (1½ cups): 28 Cal, 1 g Fat, 0 g Sat Fat, 0 mg Chol, 116 mg Sod, 3 g Carb, 2 g Fib, 2 g Prot, 62 mg Calc. ***POINTS: 0.***

*Chef's Tip:* To be sure everyone gets a nice serving, divide the salad on side plates and set out at the table before the guests are seated.

# Roast Lamb with Fresh Herbs

**MAKES 8 SERVINGS**

A boneless leg of lamb seasoned with fresh herbs and garlic is the essence of spring. Have your butcher remove the excess fat from the leg of lamb; when you get it home you'll need to trim away any remaining fat. The lamb can be partially prepared the day before: Spread with the parsley mixture, sprinkle with the salt and pepper, and refrigerate, covered, overnight. Roast as directed, about 1¼ hours before you're ready to serve it.

1 cup finely chopped
flat-leaf parsley
2 shallots, minced
2 garlic cloves, minced
1½ teaspoons chopped fresh
rosemary, or ½ teaspoon
crushed dried
½ teaspoon salt
½ teaspoon freshly
ground pepper
1 (2¼-pound) boneless leg of
lamb, untied and trimmed
of all visible fat
Fresh rosemary sprigs

*1.* Preheat the oven to 400°F. Spray the rack of a roasting pan with nonstick spray and place in the pan.

*2.* Combine the parsley, shallots, garlic, rosemary, ¼ teaspoon of the salt, and ¼ teaspoon of the pepper in a medium bowl. Rub the parsley mixture on all sides of the lamb. Sprinkle with the remaining ¼ teaspoon salt and ¼ teaspoon pepper.

*3.* Set the lamb on the roasting rack and roast until an instant-read thermometer, inserted in the center, registers 160°F for medium, about 55 minutes.

*4.* Remove the lamb from the oven, cover loosely with foil, and let stand 10–15 minutes before slicing. Arrange overlapping slices of lamb on an oval platter and garnish with sprigs of fresh rosemary.

Per serving (⅛ of lamb): 201 Cal, 9 g Fat, 3 g Sat Fat, 88 mg Chol, 218 mg Sod, 1 g Carb, 0 g Fib, 28 g Prot, 24 mg Calc. ***POINTS: 5.***

*Chef's Tip:* If you like the lamb cooked medium-rare, remove it from the oven when the instant-read thermometer, inserted in the center of the roast, registers 145°F.

# Green Beans with Snow Peas and Mint

**MAKES 8 SERVINGS**

When selecting green beans, look for crisp, firm pods, free of brown spots or scars. Break one in half; it should snap easily. Snow peas, sometimes called Chinese snow peas or edible-pod peas, should be soft, flexible, and green—a sign of freshness. To prepare ahead, trim and cut the green beans and snow peas and store in the refrigerator, but don't cook them until just before you're ready to serve the meal.

1 **pound fresh green beans, trimmed and cut diagonally into 1½-inch pieces**

6 **ounces fresh snow peas, trimmed and cut diagonally in half**

2 **teaspoons butter, softened**

1½ **teaspoons finely chopped fresh mint**

1½ **teaspoons grated lemon rind**

½ **teaspoon salt**

¼ **teaspoon freshly ground pepper**

*1.* Put the beans in a steamer basket; set in a saucepan over 1 inch of boiling water. Cover tightly and steam the beans until barely crisp-tender, 8–10 minutes. Add the snow peas to the basket and steam until the snow peas are bright green and crisp-tender, about 2 minutes.

*2.* Transfer the beans and snow peas to a large bowl; add the butter, mint, lemon rind, salt, and pepper; toss to combine.

Per serving (½ cup): 30 Cal, 1 g Fat, 1 g Sat Fat, 3 mg Chol, 157 mg Sod, 5 g Carb, 2 g Fib, 1 g Prot, 32 mg Calc. ***POINTS: 0.***

*Chef's Tip:* As a pretty alternative to grated lemon rind, prepare thin strands of the rind: Peel thin yellow strips from the lemon's skin with a vegetable peeler, stack the strips one on top of another, then use a sharp knife to cut the strips into very thin strands.

*Roast Lamb with Fresh Herbs, Green Beans with Snow Peas and Mint, and Potato, Spinach, and Leek Gratin*

# Potato, Spinach, and Leek Gratin

**MAKES 8 SERVINGS**

This hearty, flavorful side dish will please potato lovers, even with its healthy dose of spinach. It takes time to put together, but it can be done a day or two ahead. Simply assemble the dish without baking, then cover and refrigerate. Bring to room temperature for about two hours before baking. If the gratin goes into the oven when the lamb comes out, it will be ready when the lamb is carved.

2 pounds Yukon Gold potatoes, unpeeled and cut into ⅛-inch slices

2 bay leaves

3 tablespoons all-purpose flour

2 cups low-sodium vegetable or chicken broth

½ teaspoon salt

¼ teaspoon ground nutmeg

¼ teaspoon freshly ground pepper

1¼ cups low-fat (2%) evaporated milk

1 tablespoon butter

1 leek, thinly sliced

2 (10-ounce) packages frozen chopped spinach, thawed and squeezed dry

1 slice white bread, made into crumbs

1 tablespoon butter, melted

1. Bring the potatoes, bay leaves, and enough water to cover to a boil in a large saucepan. Reduce the heat and simmer, uncovered, until tender, about 6 minutes. Drain and discard the bay leaves.

2. Combine the flour, broth, salt, nutmeg, and pepper in a large bowl. With a whisk, stir to dissolve the flour. Stir in the milk.

3. Melt the butter in a large nonstick skillet over medium heat, then add the leek. Cook, stirring occasionally, until softened, about 4 minutes. Add the milk mixture; cook, stirring constantly, until the mixture boils and thickens, about 5 minutes. Remove from the heat.

4. Preheat the oven to 450°F. Spray a 9 × 13-inch baking dish with nonstick spray. Spread half the potatoes over the bottom, then top with the spinach and about 1½ cups of the leek sauce. Repeat with the remaining potatoes and leek sauce.

5. Combine the bread crumbs and melted butter; sprinkle over the top. Bake, uncovered, until golden brown and heated through, about 20 minutes.

Per serving (about 1 cup): 208 Cal, 5 g Fat, 3 g Sat Fat, 14 mg Chol, 289 mg Sod, 35 g Carb, 4 g Fib, 8 g Prot, 204 mg Calc. *POINTS: 4.*

# *Carrot Cake with Cream Cheese Frosting*

**MAKES 16 SERVINGS**

While carrot cake with cream cheese frosting has become one of our most popular desserts, central European pastry chefs have been incorporating this plentiful and flavorful vegetable into desserts for centuries. To save time on Easter Sunday, bake and frost the cake the day before, cover loosely with plastic wrap, and refrigerate overnight.

1 cup all-purpose flour

¾ teaspoon baking powder

½ teaspoon baking soda

½ teaspoon cinnamon

¼ teaspoon ground ginger

⅛ teaspoon ground nutmeg

3 tablespoons vegetable oil

1 large egg

⅔ cup granulated sugar

2 medium carrots, finely shredded (1 cup)

1 (8-ounce) can crushed pineapple in unsweetened pineapple juice, well drained

¼ cup golden raisins

⅓ cup light cream cheese or Neufchâtel

¼ teaspoon vanilla extract

1½ cups sifted confectioners' sugar

1 tablespoon finely chopped toasted walnuts

*1.* Preheat the oven to 350°F. Spray an 8-inch round cake pan with nonstick spray; line the bottom with wax paper, and spray the paper with nonstick spray.

*2.* Combine the flour, baking powder, baking soda, cinnamon, ginger, and nutmeg in a medium bowl.

*3.* With an electric mixer at medium speed, beat the oil, egg, granulated sugar, carrots, and pineapple in a large bowl until well mixed. With the mixer at low speed, stir in the flour mixture and raisins until all the flour is just moistened. Scrape the batter into the pan. Bake until a toothpick inserted in the center comes out clean, about 35 minutes.

*4.* Cool the cake in the pan on a rack 10 minutes. Remove from the pan, peel off the wax paper, and cool completely on the rack.

*5.* With an electric mixer at medium speed, beat the cream cheese and vanilla until smooth. Gradually add the confectioners' sugar and beat until evenly blended. Transfer the cake to a serving plate; spread the frosting over the top and sides of the cake. Sprinkle the walnuts in a border around the top.

Per serving (¹⁄₁₆ of cake): 163 Cal, 4 g Fat, 1 g Sat Fat, 15 mg Chol, 77 mg Sod, 30 g Carb, 1 g Fib, 2 g Prot, 28 mg Calc. ***POINTS: 3.***

# CINCO DE MAYO CELEBRATION

*Sparkling Mock Margaritas*

—

*Grilled Pepper-and-Black-Bean Quesadillas*

—

*Tortilla Soup*

—

*Braised Pork with Green Chiles and Potatoes*

—

*Chicken and Red Chile Tamales*

—

*Jicama and Sweet Red Pepper Salad*

—

*Corn Cakes with Manchego Cheese*

—

*Orange Custards with Burnt Sugar Tortilla Strips*

## *Sparkling Mock Margaritas*

**MAKES 8 SERVINGS**

Kick off the festivities in style with a pitcher of this tangy, non-alcoholic sparkler. Coating the rims of large margarita or martini glasses with salt will give these "mocktails" an authentic look, but remember to serve them with straws if you prefer not to drink your entire day's sodium allotment!

Juice of 4 limes (about ⅓ cup)
6 tablespoons fresh
   grapefruit juice
½ teaspoon salt
Ice
1 (1-liter) bottle lime-flavored
   tonic water
8 lime wedges, for garnish

*1.* Combine the lime juice, grapefruit juice, and salt in a large pitcher; stir until the salt is completely dissolved.

*2.* Fill 8 tall glasses with ice. Divide the juice mixture between the glasses; slowly fill each glass with tonic water. Garnish each serving with a lime wedge.

Per serving (1 drink): 70 Cal, 0 g Fat, 0 g Sat Fat, 0 mg Chol, 7 mg Sod, 19 g Carb, 0 g Fib, 0 g Prot, 6 mg Calc. *POINTS: 1.*

◆

*Chef's Tip:* To coat the glass rims with salt, rub the rims with a lime wedge. Pour a layer of coarse salt on a plate; press each rim into the salt. Turn the glasses right side up; use immediately or let stand for up to an hour.

# Grilled Pepper-and-Black-Bean Quesadillas

**MAKES 8 SERVINGS**

These savory little wedges are perfect for serving with drinks. Feel free to mix and match filling ingredients to suit your taste. Substituting a few roasted peppers for the minced bell peppers, or two tablespoons minced grilled meat for the beans, are just some of the intriguing possibilities.

2 tablespoons fat-free
  sour cream
2 tablespoons cooked or
  canned black beans, rinsed
  and drained
2 tablespoons minced
  red bell pepper
2 tablespoons minced
  green bell pepper
1 tablespoon minced scallions
¼ teaspoon salt
Freshly ground pepper, to taste
8 (10-inch) fat-free flour tortillas

*1.* To prepare the filling, combine the sour cream, beans, bell peppers, scallions, salt, and pepper in a small bowl.

*2.* Spread 2 tablespoons of the filling on 1 tortilla. Place another tortilla on top and press lightly. Lightly spray both sides of the quesadilla with nonstick spray. Repeat with the remaining tortillas, filling, and nonstick spray to make 4 quesadillas.

*3.* Spray a nonstick ridged grill pan or nonstick skillet with nonstick spray and set over medium heat. Cook the quesadillas until crisp and heated through, 2–3 minutes on each side. Cut into quarters, making a total of 16 wedges.

Per serving (2 wedges): 80 Cal, 2 g Fat, 0 g Sat Fat, 0 mg Chol, 135 mg Sod, 14 g Carb, 0 g Fib, 3 g Prot, 55 mg Calc. *POINTS: 2.*

*Chef's Tip:* If you want to prepare the quesadillas ahead of time, follow the directions through Step 2. Stack each quesadilla between a layer of wax or parchment paper, wrap tightly in plastic wrap, and refrigerate for up to four hours.

# Tortilla Soup

This classic Mexican soup is a lively combination of garlic, cilantro, scallions, and lime in a zesty tomato-, chile-, and cumin-seasoned broth. The crisp tortilla strips add delightful crunch.

5 (6-inch) corn tortillas, cut into matchstick-thin strips
1 tablespoon vegetable oil
1 onion, minced
1 garlic clove, minced
¾ cup tomato puree
2 tablespoons chopped fresh cilantro
1½ teaspoons chili powder
1 teaspoon ground cumin
6 cups low-sodium chicken broth
1 bay leaf
Lime slices, minced scallion, and fresh cilantro leaves, for garnish

*1.* Preheat the oven to 350°F. Place the tortilla strips in an even layer on a baking sheet. Bake until toasted, about 15 minutes; let cool. Reserve about ½ cup of the strips; set aside.

*2.* Transfer the remaining tortilla strips to a food processor or blender; pulse until crushed. Set aside.

*3.* Heat a large nonstick Dutch oven over medium-high heat. Swirl in the oil, then add the onion and garlic. Cook, stirring frequently, until softened, 3–4 minutes. Add the tomato puree, cilantro, chili powder, and cumin; cook until fragrant and slightly thickened, about 5 minutes. Add the broth, crushed tortillas, and bay leaf; bring to a boil. Reduce the heat and simmer until the flavors are blended, 25–30 minutes.

*4.* Pour the soup through a sieve set over a large bowl; discard the bay leaf. Ladle the soup into heated serving bowls; garnish each serving with the reserved tortilla strips, lime slices, scallion, and cilantro leaves.

Per serving (½ cup): 80 Cal, 2 g Fat, 0 g Sat Fat, 0 mg Chol, 135 mg Sod, 14 g Carb, 0 g Fib, 3 g Prot, 55 mg Calc. *POINTS: 2.*

*Chef's Tip:* To make this soup ahead, prepare as directed, omitting the garnishes. Cool completely; refrigerate for up to three days or freeze for up to two months in an airtight container. To reheat the soup, return it to a full boil; simmer 3 minutes. Store the tortilla strips in an airtight container at room temperature for up to three days; re-crisp the strips in a 350°F oven about 2 minutes.

# Braised Pork with Green Chiles and Potatoes

**MAKES 8 SERVINGS**

Pork tenderloin gets a great flavor boost from marinating with a hot and spicy dry rub. Like any braised dish, its flavor improves with time, so consider making it up to four days ahead of time. We select canned green chiles because they're mild. You'll need about half of a 4-ounce can for this recipe. But if you want more heat, include the optional poblano chile and jalapeño pepper on your shopping list.

4 teaspoons chili powder

1 teaspoon white vinegar

1 teaspoon ground cumin

1 teaspoon dried oregano

1 teaspoon salt

Freshly ground pepper, to taste

1½ pounds pork tenderloin, trimmed of all visible fat, cut into 8 pieces

1 tablespoon vegetable oil

1 onion, chopped

3 garlic cloves, minced

2 cups low-sodium chicken broth

6 small Yukon Gold potatoes (about 1¼ pounds), scrubbed and cut into ½-inch slices

2 poblano chiles, roasted, peeled, seeded, and chopped (optional)

½ cup chopped tomato

1 whole canned green chile, drained and cut into strips

1 jalapeño pepper, seeded and minced (wear gloves to prevent irritation) (optional)

2 teaspoons green hot pepper sauce

*1.* To prepare the spice rub, combine the chili powder, vinegar, cumin, oregano, ½ teaspoon of the salt, and pepper in a large zip-close plastic bag; add the pork. Squeeze out the air and seal the bag; turn to coat all sides of the meat. Refrigerate, turning the bag occasionally, at least 2 hours or up to 12 hours.

*2.* Preheat the oven to 325°F. Heat a large nonstick Dutch oven over high heat. Swirl in the oil, then add the pork. Cook on all sides until the meat is browned, 2–3 minutes. Transfer the pork to a plate. Reduce the heat to medium; add the onion and garlic and cook until golden brown, about 10 minutes.

*3.* Add the broth; bring to a boil, scraping up any browned bits from the bottom of the pan with a wooden spoon. Add the pork, potatoes, poblanos (if using), tomato, and green chile; bring to a boil. Cover and bake until an instant-read thermometer inserted in the thickest part of the pork registers 160°F, 35–40 minutes. Uncover and bake the pork, stirring occasionally, until the meat is very tender when pierced with a fork and the liquid has reduced slightly, about 15 minutes longer.

*4.* Transfer the Dutch oven to the stovetop. With a slotted spoon, place the pork on a plate; cover loosely with foil and keep warm. Bring the sauce to a boil. Reduce the heat and simmer, skimming off any excess fat with a spoon. Add the jalapeño (if using), hot pepper sauce, and remaining ½ teaspoon salt. Return the pork to the sauce and heat through.

Per serving (1 piece pork with 1 cup sauce): 220 Cal, 5 g Fat, 1 g Sat Fat, 40 mg Chol, 300 mg Sod, 28 g Carb, 4 g Fib, 16 g Prot, 33 mg Calc. *POINTS: 4.*

# Chicken and Red Chile Tamales

**MAKES 8 SERVINGS**

Tamales are wonderful party fare, in part because they freeze beautifully and let you plan ahead. Dried corn husks are the traditional wrapping, but you can also wrap tamales in foil or banana leaves for an unusual and beautiful presentation. It's fun to serve tamales directly from the steamer in their wrappers so guests can open their own. Masa harina gives these tamales their unique flavor. It is different from ordinary cornmeal and worth hunting down. If you don't find it in your supermarket, try a Latin-American market.

½ pound skinless boneless chicken breast, cut into 1-inch pieces

1 small onion, peeled and left whole

6 garlic cloves, minced

1 teaspoon salt

1 teaspoon vegetable oil

1 small onion, chopped

1 dried ancho chile, stemmed and seeded

1 cup water

1 plum tomato, chopped

1 tablespoon raisins

1 tablespoon sliced almonds, toasted

¼ teaspoon cinnamon

2 whole cloves

About 20 dried corn husks

¾ cup masa harina

1 tablespoon vegetable shortening

*1.* To prepare the filling, combine the chicken, the whole onion, 1 of the garlic cloves, ½ teaspoon of the salt, and enough water to barely cover the chicken in a saucepan; bring to a boil. Reduce the heat and simmer, covered, until the chicken is cooked through, 15–20 minutes. Discard the onion. With a slotted spoon, transfer the chicken to a plate. Reserve the broth and set aside.

*2.* When the chicken is cool enough to handle, thinly slice or shred, moisten with a little of the reserved broth, and set aside.

*3.* Heat a large nonstick saucepan over medium-high heat. Swirl in the oil, then add the chopped onion. Cook, stirring frequently, until golden brown, about 10 minutes. Add the remaining 5 garlic cloves and the chile; cook until the garlic is golden and the chile is toasted, about 3 minutes. Add the water, tomato, raisins, almonds, cinnamon, cloves, and ¼ teaspoon of the salt; bring to a boil. Reduce the heat and simmer, stirring occasionally, until the flavors are blended, about 15 minutes. Discard the cloves.

*4.* Puree the mixture in batches in a food processor or blender; return to the saucepan and add the chicken. Simmer over medium heat until the sauce thickens, about 5 minutes.

5. Combine the corn husks and enough hot water to cover in a large bowl. Soak, turning occasionally, until pliable, about 30 minutes.

6. Meanwhile, to prepare the masa dough, with an electric mixer at medium speed, beat the masa harina, shortening, and the remaining $\frac{1}{4}$ teaspoon salt until mixture comes together. Add $\frac{3}{4}$ cup of the reserved broth; beat on low speed until light and spongy, about 5 minutes. Cover and refrigerate the dough about 20 minutes.

7. Drain and rinse the corn husks; keep covered with a damp towel. Cut 2 or 3 of the husks lengthwise into 16 ($\frac{1}{4}$-inch wide) strips, set aside. Flatten a corn husk on a work surface; spread 2 tablespoons dough over the husk, leaving a $\frac{3}{4}$-inch margin on all sides. Spoon $1\frac{1}{2}$ tablespoons filling on top of the dough. Roll up lengthwise into a cylinder; secure each end by tying with a strip of husk. Repeat with the remaining husks, dough, and filling making a total of 16 tamales.

8. Place the tamales in a steamer basket; set in a saucepan over 1 inch of boiling water. Cover tightly; reduce the heat to low and steam until very hot, about 45 minutes.

Per serving (2 tamales): 120 Cal, 4 g Fat, 1 g Sat Fat, 15 mg Chol, 320 mg Sod, 13 g Carb, 2 g Fib, 9 g Prot, 39 mg Calc. *POINTS: 2.*

—◆—

*Chef's Tip:* Tamales can be assembled in stages. Make the filling one day; cover and refrigerate. The next day, make the dough while the corn husks soak, then assemble the tamales. You can freeze the uncooked tamales for up to a month. To cook frozen tamales, do not thaw but increase the steaming time to about one hour, checking the water periodically to be sure it does not evaporate.

## Making Tamales

Corn husks are one of several types of wrappers used throughout Mexico to prepare tamales—
savory steamed packets with a variety of tasty fillings. Soak the husks in hot water
for about 30 minutes to make them pliable. With kitchen shears, cut thin strips from two or three
of the husks and use them to tie up the filled and folded tamales.

*1.* Spread about 2 tablespoons of masa dough down the center of the corn husk and top with 1 to 2 tablespoons of the filling.

*2.* Roll the husk completely around the masa and filling, overlapping the seam. Use thin corn husk strips to tie the ends of the tamale.

*3.* Serve the steamed tamales in their wrappers, so they stay hot. Untie them before eating.

# Jicama and Sweet Red Pepper Salad

Jicama is a vegetable often found in Mexican salads and salsas. No wonder! Its crunchy texture and sweet, nutty flavor tames the heat of the fieriest dishes. Jicama is available in the produce section of many supermarkets. But if you have trouble finding it, substitute 2 cups shredded green or red cabbage and 1 cup chopped cucumber.

1 (½-pound) jicama, peeled and coarsely grated

1 red bell pepper, seeded and cut into strips

2 scallions, thinly sliced

2 teaspoons chopped fresh cilantro

Juice of 1 lime

1 teaspoon sugar

½ teaspoon salt

½ teaspoon hot pepper sauce

1 tablespoon vegetable oil

*1.* Combine the jicama, bell pepper, scallions, and cilantro in a salad bowl.

*2.* To prepare the dressing, whisk together the lime juice, sugar, salt, and hot pepper sauce in a bowl; gradually whisk in the oil until blended.

*3.* Drizzle the dressing over the salad; toss to coat. Cover and refrigerate at least 1 hour or up to 4 hours before serving to allow the flavors to blend.

Per serving (⅓ cup): 35 Cal, 2 g Fat, 0 g Sat Fat, 0 mg Chol, 150 mg Sod, 4 g Carb, 2 g Fib, 0 g Prot, 8 mg Calc. *POINTS: 0.*

*Chef's Tip:* To retain this salad's vibrant taste and texture, it's best to serve it within an hour of preparation. If you *must* make it ahead, you can keep it refrigerated up to 12 hours before serving.

# Corn Cakes with Manchego Cheese

How could something this crunchy, cheesy, and totally addictive be good for you? It's the combo of fiber-rich nutty brown rice, sweet kernel corn, bell pepper, cilantro, and Spanish manchego cheese that makes all the difference. Not only does manchego have a full, mellow flavor, it also melts beautifully.

1½ cups cooked brown rice
½ cup fresh or thawed frozen corn kernels
¼ cup seeded and minced red bell pepper
1 egg white, lightly beaten
2 teaspoons chopped fresh cilantro
½ teaspoon salt
Freshly ground pepper, to taste
3–4 tablespoons cornmeal
3 tablespoons crumbled manchego or feta cheese
1 tablespoon vegetable oil

*1.* To prepare the batter, combine the rice, corn, bell pepper, egg white, cilantro, salt, and pepper in a medium bowl. Stir in enough cornmeal to make a thick batter; fold in the cheese.

*2.* Heat an extra-large nonstick skillet over medium-high heat. Swirl in the oil, then drop the batter by spoonfuls into the skillet, making a total of 16 (1½-inch) round cakes. Cook until browned and crisp, 3–4 minutes on each side. Serve at once.

Per serving (2 cakes): 90 Cal, 2 g Fat, 1 g Sat Fat, 5 mg Chol, 250 mg Sod, 14 g Carb, 1 g Fib, 4 g Prot, 25 mg Calc. *POINTS: 2.*

———◆———

*Chef's Tip:* These cakes can easily be made ahead and reheated. Prepare the recipe as directed, except cook the cakes until just crisp, about 2 minutes on each side. Transfer to a large plate and let cool. Cover and refrigerate for up to 24 hours. To reheat, transfer the cakes to a baking sheet sprayed with nonstick spray; bake in a 350°F oven until very hot and crisp, about 8 minutes.

*Sparkling Mock Margaritas, Braised Pork with Green Chiles and Potatoes, and Corn Cakes with Manchego Cheese*

# Orange Custards with Burnt Sugar Tortilla Strips

**MAKES 8 SERVINGS**

Don't let the words *burnt sugar* scare you. Broiling the sugar-coated tortilla strips caramelizes the sugar, making each strand super-crunchy and wonderfully sweet.

3 large eggs, lightly beaten
½ cup sugar
1 cup orange juice
1 cup pineapple juice
½ cup evaporated fat-free milk
¼ teaspoon vanilla or
    almond extract
⅛ teaspoon salt
2 (8-inch) fat-free flour tortillas,
    cut into ¼-inch strips
2 tablespoons cinnamon-sugar

*1.* Preheat the oven to 350°F. Spray 8 (4-ounce) custard cups with nonstick spray; set aside.

*2.* Bring a large saucepan or tea kettle filled with water to a boil. Meanwhile, whisk the eggs and ¼ cup of the sugar in a medium bowl; set aside.

*3.* Combine the remaining ¼ cup sugar, the orange juice, pineapple juice, milk, vanilla, and salt in a medium saucepan; bring to a boil, stirring to dissolve the sugar. Whisking constantly, gradually add the hot juice mixture to the egg mixture until blended. Divide the mixture evenly among the prepared cups.

*4.* Arrange the cups in a roasting pan. Place the pan in the oven, then carefully fill the roasting pan with enough boiling water until it reaches 1 inch up the sides of the cups. Bake until a knife inserted in the center of each custard comes out clean, 20–30 minutes. Carefully remove the custards from the water bath. Refrigerate on a rack until completely cooled, about 2 hours.

*5.* Preheat the broiler. Place the tortilla strips in one layer on a large baking sheet. Spray the strips lightly with nonstick spray; sprinkle evenly with cinnamon-sugar. Broil the strips 5 inches from the heat, turning once, until the sugar is evenly browned, about 3 minutes; cool on a rack. Serve with the custards.

Per serving (1 custard with 5-6 tortilla strips): 147 Cal, 3 g Fat, 1 g Sat Fat, 80 mg Chol, 87 mg Sod, 26 g Carb, 1 g Fib, 5 g Prot, 64 mg Calc. **POINTS: 3.**

———◆———

*Chef's Tip:* To prepare the dessert ahead, make the tortilla strips as directed. Store in an airtight container for up to five days. Prepare the custards as directed; cover and refrigerate for up to three days. Just before serving, re-crisp the tortillas in a 350°F oven, 2 to 3 minutes.

# MOTHER'S DAY BRUNCH

*Red Pepper Soup*
—
*Spinach and Ricotta Tart*
—
*Garden-Style Baked Chicken*
—
*Pasta with Seafood and Pesto*
—
*Asparagus with Lemon-Herb Topping*
—
*Grapefruit and Avocado Salad*
—
*Champagne and Lemon Sorbet*
—
*Individual Fresh-Berry Trifles*

## Red Pepper Soup

**MAKES 12 SERVINGS**

If it's a blustery day outside, serve this vibrant red soup hot, but if you live in a warmer climate, it is equally good served chilled. Because the flavors in foods diminish when they are chilled, serve the cold soup with a sprinkling of white-wine vinegar and freshly ground pepper. To make ahead: Prepare the soup, let cool one to two hours, then refrigerate, covered, for up to three days.

1½ tablespoons butter
1 bunch scallions, sliced
2 garlic cloves, minced
7 cups low-sodium chicken or vegetable broth
6 red bell peppers, seeded and cut into eighths
2 Granny Smith apples, unpeeled and cut into chunks
1 large baking potato, scrubbed and cubed
1½ teaspoons salt
¼ teaspoon crushed red pepper
¼ cup light sour cream
12 fresh mint sprigs

*1.* Melt the butter in a large nonstick Dutch oven over medium-high heat, then add the scallions and garlic. Cook, stirring occasionally, until golden, 8–10 minutes.

*2.* Add the broth, bell peppers, apples, potato, salt, and crushed red pepper; bring to a boil. Reduce the heat and simmer, covered, until the vegetables are tender, 20–25 minutes.

*3.* Pour the soup, in batches, into a food processor or blender, filling the container no more than half full, and puree. Return the pureed soup to the Dutch oven and reheat. Garnish with the sour cream and mint sprigs and serve.

Per serving (scant 1 cup): 85 Cal, 3 g Fat, 1 g Sat Fat, 6 mg Chol, 342 mg Sod, 14 g Carb, 2 g Fib, 3 g Prot, 32 mg Calc. ***POINTS: 2.***

# Spinach and Ricotta Tart

**MAKES 12 SERVINGS**

Do real men eat quiche? Well, moms sure do, especially when it's as delicate and sophisticated as this stunning quiche-like tart. The crust is a wonderfully crunchy combination of wild rice, bread crumbs, and toasted nuts; the rich, custard-like filling is chock-full of good-for-you spinach, carrots, fresh herbs, and a sprinkling of cheese.

⅓ cup wild rice

1¼ teaspoons salt

¼ cup plain dry bread crumbs

3 tablespoons chopped pecans or walnuts, toasted

1 tablespoon low-sodium vegetable broth or water

1 tablespoon vegetable oil

2 (10-ounce) bags triple-washed spinach, torn

1 onion, minced

1 cup grated carrots

2 garlic cloves, minced

1 cup part-skim ricotta cheese

1 large egg, lightly beaten

1 egg white, lightly beaten

1 tablespoon minced fresh chives

⅛ teaspoon freshly grated nutmeg

Freshly ground pepper, to taste

¼ cup grated Parmesan cheese

*1.* Bring a medium saucepan half-full of water to a boil, then add the rice and ½ teaspoon of the salt. Reduce the heat and simmer, partially covered, until the kernels just start to pop and the rice is tender, 35–40 minutes. Drain.

2. Meanwhile, adjust the racks to divide the oven into thirds. Preheat the oven to 375°F. Spray a 10-inch quiche pan or pie plate with nonstick spray.

*3.* To make the crust, in a large bowl, combine the cooked wild rice, bread crumbs, pecans, broth, and ¼ teaspoon of the salt. Press into the quiche pan. Cover with plastic wrap and refrigerate while preparing the filling.

*4.* To make the filling, heat a large nonstick skillet over medium heat. Swirl in 2 teaspoons of the oil, then add the spinach, by handfuls if necessary. Cook until wilted and a deep green, about 2 minutes. Drain the spinach in a colander then transfer to a bowl.

*5.* Swirl the remaining 1 teaspoon oil into the same skillet, then add the onion, carrots, and garlic. Cook, stirring occasionally, until the onions are golden. Transfer the onion mixture to the bowl with the spinach; stir in the ricotta, egg, egg white, chives, nutmeg, pepper, and the remaining ½ teaspoon salt.

*6.* Scrape the filling into the crust and spread in an even layer. Sprinkle with the Parmesan cheese. Bake in the bottom third of the oven until the crust is golden and the filling is set, about 20 minutes. Let the tart stand for 10 minutes before serving.

Per serving (¹⁄₁₂ of tart): 118 Cal, 5 g Fat, 2 g Sat Fat, 26 mg Chol, 400 mg Sod, 12 g Carb, 2 g Fib, 7 g Prot, 115 mg Calc. **POINTS: 2.**

# Garden-Style Baked Chicken

## MAKES 12 SERVINGS

To lock in maximum flavor and moisture, we top the chicken breasts with a savory crumb topping, then bake them on a bed of zucchini and tomatoes. Best of all, everything bakes in one oven-to-table casserole, making clean up a breeze.

**6** cups sliced zucchini

**4** medium tomatoes, peeled, seeded, and chopped

**1** tablespoon unsalted butter, melted

**1** teaspoon salt

Freshly ground pepper, to taste

**12** (4-ounce) skinless boneless chicken breasts

**½** cup dry white wine or low-sodium chicken broth

**1** cup plain dry bread crumbs

**½** cup chopped fresh parsley, chives, or dill (use one or a combination)

**3** tablespoons grated Parmesan cheese

**2** tablespoons Dijon mustard

*1.* Preheat the oven to 350°F. Spray a 9 × 13-inch baking pan with nonstick spray.

*2.* Place the zucchini in a single layer in the baking dish and top with the tomatoes. Drizzle the vegetables with the butter, then sprinkle with ¼ teaspoon of the salt and the pepper.

*3.* Sprinkle the chicken with the remaining ¾ teaspoon salt and more pepper. Place the chicken in a single layer on top of the vegetables then pour the wine around the edge of the dish.

*4.* Combine the bread crumbs, parsley, Parmesan cheese, and mustard in a small bowl. Press the mixture on top of the chicken. Cover the pan loosely with foil and bake until the chicken is cooked through, about 25 minutes. If you like, increase the oven temperature to broil and broil the chicken 5 inches from the heat, until the bread crumbs are browned.

Per serving (1 chicken breast with ⅓ cup vegetables): 240 Cal, 4 g Fat, 1 g Sat Fat, 70 mg Chol, 380 mg Sod, 18 g Carb, 2 g Fib, 31 g Prot, 103 mg Calc. ***POINTS: 5.***

*Pasta with Seafood and Pesto*

# Pasta with Seafood and Pesto

### MAKES 12 SERVINGS

If you adore pasta with pesto (that perfect puree of fresh basil, Parmesan cheese, olive oil, and nuts) but you're also crazy about pasta with seafood, this recipe combines the best of both—all in one bowl. You can use any medium size pasta in the dish: Penne, ziti, and fusilli are all good choices. For a dramatic presentation, keep the clams in their shells.

½ **pound rigatoni pasta**
1 **teaspoon vegetable oil**
1 **small onion, minced**
1 **garlic clove, minced**
24 **cherrystone clams, scrubbed**
½ **cup water**
½ **pound medium cooked**
    **shrimp, shelled and deveined**
2 **tablespoons prepared pesto**
1 **teaspoon salt**
**Freshly ground pepper, to taste**

*1.* Cook the pasta according to package directions until just al dente. Drain; toss in a bowl with the oil and set aside.

*2.* Spray a large nonstick saucepan with nonstick spray and set over low-medium heat. Add the onion and garlic. Cook, stirring frequently, until softened, 3–5 minutes. Add the clams and the water. Increase the heat to high and cook, covered, until the clams open, 4–8 minutes.

*3.* Transfer the clams to a bowl with a slotted spoon. Discard any clams that do not open. Cover the pan and keep the cooking liquid warm.

*4.* When the clams are cool enough to handle, remove the meat and discard the shells (if desired). Return the clams to the cooking liquid; add the shrimp and pesto and bring to a simmer. Add the pasta and simmer until the pasta is very hot and evenly coated with the pesto sauce. Season with the salt and pepper; serve at once.

Per serving (¾ cup): 120 Cal, 2 g Fat, 0 g Sat Fat, 45 mg Chol, 270 mg Sod, 15 g Carb, 0 g Fib, 9 g Prot, 36 mg Calc. ***POINTS: 3.***

*Chef's Tip:* For this dish, or in any recipe where the pasta will be reheated, cook the pasta a minute or two less than directed so it won't overcook when reheated. Drain the hot pasta in a colander as directed in Step 1, then immediately rinse under running cold water to stop the cooking.

# *Asparagus with Lemon-Herb Topping*

**MAKES 12 SERVINGS**

Nothing says spring like asparagus and lemon, and this simple dish will surely put mom in a festive mood. We use fresh parsley and basil in the sauce, but feel free to try whatever fresh herbs look best at the market. The easy skillet sauce is equally delicious served with steamed green beans or artichokes.

1½ **pounds fresh asparagus, trimmed**

1 **teaspoon vegetable oil**

3 **garlic cloves, minced**

½ **cup chopped flat-leaf parsley**

½ **cup lightly packed fresh basil leaves, chopped**

2 **tablespoons fresh lemon juice**

½ **teaspoon salt**

**Freshly ground pepper, to taste**

*1.* Put the asparagus in a steamer basket; set in a saucepan over 1 inch of boiling water. Cover tightly and steam until tender, about 5 minutes.

*2.* Meanwhile, heat a nonstick skillet over medium heat. Swirl in the oil, then add the garlic. Cook until fragrant, about 30 seconds. Remove from the heat; add the parsley, basil, lemon juice, salt, and pepper.

*3.* Transfer the asparagus to a platter; sprinkle with the topping. Serve warm or at room temperature.

Per serving (about 3 spears with 1 tablespoon topping): 53 Cal, 2 g Fat, 0 g Sat Fat, 1 mg Chol, 43 mg Sod, 7 g Carb, 3 g Fib, 3 g Prot, 135 mg Calc. ***POINTS: 1.***

*Chef's Tip:* The asparagus can be steamed, then refrigerated overnight, but for maximum flavor prepare the topping no more than a couple of hours ahead. Allow the asparagus to stand at room temperature 20 minutes before serving.

# Grapefruit and Avocado Salad

**MAKES 12 SERVINGS**

Juicy, tangy grapefruit, creamy avocado, and crisp romaine lettuce make this simple salad a wonderful combination of tastes and textures. There's no oil in the grapefruit juice dressing—just a touch of brown sugar to heighten the sweetness of the fruit.

⅓ cup fresh grapefruit juice
¾ teaspoon packed light
  brown sugar
¼ teaspoon salt
Freshly ground pepper, to taste
2 hearts of romaine lettuce,
  separated into leaves
2 grapefruits, peeled and sliced
  or cut into segments
1 avocado, peeled, pitted, and
  sliced or cubed
1 red onion, thinly sliced and
  separated into rings

*1.* To make the dressing, combine the grapefruit juice, brown sugar, salt, and pepper in a medium bowl. Let the dressing stand 15 minutes to allow the flavors to blend.
*2.* Place the romaine leaves on a large serving plate. Add the grapefruit slices and avocado to the dressing; toss gently to coat. Place the avocado and grapefruit mixture on the romaine; drizzle with any remaining dressing, then top with the onion.

Per serving (about ½ cup): 51 Cal, 3 g Fat, 0 g Sat Fat, 0 mg Chol, 52 mg Sod, 7 g Carb, 2 g Fib, 0 g Prot, 17 mg Calc. *POINTS: 1.*

*Chef's Tip:* This dressing can be refrigerated for up to two days. Just allow it to warm to room temperature for 15 to 20 minutes, then stir or shake it vigorously before adding to the salad. To cut the sharp flavor of sliced raw onions, rinse them in a sieve under cold water, then pat dry.

# Champagne and Lemon Sorbet

### MAKES 12 SERVINGS

A lively burst of lemon and the slightly fizzy taste of champagne make a delightful taste duet in this refreshing sorbet. Serve it between courses to cleanse the palate or as dessert. It keeps very well in the freezer for up to two months.

2 cups water
1½ cups sugar
1½ cups champagne, sparkling dry white wine, or selzter
1 tablespoon grated lemon rind
½ cup fresh lemon juice

*1.* Bring 1 cup of the water and the sugar to a boil in a medium saucepan, stirring occasionally, until the sugar is dissolved. Remove from the heat and let cool to room temperature, about 1 hour.

*2.* Stir in the remaining 1 cup water, the champagne, lemon rind, and lemon juice. Pour the mixture into a 9-inch square baking dish and freeze until frozen 1 inch around the edges, about 3 hours.

*3.* Transfer the mixture to a food processor or blender, in batches, filling the container no more than one-third full, and puree. Return the mixture to the baking dish and freeze until firm, at least 8 hours.

*4.* Let the mixture soften at room temperature, 5 minutes, then return to a food processor or blender and pulse until smooth and creamy looking. Pour the mixture into freezer containers and freeze until firm, at least 8 hours.

Per serving (scant ½ cup): 120 Cal, 0 g Fat, 0 g Sat Fat, 0 mg Chol, 5 mg Sod, 26 g Carb, 0 g Fib, 0 g Prot, 5 mg Calc. ***POINTS: 2.***

*Chef's Tip:* Because alcohol freezes at a lower temperature than other liquids, sorbets with alcohol may not freeze as solidly as sorbets without alcohol. Here's a handy remedy: For a "keep cool" presentation, serve the sorbet on individual blocks of ice, made by freezing 2 to 3 inches of water in ½-pint plastic storage containers or plastic tumblers with a 3-inch base.

*Champagne and Lemon Sorbet*

# Individual Fresh-Berry Trifles

**MAKES 12 SERVINGS**

Trifle, a classic English dessert, is a layered confection of sherry-soaked sponge cake, jam, custard, whipped cream, and fruit—not exactly what mom would choose if she were trying to watch her **POINTS!** So offer her our version, with double the fruit, tender ladyfingers, and deliciously light orange custard.

¼ cup cornstarch

⅓ cup fresh orange juice (about 1 orange)

¼ cup Vin Santo or other dessert wine

2 cups fat-free milk

½ cup sugar

12 ladyfingers, split

3 cups whole or sliced fresh berries (raspberries, blackberries, blueberries, or strawberries)

¾ cup fat-free whipped topping

6 fresh strawberries, halved

*1.* To make the custard, combine the cornstarch, orange juice, and wine in a small bowl until the cornstarch dissolves. Bring the milk and sugar to a simmer in a medium saucepan over medium heat. Drizzle the cornstarch mixture into the simmering milk, whisking constantly. Bring to a boil, then reduce the heat and simmer, whisking constantly, until thickened, about 5 minutes. Let the custard cool, stirring from time to time to release the heat.

*2.* To assemble, place 1 split ladyfinger half in each of 12 individual dessert bowls or sundae glasses. Top each with 2 tablespoons berries and 2 tablespoons custard. Top with another split ladyfinger half, 2 tablespoons berries, and 2 tablespoons custard, making 12 individual trifles.

*3.* Add 1 tablespoon of whipped topping to each trifle, then garnish with a strawberry half.

Per serving (1 trifle): 112 Cal, 0 g Fat 0 g Sat Fat, 3 g Prot, 25 g Carb, 2 g Fib, 1 mg Chol, 128 mg Sod, 77 mg Calc. **POINTS: 2.**

———◆———

*Chef's Tip:* To make a large trifle, arrange enough split ladyfinger halves to fit around the side of a large glass bowl or soufflé dish, then layer the remaining ladyfingers, berries, and custard in the center as directed. The custard can be prepared and refrigerated up to a day ahead and the trifle(s) can be assembled up to four hours before serving.

# DERBY DAY BUFFET DINNER

*Ginger Mint Juleps*
—
*Shrimp and Penne Salad with Creamy Tarragon Dressing*
—
*Chicken Burgoo*
—
*Kentucky Barbecued Beef*
—
*Brown Sugar–Glazed Carrots*
—
*Garlicky Green Bean Salad with Shallots*
—
*Strawberry-Rhubarb Cobbler*
—
*Derby Pecan Pie*

## Ginger Mint Juleps

**MAKES 8 SERVINGS**

No Kentucky celebration would be complete without this drink! Here, fresh lime juice and ginger ale give our Juleps sparkle and a different twist. For an alcoholic version and *1 POINT* extra per serving, substitute ¾ cup bourbon for ¾ cup of the club soda.

⅔ cup superfine sugar
½ cup fresh mint leaves
1 tablespoon water
1 cup club soda
⅔ cup fresh lime juice
4 cups ice cubes or crushed ice
2½ cups diet ginger ale

*1.* Mash the sugar, mint, and water with a wooden spoon in a small bowl to release some of the flavor and fragrance of the mint. Transfer to a large pitcher.

*2.* Stir in the club soda, lime juice, and ice. Slowly pour in the ginger ale. Serve at once.

Per serving (¾ cup): 71 Cal, 0 g Fat, 0 g Sat Fat, 0 mg Chol, 18 mg Sod, 18 g Carb, 0 g Fib, 0 g Prot, 13 mg Calc. *POINTS: 1.*

———◆———

*Chef's Tip:* To keep with tradition, serve this refreshing favorite in a chilled silver or pewter pitcher.

# Shrimp and Penne Salad with Creamy Tarragon Dressing

**MAKES 8 SERVINGS**

This colorful side salad is a make-ahead dream. Up to two days ahead, make and refrigerate the dressing; cook the pasta, rinse well under cold running water, pat dry with paper towels, then refrigerate in a large zip-close plastic bag (no oil is needed to coat the pasta as rinsing removes most of the starch that causes it to stick). Refrigerate the stemmed arugula, bell pepper strips, and chopped olives in separate zip-close plastic bags. To save time, buy already peeled, deveined, and cooked shrimp the day of the party.

⅓ cup reduced-calorie mayonnaise

⅓ cup fat-free sour cream

¼ cup low-fat (1%) milk

1 tablespoon cider vinegar

1 tablespoon chopped fresh tarragon, or 1 teaspoon dried

1 teaspoon Worcestershire sauce

1 teaspoon Dijon mustard

¾ teaspoon sugar

½ teaspoon salt

¼ teaspoon hot pepper sauce

½ pound penne pasta

½ pound large shrimp, peeled and deveined

4 cups loosely packed arugula leaves, stemmed

1 cup grape or cherry tomatoes, halved

1 red bell pepper, seeded and cut into ¼-inch strips

1 green bell pepper, seeded and cut into ¼-inch strips

1 yellow bell pepper, seeded and cut into ¼-inch strips

12 kalamata olives, pitted and chopped

1. To prepare the dressing, whisk together the mayonnaise, sour cream, milk, vinegar, tarragon, Worcestershire sauce, mustard, sugar, salt, and hot pepper sauce in a small bowl. Refrigerate, covered, at least 20 minutes or up to 2 days.

2. Cook the penne according to package directions. With a large strainer or slotted spoon, transfer the penne (reserving the water in the pot) to a colander. Rinse under cold water, and transfer to a large bowl.

3. Cook the shrimp in the same pot of boiling water, until they are just opaque in the center, about 3 minutes; drain. Rinse under cold water to stop the cooking; drain and add to the bowl with the penne. Stir in the arugula, tomatoes, bell peppers, and olives. Add the dressing and toss well to coat. Serve at once.

Per serving (1⅓ cups): 190 Cal, 5 g Fat, 1 g Sat Fat, 31 mg Chol, 449 mg Sod, 28 g Carb, 2 g Fib, 8 g Prot, 70 mg Calc. *POINTS: 4.*

# Chicken Burgoo

A Kentucky Derby classic, burgoo is a slow-simmering stew, usually made from a combination of meats such as beef, lamb, chicken, and pork, along with just about any vegetable you can imagine— potatoes, carrots, corn, okra, lima beans, and cabbage. It's a simple, one-pot dish, making it perfect for large crowds. You can make it ahead of time and freeze it for up to three months; it tastes even better when reheated. If necessary, add a little water to the saucepan when reheating.

6 cups fat-free low-sodium chicken broth

2 pounds chicken thighs, bone-in, skin removed, trimmed of all visible fat

4 large carrots, peeled

1 large onion, quartered

1 (14½-ounce) can stewed tomatoes

2 russet potatoes, peeled and cut into ½-inch chunks

2 cups frozen pearl onions

1 (10-ounce) package frozen corn kernels, thawed

¼ cup water

3 tablespoons all-purpose flour

1 tablespoon hot pepper sauce

3 tablespoons chopped fresh parsley

*1.* Combine the broth, chicken, carrots, and onion in a large saucepan; bring to a boil. Reduce the heat and simmer, covered, until the chicken is fork-tender, about 1 hour.

*2.* With a slotted spoon, transfer the chicken and carrots to a plate. When the chicken is cool enough to handle, remove the bones and shred the meat. Cut the carrots into ½-inch thick slices; set aside.

*3.* Add the tomatoes, potatoes, and pearl onions to the simmering broth; bring to a boil. Reduce the heat and simmer, covered, until the vegetables are tender, about 10 minutes. Add the chicken, carrots, and corn; simmer 5 minutes to heat through.

*4.* Whisk together the water, flour, and hot pepper sauce in a small bowl; stir in about ½ cup of the simmering liquid. Stir the flour mixture into the simmering stew along with the parsley. Cook, stirring constantly, until the mixture boils and thickens, about 3 minutes.

Per serving (1½ cups): 239 Cal, 5 g Fat, 2 g Sat Fat, 50 mg Chol, 210 mg Sod, 28 g Carb, 5 g Fib, 21 g Prot, 65 mg Calc. ***POINTS: 4.***

*Ginger Mint Julep, Kentucky Barbecued Beef, and Brown Sugar–Glazed Carrots*

# Kentucky Barbecued Beef

Beef tenderloin served with tangy barbecue sauce is a traditional Derby Day favorite. Good either hot or at room temperature, this tenderloin can be made early in the day or even the night before your party, left whole, covered, and refrigerated. Just make sure to allow the meat to come to room temperature before slicing and serving. The barbecue sauce can be made up to a week ahead and stored in a jar in the refrigerator.

¼ cup minced fresh parsley
2 garlic cloves, minced
1 tablespoon dried oregano
1 tablespoon olive oil
½ teaspoon salt
1 (2-pound) beef tenderloin, trimmed of all visible fat
½ cup bottled steak sauce
¼ cup bottled chili sauce
2 tablespoons packed dark brown sugar
2 tablespoons honey
2 tablespoons cider vinegar
1 tablespoon Worcestershire sauce
4–6 drops hot pepper sauce

1. Preheat the oven to 425°F. Spray a shallow roasting pan with nonstick spray.
2. Combine the parsley, garlic, oregano, oil, and salt in a small bowl and blend to a paste. Rub the tenderloin with the parsley mixture and place in the pan. Roast until an instant-read thermometer, inserted in the center of the beef, registers 145°F for medium-rare, 35–40 minutes. Let stand 10 minutes, then slice and arrange on a platter.
3. Meanwhile, combine the steak sauce, chili sauce, sugar, honey, vinegar, Worcestershire sauce, and hot pepper sauce in a small bowl. Drizzle the sauce over the beef.

Per serving (⅛ of beef with 1 tablespoon sauce): 196 Cal, 8 g Fat, 3 g Sat Fat, 48 mg Chol, 526 mg Sod, 13 g Carb, 1 g Fib, 19 g Prot, 23 mg Calc. *POINTS: 4.*

*Chef's Tip:* You won't want to overcook this buttery piece of meat—medium-rare is our favorite way to serve it. Since all meats continue to cook after they are removed from the oven, with their internal temperature rising from 5 to 10 degrees, it's best to remove the meat when its temperature is slightly lower than actually desired.

# Brown Sugar–Glazed Carrots

They're as yummy as they sound—and so simple. For best flavor, make them right before you're ready to serve them. Baby carrots are sold in large bags, already peeled and pared, making them very convenient for cooking for a crowd.

1 tablespoon butter

1 (2-pound) bag baby carrots

1 tablespoon packed light
    brown sugar

1 tablespoon chopped
    candied ginger

½ teaspoon ground nutmeg

½ teaspoon salt

½ cup water

*1.* Melt the butter in a large skillet over low heat, then add the carrots, sugar, ginger, nutmeg, salt, and water; bring to a boil. Cover and cook over medium-high heat, shaking the pan occasionally, until the water has evaporated and the carrots are just tender, about 10 minutes.

*2.* Remove the cover and cook over high heat, stirring occasionally, until the carrots are golden brown and glazed, about 5 minutes.

Per serving (¾ cup): 73 Cal, 2 g Fat, 1 g Sat Fat, 4 mg Chol, 199 mg Sod, 14 g Carb, 3 g Fib, 1 g Prot, 34 mg Calc. *POINTS: 1.*

# Garlicky Green Bean Salad with Shallots

**MAKES 8 SERVINGS**

This simple green bean salad makes the perfect accompaniment to the Chicken Burgoo or the Kentucky Barbecued Beef. The green beans can be blanched the day before, placed in a zip-close plastic bag, and refrigerated. The dressing can be mixed and refrigerated up to two days ahead. Add the dressing right before you are ready to serve the beans. If added too soon, the vinegar in the dressing will turn these vibrant green beans a drab olive color.

1½ **pounds fresh green beans, trimmed**

1 **tablespoon extra-virgin olive oil**

4 **garlic cloves, finely chopped**

¼ **cup chopped fresh basil**

2 **oil-packed sun-dried tomatoes, rinsed, patted dry, and cut into thin slivers**

3 **tablespoons balsamic vinegar**

2 **tablespoons minced shallot**

¼ **teaspoon salt**

¼ **teaspoon coarsely ground pepper**

*1.* Bring a large pot of lightly salted water to a boil. Add the green beans, return to a boil and cook until just crisp-tender, 4–5 minutes. Rinse under cold running water; drain and place in a large bowl.

*2.* Meanwhile, heat a small nonstick skillet over low heat. Swirl in 1 teaspoon of the oil, then add the garlic. Cook, stirring constantly, until fragrant and just beginning to turn golden, about 1 minute. Combine the garlic with the remaining 2 teaspoons oil, the basil, sun-dried tomatoes, vinegar, shallot, salt, and pepper. Add to the green beans; toss to coat. Serve at once.

Per serving (¾ cup): 41 Cal, 2 g Fat, 0 g Sat Fat, 0 mg Chol, 82 mg Sod, 6 g Carb, 2 g Fib, 1 g Prot, 42 mg Calc. ***POINTS: 1.***

# Strawberry-Rhubarb Cobbler

**MAKES 8 SERVINGS**

Nothing says spring like the delicious combination of fresh strawberries and rhubarb. If you can't find fresh, substitute 4 cups frozen strawberries and 2 cups frozen rhubarb. Make this simple dessert early in the day to serve at room temperature or reheat in the oven to serve warm. It's delicious as is or with a dollop of fat-free whipped topping.

2 **pints fresh strawberries, rinsed and quartered**
¾ **pound fresh rhubarb, cut into ½-inch pieces**
¾ **cup + 1 tablespoon sugar**
3 **tablespoons quick-cooking tapioca**
½ **teaspoon cinnamon**
¼ **teaspoon salt**
1¼ **cups reduced-fat all-purpose baking mix**
½ **cup fat-free milk**

*1.* Preheat the oven to 400°F. Spray an 8-inch square baking dish with nonstick spray.

*2.* Combine the strawberries, rhubarb, ¾ cup of the sugar, the tapioca, cinnamon, and salt in a large bowl. Let stand 15 minutes to allow the tapioca beads to soften and swell. Pour into the baking dish.

*3.* Stir together the baking mix, milk, and remaining 1 tablespoon sugar in a small bowl until blended. Spoon the batter in 8 dollops onto the fruit mixture. Bake until the topping is golden and the filling is bubbly, about 35 minutes.

Per serving (about ¾ cup): 192 Cal, 2 g Fat, 0 g Sat Fat, 0 mg Chol, 287 mg Sod, 43 g Carb, 3 g Fib, 3 g Prot, 130 mg Calc. *POINTS: 3.*

# *Derby Pecan Pie*

**MAKES 24 SERVINGS**

Pecan pie is a true southern favorite. The legendary Derby Pie, made with chocolate and walnuts
or pecans, is a Kentucky tradition and favorite, created nearly 50 years ago as a special dessert at the
Melrose Inn in Prospect, Kentucky. We cut the fat in this recipe by using egg substitute and just
a sprinkling of chocolate chips. If you like, prepare the pie shell, without baking it, the night before
and keep it covered in the refrigerator.

| | |
|---|---|
| 1 cup all-purpose flour | |
| ¼ teaspoon salt | |
| ¼ cup vegetable shortening | |
| 3½ tablespoons ice water | |
| 1 cup light corn syrup | |
| ¾ cup fat-free egg substitute | |
| ⅔ cup packed light brown sugar | |
| 1 teaspoon vanilla extract | |
| 1 cup pecan halves | |
| 2 tablespoons semisweet chocolate chips | |

*1.* Combine the flour and salt in a medium bowl. With a pastry
blender, cut in the shortening until the mixture is crumbly. Add
the water and mix with a knife just until the mixture forms a ball.
On a lightly floured surface, roll the pastry into a 12-inch circle,
then fit into a 9-inch pie plate. Fold the pastry edges under and
flute. Cover and refrigerate until ready to use.

*2.* Preheat the oven to 350°F.

*3.* Combine the corn syrup, egg substitute, sugar, and vanilla in a
medium bowl until blended. Stir in the pecans and chocolate
chips. Pour into the prepared crust. Bake until the filling is set and
a knife inserted 1 inch from the edge comes out clean, about
50 minutes. Cool on a rack. Serve warm or at room temperature.

Per serving (¹⁄₂₄ of pie): 137 Cal, 5 g Fat, 1 g Sat Fat, 0 mg Chol, 53 mg Sod,
22 g Carb, 1 g Fib, 2 g Prot, 11 mg Calc. **POINTS: 3.**

# BRIDAL SHOWER BUFFET

*Bridal Punch*
—
*Caponata Crostini*
—
*Warm Fingerling Potato and Arugula Salad*
—
*Lemon-Herb Chicken*
—
*Asparagus with Toasted Walnuts*
—
*Roasted-Pepper Rolls with Ricotta Pesto*
—
*Iced Heart Cookies*
—
*Chocolate-Dipped Strawberries*

## *Bridal Punch*

**MAKES 12 SERVINGS**

This frothy punch with Caribbean flavors is non-alcoholic. If you like, and for an extra *1 POINT* per serving, spike it with 9 fluid ounces (a generous cup) of white rum for a little extra "punch."

4 cups pineapple-orange
 banana juice, chilled
1 pint nonfat mango sorbet,
 softened
½ cup canned crushed pineapple
1 teaspoon rum extract
½ teaspoon vanilla extract
4 cups diet lemon-lime soda,
 chilled
4 cups ice cubes or crushed ice
12 maraschino cherries

Combine the juice, sorbet, pineapple, and rum and vanilla extracts in a large punch bowl. Slowly pour in the soda, then add the ice. Garnish with the cherries. Serve at once.

Per serving (scant 1 cup): 92 Cal, 0 g Fat, 0 g Sat Fat, 0 mg Chol, 17 mg Sod, 22 g Carb, 0 g Fib, 1 g Prot, 16 mg Calc. *POINTS: 2.*

◆

*Chef's Tip:* Make decorative ice cubes the day before the party by adding bits of crushed pineapple and chopped maraschino cherries to the water in the ice-cube trays.

# *Caponata Crostini*

Caponata, a tasty Italian condiment made with eggplant, is perfect for serving on these little toasts. Our version can be made up to two days ahead and kept in the refrigerator. The baguette can be toasted and kept in a zip-close plastic bag for one to two days. Bring the caponata to room temperature and assemble just before serving.

1 (1¼-pound) eggplant, cut into
   ½-inch pieces

2 onions, cut into 1-inch chunks

6 garlic cloves, halved

4 plum tomatoes, seeded and
   cut into ¾-inch chunks

½ teaspoon salt

½ teaspoon coarsely
   ground pepper

¼ cup golden raisins

¼ cup chopped fresh basil

8 kalamata olives, pitted
   and chopped

2 tablespoons chopped capers

2 tablespoons pine nuts

2 tablespoons red-wine vinegar

1 tablespoon extra-virgin
   olive oil

2 teaspoons sugar

1 (8-ounce) French baguette,
   cut into 24 slices, toasted

*1.* Preheat the oven to 425°F. Spray 2 large shallow roasting pans with nonstick spray.

*2.* Combine the eggplant, onions, and garlic in a large bowl; spray the vegetables lightly with olive-oil nonstick spray. Spread the eggplant mixture in one roasting pan. Spread the tomatoes in the other roasting pan. Sprinkle the tomatoes with the salt and pepper; spray lightly with olive-oil nonstick spray. Roast, switching the pans from higher shelf to lower shelf halfway through the baking time, stirring occasionally, until the vegetables are tender and browned, about 40 minutes. Let stand 15 minutes to cool slightly.

*3.* Transfer the vegetables to a large bowl. Stir in the raisins, basil, olives, capers, pine nuts, vinegar, oil, and sugar; toss to coat.

*4.* Spoon about 2 tablespoons of the caponata on each piece of toast. Serve immediately.

Per serving (2 crostini): 113 Cal, 4 g Fat, 1 g Sat Fat, 0 mg Chol, 273 mg Sod, 19 g Carb, 3 g Fib, 3 g Prot, 30 mg Calc. *POINTS: 2.*

---

*Chef's Tip:* An easy way to slice eggplant is to use a serrated knife. It glides right through the tough outer skin of the eggplant. For a striking presentation, arrange the crostini on a platter with a mound of fresh basil leaves in the center.

# Warm Fingerling Potato and Arugula Salad

**MAKES 12 SERVINGS**

Fingerling potatoes are small white or red potatoes. They are thin-skinned and have a delicious, buttery texture. If fingerlings are not available, cut-up Yukon Gold or any other waxy potato will do. You can prepare this salad the day of the buffet and serve it warm, or make it a day ahead, cover and refrigerate, then serve it cold.

3 pounds fingerling potatoes, scrubbed and left whole
2 tablespoons cider vinegar
1 tablespoon coarse-grained Dijon mustard
1 tablespoon extra-virgin olive oil
¾ teaspoon salt
2 cups arugula
2 large shallots, chopped
3 scallions, chopped

*1.* Place the potatoes and enough water to cover in a large saucepan; bring to a boil. Reduce the heat and simmer, covered, until tender, 15–20 minutes; drain. When the potatoes are cool enough to handle, cut them into ½-inch slices.
*2.* Whisk together the vinegar, mustard, oil, and salt in a large bowl. Add the warm potatoes and gently toss to coat. Add the arugula, shallots, and scallions; toss gently. Serve at once.

Per serving (¾ cup): 113 Cal, 1 g Fat, 0 g Sat Fat, 0 mg Chol, 171 mg Sod, 24 g Carb, 2 g Fib, 2 g Prot, 22 mg Calc. *POINTS: 2.*

*Lemon-Herb Chicken, Warm Fingerling Potato and Arugula Salad,*
*and Asparagus with Toasted Walnuts*

# Lemon-Herb Chicken

**MAKES 12 SERVINGS**

Succulent and flavorful, this chicken is good served hot or cold. If you want to make it the day before, do so and keep it in the refrigerator, then serve it cold on a bed of leafy greens. Either way, make the lemon dressing the day before and refrigerate it separately until you're ready to spoon it over the chicken, just before serving.

12 (½-pound) skinless boneless chicken breasts
2 tablespoons Cajun seasoning
½ cup fresh lemon juice
6 scallions, chopped
2 tablespoons olive oil
1 tablespoon chopped fresh rosemary, or 1 teaspoon dried
1 tablespoon chopped fresh oregano, or 1 teaspoon dried
1 tablespoon chopped fresh thyme, or 1 teaspoon dried
3 garlic cloves, minced

*1.* Sprinkle both sides of the chicken with the Cajun seasoning. Spray a nonstick skillet with nonstick spray and set over medium-high heat. Add the chicken, in batches, and cook until golden on the outside and cooked through, about 4 minutes on each side. Transfer the chicken to a cutting board; let stand 5 minutes.

*2.* Meanwhile, whisk together the lemon juice, scallions, oil, rosemary, oregano, thyme, and garlic in a medium bowl.

*3.* Arrange the chicken breasts on a platter. Spoon the lemon-herb mixture over the chicken. Serve at once.

Per serving (1 chicken breast with 1 tablespoon dressing): 160 Cal, 5 g Fat, 1 g Sat Fat, 62 mg Chol, 326 mg Sod, 2 g Carb, 0 g Fib, 25 g Prot, 25 mg Calc. ***POINTS: 4.***

*Chef's Tip:* Make appealing grill marks on the chicken breasts by using a nonstick ridged grill pan to cook them. If you have a large grill pan that fits over two burners you can cook all the chicken in one batch. For an attractive presentation, slice the cooked chicken in fourths, leave one end uncut, then fan the chicken out.

# *Asparagus with Toasted Walnuts*

**MAKES 12 SERVINGS**

Walnut oil and toasted walnuts give a nutty flavor and aroma to this asparagus dish. There are several varieties of walnut oil, including those imported from France (known as *huile de noix*), as well as several from California. They can be found in specialty food and gourmet markets. If you can't find walnut oil, use olive or canola oil instead.

2 **pounds asparagus, trimmed and fibrous stalks peeled**

2 **tablespoons white balsamic vinegar**

1 **tablespoon walnut oil**

1 **teaspoon Dijon mustard**

¾ **teaspoon salt**

¼ **cup walnut pieces, toasted**

½ **teaspoon coarsely ground pepper**

*1.* Blanch the asparagus in a large pan of salted boiling water until just crisp-tender, about 4 minutes. Using tongs, transfer the asparagus to a large bowl of ice water. Cool the asparagus for 1 minute, then drain on layers of paper towels. Place the asparagus in a large bowl.

*2.* To make the dressing, whisk together the vinegar, oil, mustard, and salt in a small bowl. Drizzle the dressing over the asparagus, tossing gently to coat.

*3.* Arrange the asparagus on a serving platter. Sprinkle with the walnuts and the pepper.

Per serving (¹⁄₁₂ of asparagus): 37 Cal, 3 g Fat, 0 g Sat Fat, 0 mg Chol, 153 mg Sod, 3 g Carb, 1 g Fib, 1 g Prot, 12 mg Calc. *POINTS: 1.*

*Chef's Tip:* The asparagus can be blanched the day before and kept between layers of paper towels in a plastic bag in the refrigerator. Make the dressing a day ahead and keep it refrigerated. Drizzle the asparagus with the dressing just before serving.

# Roasted-Pepper Rolls with Ricotta Pesto

**MAKES 12 SERVINGS**

Stuffed sweet red-pepper rolls give a colorful splash to this menu. Roast the peppers and make the ricotta pesto the night before. If you don't have time to roast peppers, use roasted red peppers from a jar. Just be sure to drain them well and pat dry with paper towels before using.

12 **red bell peppers**
 2 **cups fresh basil leaves,**
   **coarsely chopped**
 1 **tablespoon extra-virgin**
   **olive oil**
 ½ **teaspoon salt**
 3 **cups fat-free ricotta cheese**
 ¼ **cup grated Parmesan cheese**
 ½ **teaspoon ground nutmeg**
 2 **tablespoons dried oregano**
 1 **teaspoon coarsely**
   **ground pepper**
 **Fresh basil sprigs**

*1.* Preheat the boiler. Line the broiler pan with foil; place the peppers on the pan. Broil 5 inches from the heat, turning frequently with tongs, until the skins are lightly charred, 10–20 minutes. Place the peppers in a large roasting pan; cover with foil and let steam 10 minutes. When cool enough to handle, peel them. Then cut each pepper, from stem to bottom, in half and remove the seeds, making 24 halves.

*2.* Meanwhile, puree the basil, oil, and salt in a food processor or blender. Transfer to a large bowl. Stir in the ricotta, Parmesan cheese, and nutmeg.

*3.* To assemble the rolls, place about 2 tablespoons of the ricotta pesto on each pepper half. Roll up and arrange, seam-side down, on a large platter. Sprinkle with the oregano and pepper. Garnish with the basil sprigs.

Per serving (2 rolls): 95 Cal, 2 g Fat, 1 g Sat Fat, 2 mg Chol, 184 mg Sod, 10 g Carb, 1 g Fib, 10 g Prot, 153 mg Calc. ***POINTS: 2.***

*Chef's Tip:* For a colorful display, use a combination of yellow, red, and green bell peppers.

# Iced Heart Cookies

Light and lemony, with icing that hardens, these cookies can be baked, iced, and stored in an airtight container, at room temperature, for up to three days. Or the dough can be made up to two months in advance and kept in the freezer. Simply allow to thaw overnight in the refrigerator before using.

1 cup all-purpose flour
¼ teaspoon baking soda
¼ teaspoon salt
4 tablespoons margarine
½ cup sugar
2 tablespoons fat-free
   egg substitute
1 grated lemon rind
1 teaspoon lemon extract
1¼ cups confectioners' sugar
3 tablespoons water
Red food coloring

1. Combine the flour, baking soda, and salt in a small bowl. With an electric mixer at medium speed, beat the margarine and sugar until creamy. Add the egg substitute, lemon rind, and lemon extract; beat until blended. With the mixer at low speed, stir in the flour mixture, until all the flour is just moistened. On a lightly floured surface, roll out the dough to a 6-inch disk; refrigerate at least 30 minutes.

2. Preheat the oven to 375°F. Spray 2 nonstick baking sheets with nonstick spray.

3. On a lightly floured surface, roll the dough ⅛-inch thick. Using a 3-inch heart-shaped cookie cutter, cut out cookies, gathering and re-rolling the scraps of dough to make 36 cookies. With a metal spatula, carefully place cookies ½ inch apart on the baking sheets. Bake until the cookies are set but not browned, about 10 minutes. Cool the cookies on the baking sheet on a rack about 1 minute; remove from the baking sheet and cool completely on the rack.

4. To make the icing, combine the confectioners' sugar and water in a small bowl until blended. Add the red food coloring, a drop at a time, until the icing is light pink. Place a sheet of wax paper underneath the rack of cookies to catch the drips. Drizzle the icing on the cookies (about ½ teaspoon per cookie) to cover. Let dry completely.

Per serving (1 cookie): 52 Cal, 1 g Fat, 0 g Sat Fat, 0 mg Chol, 43 mg Sod, 10 g Carb, 0 g Fib, 0 g Prot, 1 mg Calc. **POINTS: 1.**

---

*Chef's Tip:* Transform these yummy cookies into shower favors. While they're still warm, take a wooden skewer and poke a hole in the top of each cookie. After they've cooled, tie a pretty ribbon through each. You can even personalize the cookies by piping the names of your guests on each cookie with tubes of writing gel found in the baking section of most supermarkets.

*Bridal Punch, Iced Heart Cookies, and Chocolate-Dipped Strawberries*

# Chocolate-Dipped Strawberries

**MAKES 12 SERVINGS**

These showstoppers will dazzle and delight your guests. The chocolate melting wafers are good for coating the berries, as they harden nicely and hold up well. The wafers can be found in some supermarkets in the produce section, often right alongside the berries. You can also find them in candy shops. These strawberries are too delicate to be made the night before, so it's best to make them the day of your party. They will hold up at room temperature for three to four hours.

12 **large strawberries (about ½ pound)**

2 **ounces chocolate melting wafers**

2 **ounces white melting wafers**

1½ **tablespoons shredded sweetened coconut,**

1 **tablespoon finely chopped pecans**

1. Line a large baking sheet with wax paper. Rinse and completely dry the strawberries.

2. Melt the chocolate wafers in a small pan over low heat, stirring frequently, until melted and smooth. Melt the white wafers in another small pan over low heat, stirring frequently, until melted and smooth. To prevent the melting wafers from getting too hard while dipping the berries, return them to low heat occasionally and stir frequently.

3. Place the coconut on 1 sheet of wax paper and the pecans on another.

4. Dip 1 strawberry at a time into one of the melted coatings so that the coating comes up about halfway. Shake off the excess or gently scrape the bottom of the berry across the rim of the pan, being careful not to scrape off too much coating. Roll in one of the toppings or leave plain and place on the baking sheet. Repeat with the remaining berries, coatings, and toppings, making a total of 6 chocolate- and 6 white-dipped berries. Let stand at least 20 minutes to dry completely. Serve at room temperature.

Per serving (1 strawberry): 62 Cal, 4 g Fat, 2 g Sat Fat, 1 mg Chol, 7 mg Sod, 8 g Carb, 1 g Fib, 1 g Prot, 15 mg Calc. **POINTS: 1.**

*Chef's Tip:* Make sure to buy large strawberries with the stems attached. They must be completely dry before dipping. To do this, rinse the berries, place them on a tray lined with several sheets of paper towels, blot the tops of the berries with paper towels, then let them air dry completely.

# *summer*

# A SUMMER WEDDING

*Thyme-Flavored Mini Crab Cakes*
—
*Jerk Chicken Kebabs with Pineapple Dipping Sauce*
—
*Savory Flatbread Spirals*
—
*Warm Tomato And Mesclun Salad with Goat Cheese Croutons*
—
*Slow-Baked Salmon with Cucumber-Chive Raita*
—
*Sugar Snap Peas and Asparagus with Tarragon Butter*
—
*Poppy and Sesame Seed Dinner Rolls*
—
*Almond Dove Cookies*

## Thyme-Flavored Mini Crab Cakes

**MAKES 12 SERVINGS**

It's a celebration! While lump crabmeat is a splurge, it's worth it to get the wonderful sweet flavor in these mini cakes. Small enough to eat in two bites, these crab cakes can be made ahead, cooled, then stored in an airtight container in the refrigerator for up to 24 hours. To reheat, bring the crab cakes to room temperature, then heat in a 350°F oven until hot, about 8 minutes.

¼ cup light mayonnaise

1 large egg

⅓ cup minced shallots

⅓ cup minced red bell pepper

2 tablespoons fresh lemon juice

2 teaspoons minced fresh thyme

1½ teaspoons hot pepper sauce

½ teaspoon salt

6 slices firm white bread, made into fine crumbs

1 pound cooked lump crabmeat, picked over

1¼ tablespoons olive or vegetable oil

*1.* Combine the mayonnaise, egg, shallots, bell pepper, juice, thyme, hot pepper sauce, and salt in a bowl. Stir in ⅓ cup of the bread crumbs and the crab. Cover and refrigerate about 2 hours.
*2.* Form the crab mixture into 24 (2-inch) cakes. Coat with remaining bread crumbs; place on wax paper. Preheat oven to 350°F. Spray a large nonstick baking sheet with nonstick spray.
*3.* Heat a nonstick skillet over medium-high heat. Swirl in 1½ teaspoons of the oil, then add 8 of the crab cakes and cook until golden, 1½–2 minutes on each side. Transfer to the baking sheet. Repeat twice more with the remaining oil and crab cakes. Bake the crab cakes until cooked through, 8–10 minutes.

Per serving (2 crab cakes): 106 Cal, 5 g Fat, 1 g Sat Fat, 57 mg Chol, 309 mg Sod, 6 g Carb, 1 g Fib, 9 g Prot, 54 mg Calc. ***POINTS: 2.***

# Jerk Chicken Kebabs with Pineapple Dipping Sauce

**MAKES 12 SERVINGS**

Aromatic jerk seasoning and a rum-spiked pineapple dipping sauce transform everyday chicken chunks into delicious appetizers. You can toss the chicken chunks with the dry seasonings and refrigerate them in the zip-close plastic bag for up to a day. The dipping sauce can be made ahead and kept in the refrigerator for up to two days (stir in the jalapeño just before serving).

1 **(20-ounce) can crushed pineapple in juice**
½ **cup sugar**
⅓ **cup chopped red onion**
2 **tablespoons rum**
2 **teaspoons white vinegar**
1 **teaspoon salt**
½ **jalapeño pepper, seeded and chopped (wear gloves to prevent irritation)**
2 **teaspoons jerk seasoning**
2 **teaspoons onion powder**
2 **teaspoons paprika**
1½ **pounds skinless boneless chicken thighs, cut into 36 (about 1½-inch) chunks**
1 **teaspoon vegetable oil**

*1.* To prepare the dipping sauce, drain the pineapple through a sieve over a medium saucepan to reserve the juice. Set the pineapple aside. Stir the sugar into the juice and bring to a boil. Reduce the heat and simmer, uncovered, until thickened, 7–8 minutes.

*2.* Add the onion and simmer 2 minutes. Remove from the heat; add the pineapple and let cool. Transfer the mixture to a food processor. Add the rum, vinegar, and ½ teaspoon of the salt; pulse to a coarse applesauce consistency. Stir in the jalapeño.

*3.* Combine the jerk seasoning, onion powder, paprika, and remaining ½ teaspoon salt in a zip-close plastic bag. Dry the chicken with paper towels and add to the bag; toss to coat.

*4.* Preheat the oven to 350°F. Heat a large nonstick skillet over medium-high heat. Swirl in the oil, then add half the chicken and cook until well browned, turning occasionally, about 5 minutes. Transfer the chicken to a jelly-roll pan. Repeat with the remaining chicken. Skewer 1 piece of chicken onto each of 36 wooden sandwich picks. Bake on the jelly-roll pan until the chicken is cooked through, 10–12 minutes. Serve with the dipping sauce.

Per serving (3 pieces chicken with 2 tablespoons dipping sauce): 159 Cal, 4 g Fat, 1 g Sat Fat, 38 mg Chol, 232 mg Sod, 17 g Carb, 1 g Fib, 12 g Prot, 23 mg Calc. *POINTS: 3.*

———◆———

*Chef's Tip:* If you have access to fresh grape leaves, rinse them and use to line a large platter. Arrange the kebabs on top. Serve the sauce in a bowl alongside the kebabs.

# Savory Flatbread Spirals

**MAKES 36 SERVINGS**

To make these tasty bites ahead of time, cool the baked spirals completely
on a rack, then wrap and freeze for up to two weeks. To serve warm, heat the frozen
spirals on a baking sheet in a 350°F oven, 6 to 8 minutes.

**DOUGH**

- ½ cup warm (105–115°F) water
- ½ teaspoon sugar
- 1 package active dry yeast
- ½ cup low-fat (1%) milk
- 1 tablespoon extra-virgin olive oil
- 2⅓–2½ cups all-purpose flour
- ½ teaspoon kosher salt
- 2 tablespoons cornmeal

**FILLING**

- 1½ teaspoons extra-virgin olive oil
- 4–5 large shallots, finely chopped
- ⅓ cup sun-dried tomato strips in oil, drained well and finely chopped
- 1 tablespoon fresh thyme, minced
- 1 tablespoon fresh rosemary, minced
- 1 large garlic clove, minced
- ¾ teaspoon kosher salt
- ½ cup shredded pepperjack cheese
- 1 egg white, lightly beaten

*1.* To make the dough, combine the water and sugar in a 2-cup measuring cup; sprinkle in the yeast and let stand until foamy, about 5 minutes. Stir in the milk and oil. Combine the flour and salt in a food processor. With the machine running, pour the yeast mixture through the feed tube; pulse about 1 minute, until the dough forms a ball. Turn the dough onto a lightly floured surface and knead a few times until smooth. Cover the dough lightly with plastic wrap; let stand 15 minutes. Arrange the oven racks in the top third and middle of the oven. Preheat the oven to 425°F. Sprinkle 2 large baking sheets with the cornmeal.

*2.* Meanwhile, to make the filling, heat a large nonstick skillet over medium heat. Swirl in the oil, then add the shallots and cook, stirring occasionally, until lightly browned, 3–4 minutes; let cool. Combine the shallots, sun-dried tomato, thyme, rosemary, garlic, and ¼ teaspoon of the salt in a small bowl.

*3.* Sprinkle a work surface lightly with flour. Turn the dough onto the surface and cut in two. Roll each piece of dough to a 10 × 20-inch rectangle. Spread the shallot mixture over both rectangles, then sprinkle each with ¼ cup of the cheese. Starting from one long end, roll up each rectangle tightly. Pinch the seams closed and place seam-side down on a board. Cut each roll into 18 (½-inch) slices, making a total of 36 pieces. Using a small spatula, transfer the slices, cut-side up, about ½ inch apart, onto the baking sheets. Lightly brush the tops with the egg white and sprinkle with the remaining ½ teaspoon salt.

*4.* Bake the spirals until deep golden, 12–14 minutes. Serve at once, or transfer to a rack to cool and serve at room temperature.

Per serving (1 spiral): 48 Cal, 1 g Fat, 0 g Sat Fat, 2 mg Chol, 70 mg Sod, 7 g Carb, 0 g Fib, 2 g Prot, 20 mg Calc. **POINTS: 1.**

# *Warm Tomato and Mesclun Salad with Goat Cheese Croutons*

**MAKES 12 SERVINGS**

A marriage made in heaven—warm tomatoes, creamy goat-cheese croutons, and mesclun greens mingled with a fruity, piquant dressing—this salad will dazzle your guests. The croutons can be made the day before, but need to be sautéed at the last minute. The vinaigrette can be prepared up to two hours ahead and kept at room temperature.

**CROUTONS**
- ¼ **pound goat cheese**
- ½ **cup farmer cheese**
- 1 **garlic clove, minced**
  **Pinch dried thyme**
- 1 **large egg, lightly beaten**
- ½ **cup dry bread crumbs**

**VINAIGRETTE**
- 1 **cup seedless red grapes**
- 2 **tablespoons white balsamic vinegar**
- 1½ **tablespoons extra-virgin olive oil**
- 1 **garlic clove**
- 2 **teaspoons Dijon mustard**
- ¾ **teaspoon salt**
- ¼ **teaspoon white pepper**

**SALAD**
- 1 **teaspoon extra-virgin olive oil**
- 2 **pints red grape tomatoes**
- 1 **pint golden grape tomatoes**
- ⅓ **cup snipped fresh chives**
- 1 **pound (about 12 cups) mesclun greens**

*1.* To make the croutons, puree the goat cheese, farmer cheese, garlic, and thyme in a food processor. Form into 12 (½ -inch) disks; place on a sheet of wax paper. Dip each disk into the egg and then coat lightly with the breadcrumbs. Place on a large flat plate, cover lightly with plastic wrap, and refrigerate until firm, at least 1 hour or up to 24 hours.

*2.* To make the vinaigrette, puree the grapes, vinegar, oil, garlic, mustard, salt, and pepper in a blender.

*3.* To make the salad, heat a large nonstick skillet over medium-high heat. Swirl in the oil, then add the tomatoes and heat just until very warm. Add the chives, transfer to a bowl, and keep warm. Wipe the skillet with a paper towel.

*4.* Spray the same skillet with nonstick spray and set over medium-high heat. Add the cheese disks and cook until browned, 1–2 minutes on each side.

*5.* Toss the mesclun greens with the vinaigrette in a large bowl; divide among 12 side plates. Top each with ⅓ cup tomatoes and 1 goat cheese crouton. Serve at once.

Per serving (1 cup mesclun with ⅓ cup tomatoes and 1 crouton): 106 Cal, 6 g Fat, 2 g Sat Fat, 27 mg Chol, 269 mg Sod, 11 g Carb, 2 g Fib, 5 g Prot, 96 mg Calc. ***POINTS: 2.***

# Slow-Baked Salmon with Cucumber-Chive Raita

**MAKES 12 SERVINGS**

Baking salmon slowly at a low temperature ensures that it will stay moist and a little rosy in the center. You can make the raita up to eight hours ahead and keep it in the refrigerator until serving time.

3 cups plain fat-free yogurt
1 large seedless cucumber, peeled and diced
1 bunch fresh chives, snipped
1¼ teaspoons salt
12 (4-ounce) center-cut salmon fillets
¼ teaspoon freshly ground pepper

*1.* Combine the yogurt, cucumber, chives, and ¼ teaspoon of the salt in a medium bowl. Cover and refrigerate at least 20 minutes or up to 8 hours.

*2.* Preheat the oven to 300°F. Spray a large broiler pan with nonstick spray.

*3.* Sprinkle the salmon with the remaining 1 teaspoon salt and the pepper; arrange almost touching in the pan. Bake until opaque on the outside with a rosy center, 15–17 minutes. Continue baking, checking every 1–2 minutes for more well-cooked fish. Serve with the raita.

Per serving (1 salmon fillet with generous ⅓ cup raita): 200 Cal, 7 g Fat, 2 g Sat Fat, 76 mg Chol, 357 mg Sod, 6 g Carb, 0 g Fib, 28 g Prot, 141 mg Calc. ***POINTS: 5.***

———◆———

*Chef's Tip:* For a large-platter presentation, thinly slice an unpeeled seedless cucumber and overlap on the platter to cover the bottom. Arrange the salmon on the cucumber, top each fillet with two crisscrossed chives, and garnish the platter with lime wedges. Serve the raita in a bowl alongside.

*Slow-Baked Salmon with Cucumber-Chive Raita, Sugar Snap Peas and Asparagus with Tarragon Butter, and Poppy and Sesame Seed Dinner Roll*

# Sugar Snap Peas and Asparagus with Tarragon Butter

### MAKES 12 SERVINGS

Crisp sugar snap peas and tender spring asparagus dressed with buttered tarragon and chives combine for an elegant side dish. To make ahead, cook the vegetables as directed, then plunge immediately into ice water; drain well. Pack in a zip-close plastic bag with paper towels and refrigerate for up to a day. To reheat, toss the vegetables with the melted-butter mixture and microwave on High, 2 to 3 minutes.

1½ tablespoons unsalted butter

1–2 tablespoons minced fresh tarragon

1 tablespoon snipped fresh chives

¾ teaspoon salt

¼ teaspoon freshly ground pepper

1 pound fresh sugar snap peas, trimmed

2 pounds fresh asparagus, fibrous stem ends trimmed

*1.* Melt the butter in a large microwavable bowl on High, 30–40 seconds. Cool to just warm. Stir in the tarragon, chives, salt, and pepper.

*2.* Meanwhile, fill a large Dutch oven two-thirds full with water; bring to a boil. Add the sugar snap peas and cook until just crisp-tender, 2–3 minutes. Transfer with a slotted spoon to the bowl with the butter. Add the asparagus to the water and cook until just crisp-tender, 3–5 minutes. Drain and add to the bowl with the sugar snap peas; toss gently to coat. Serve at once.

Per serving (¾ cup): 38 Cal, 2 g Fat, 1 g Sat Fat, 4 mg Chol, 148 mg Sod, 4 g Carb, 2 g Fib, 2 g Prot, 25 mg Calc. *POINTS: 1.*

—◆—

*Chef's Tip:* If you prefer a more subtle flavor, substitute fresh chervil for the tarragon—they each have a slightly spicy anise flavor, but tarragon tends to be stronger. Arrange the asparagus and sugar snap peas on a large oval platter and garnish with fresh tarragon leaves.

# Poppy and Sesame Seed Dinner Rolls

**MAKES 12 SERVINGS**

These soft dinner rolls are made with an old-fashioned touch by adding a small amount of rye flour. To make the rolls ahead of time, wrap the cooled rolls, then freeze for up to a month. To serve warm, place the frozen rolls on a baking sheet and heat in a 350°F oven, 8 to 10 minutes.

¾ cup warm (105–115°F) water
1 teaspoon sugar
1 package active dry yeast
2 tablespoons honey
1 tablespoon unsalted butter, melted
2 cups all-purpose flour
¼ cup rye flour
1 teaspoon kosher salt
1 egg white, lightly beaten
1½ teaspoons poppy seeds
¾ teaspoon each sesame seeds and black sesame seeds, mixed

*1.* Combine the water and sugar in a 2-cup measuring cup; sprinkle in the yeast and let stand until foamy, about 5 minutes. Stir in the honey and butter.

*2.* Combine the all-purpose flour, rye flour, and salt in a food processor. With the machine running, pour the yeast mixture through the feed tube; pulse about 1 minute until the dough forms a ball. Turn the dough out onto a lightly floured surface and knead a few times until smooth.

*3.* Spray a large bowl with nonstick spray; put the dough in the bowl. Cover lightly with plastic wrap and let the dough rise in a warm spot until it doubles in size, about 1¼ hours.

*4.* Spray a 12-cup muffin tin with nonstick spray. Punch down the dough. Sprinkle a work surface lightly with flour. Turn the dough onto the surface and cut into 12 pieces. Shape each piece into a ball and place in the muffin tins. Lightly brush the tops of the rolls with the egg white and sprinkle 6 rolls with the poppy seeds and 6 rolls with the sesame seed mixture. Cover lightly with plastic wrap and let rise in a warm spot until they double in size, about 30 minutes. Preheat the oven to 375°F.

*5.* Bake the rolls until they sound hollow when tapped, 14–16 minutes. Remove the rolls from the muffin cups and cool on a rack. Serve warm or at room temperature.

Per serving (1 roll): 111 Cal, 2 g Fat, 1 g Sat Fat, 3 mg Chol, 136 mg Sod, 21 g Carb, 1 g Fib, 3 g Prot, 11 mg Calc. **POINTS: 2.**

◆

*Chef's Tip:* To make the rolls by hand, combine the water, sugar, and yeast in a large bowl; set aside until foamy. Stir in the honey and butter. Stir in the all-purpose flour, rye flour, and salt until the dough starts to gather around the spoon. Turn out the dough on a lightly floured surface; knead until the dough is smooth and elastic, about 10 minutes.

# Almond Dove Cookies

**MAKES 24 SERVINGS**

Cake flour and almonds give these cookies a tender crispness, although we use
only half the butter called for in most butter cookie recipes. The cookies will keep in airtight
containers at room temperature for up to three weeks. If you don't have dove-shaped
cookie cutters, use any other 2¼-inch cookie cutter.

⅓ cup granulated sugar

¼ cup sliced blanched almonds,
   lightly toasted

¼ cup unsalted butter, softened

½ teaspoon almond extract

1 egg yolk

1 cup cake flour (not self-rising)

3 tablespoons confectioners'
   sugar

⅛ teaspoon salt

*1.* Pulse the granulated sugar and almonds in a food processor
until finely ground. Add the butter and almond extract; process,
scraping the bowl once, until lightly fluffy, 1 minute. Add the egg
yolk and pulse to combine. Add the flour, 2 tablespoons of the
confectioners' sugar, and the salt; pulse just until a dough forms.
*2.* Preheat the oven to 350°F. Line 2 large baking sheets with
parchment paper. Divide the dough in half. On a lightly floured
surface, roll out each piece ⅛-inch thick. Using a dove-shaped
cookie cutter or other 2¼-inch cutter, cut out the cookies,
re-rolling the scraps of dough to make a total of 24 cookies. With
a spatula, place 1 inch apart on the baking sheets. Bake 1 sheet at
a time, until the cookies are still light on top and golden on the
bottom, 8–9 minutes. Remove the cookies from the baking
sheets and cool completely on racks. Dust with the remaining
1 tablespoon confectioners' sugar.

Per serving (1 cookie): 57 Cal, 3 g Fat, 1 g Sat Fat, 14 mg Chol, 12 mg Sod,
7 g Carb, 0 g Fib, 1 g Prot, 5 mg Calc. ***POINTS: 1.***

———◆———

*Chef's Tip:* The dough may be soft, but it will roll out easily on a well-floured surface. If you're a
novice cookie baker, and the dough is too soft to manage, scrape it onto a piece of plastic wrap, flatten
to form a disk, and refrigerate until firm (about two hours); then roll out. Arrange the cookies on a
fitting bed—a red or pink rose petal–lined platter.

# Cutting a Wedding Cake

The cutting and the serving of a wedding cake symbolize the bride and groom's commitment to caring for each other. To make the job less messy, especially when you must cut the cake in full view of guests, set yourself up ahead of time. You need a knife with a long thin blade, a cake server or spatula, a pitcher filled with hot water to clean the knife as you work, and stacked plates.

*1.* After the traditional piece has been cut and consumed by the bride and groom, lift the top tier carefully from the cake and set it aside, to be frozen later. To properly freeze this cake to last until the couple's first anniversary, set the cake on a baking sheet or plate and let it freeze, uncovered, until the frosting and decorations are completely solid. Wrap the tier loosely but completely in several layers of plastic wrap.

*2.* Cut the remaining cake tiers in a specific manner, according to their diameter, so that the slices are even and attractive. Cakes that are more than 10 inches in diameter should be cut as shown in the accompanying photographs. Cut around the cake, at a distance of about 3 inches in from the edge, then cut slices from that ring.

*3.* Repeat, cutting rings from the outer portion of the cake and dividing them into slices, until the diameter of the cake is less than 6 inches. For the remaining inner 6-inch circle of cake, cut into slices, as you would for any other small cake.

# FATHER'S DAY DINNER

*Carpaccio-Wrapped Watercress with Blue Cheese Dip*
—
*Hearty Split Pea Soup*
—
*Pistachio-Crusted Tuna*
—
*Grilled Vidalia Onions*
—
*Garlic-Rosemary Potatoes*
—
*Sautéed Sesame Spinach*
—
*Black Pepper Biscuits with Smoked Trout Spread*
—
*Chocolate Cream Pie*

## Carpaccio-Wrapped Watercress with Blue Cheese Dip

**MAKES 8 SERVINGS**

Carpaccio is an Italian appetizer of paper-thin shavings of raw beef fillet. To make slicing easier, freeze the fillet until firm, about 20 minutes.

½ cup yogurt cheese*
2 tablespoons light sour cream
2 tablespoons fat-free buttermilk
2 tablespoons crumbled blue cheese
1 tablespoon minced chives
⅛ teaspoon salt
Freshly ground pepper, to taste
2 bunches watercress, trimmed to 2½-inch lengths
8 (½-ounce) paper-thin slices raw beef tenderloin, trimmed of all visible fat

*1.* To make the dip, combine the yogurt cheese, sour cream, buttermilk, blue cheese, chives, salt, and pepper in a bowl. Refrigerate at least 1 hour or up to 2 days.

*2.* Divide the watercress into 8 equal portions. Place 1 slice of the beef on a counter; place 1 portion of the watercress on top and roll up. Repeat with the remaining beef and watercress to make 8 bundles. Transfer the bundles to a cutting board. With a very sharp knife, cut each bundle crosswise in half. Serve with the dip.

*To make ½ cup yogurt cheese, spoon 1 cup plain fat-free yogurt into a coffee filter- or cheesecloth-lined strainer; set over a bowl. Refrigerate, covered, at least 24 hours. To make enough yogurt cheese for this entire menu (including the Smoked Trout Spread and the Chocolate Cream Pie), start with 3½ cups plain fat-free yogurt.

Per serving (2 pieces with 1½ tablespoons dip): 41 Cal, 3 g Fat, 1g Sat Fat, 9 mg Chol, 44 mg Sod, 1 g Carb, 0 g Fib, 2 g Prot, 12 mg Calc. *POINTS: 1.*

# Hearty Split Pea Soup

**MAKES 8 SERVINGS**

Nothing is quite as satisfying as a bowl of piping-hot pea soup. We pureed the
soup to give it a touch of elegance, and thanks to the potatoes, it's especially smooth
and creamy. The bay leaf and clove add a welcome hint of sweetness.

1 tablespoon vegetable oil
1 onion, diced
1 leek, cleaned and sliced
1 garlic clove, minced
4½ cups low-sodium chicken or
    vegetable broth
2 cups chopped, peeled
    all-purpose potatoes
1½ cups split peas, picked over,
    rinsed, and drained
1 carrot, chopped
1 celery stalk, chopped
½ teaspoon salt
Freshly ground pepper, to taste
4–5 whole black peppercorns
1 bay leaf
1 whole clove

1. Heat a large soup pot over medium-high heat. Swirl in the oil, then add the onion, leek, and garlic. Cook, stirring frequently, until softened, about 6 minutes.

2. Add the chicken broth, potatoes, split peas, carrot, celery, salt, and ground pepper; bring to a boil. Reduce the heat and simmer, covered, 20 minutes.

3. Meanwhile, combine the peppercorns, bay leaf, and clove in a double-thick piece of cheesecloth; tie the cheesecloth with a piece of kitchen string.

4. Add the spice bag to the soup and simmer until the split peas are soft, about 30 minutes longer.

5. Let the soup cool slightly. Discard the spice bag and puree the soup, in batches, in a blender or food processor. Return the soup to the pot and reheat.

Per serving (¾ cup): 142 Cal, 1 g Fat, 0 g Sat Fat, 10 mg Chol, 750 mg Sod, 21 g Carb, 7 g Fib, 12 g Prot, 71 mg Calc. *POINTS: 2.*

## Creating a Crisp Crust

Bread crumbs can give fish, poultry, and meats a crisp, crunchy coating. Instead of frying the coated foods, we bake them in a hot oven and still get that sought-after golden crispy finish—without all the fat. Soft white bread crumbs adhere best to meats, poultry, and fish. Adding fresh or dried herbs, freshly ground pepper, grated Parmesan, or even chopped nuts can give delicious variety to the flavor and color of the crust.

*1.* Combine the coating ingredients in a shallow pie plate. Blend them with your fingertips to evenly distribute any seasonings. Dip the food into the coating, pressing all sides into the mixture to coat the food completely.

*2.* Bake the coated foods on a dark, nonstick baking sheet, uncovered, until they are cooked through with a crisp, deep golden crust. A light touch of nonstick spray on both sides of the food before baking will help the browning process. Use a thin-bladed spatula to lift the food from the pan without disturbing the crust.

# Pistachio-Crusted Tuna

**MAKES 8 SERVINGS**

This dish is a welcome change from the typical butter-laden trout with almonds. We use fresh tuna for its rich, meaty color and texture, then add a sophisticated pistachio nut coating, and roast (versus pan-fry) the fish to achieve a crispy crust. For variety, try this recipe with salmon fillets or skinless boneless chicken breasts.

2 tablespoons fresh lemon juice

1 tablespoon minced
   flat-leaf parsley

2 teaspoons minced
   fresh chives

2 garlic cloves, minced

1 teaspoon vegetable oil

1 teaspoon ground coriander

½ teaspoon salt

Freshly ground pepper, to taste

8 (4-ounce) tuna steaks

¾ cup fresh white bread crumbs

½ cup unsalted pistachios,
   toasted and chopped

*1.* Combine the lemon juice, parsley, chives, garlic, oil, coriander, salt, and pepper in a large zip-close plastic bag; add the tuna. Squeeze out the air and seal the bag; turn to coat the tuna. Refrigerate, turning the bag occasionally, about 2 hours.

*2.* Preheat the oven to 400°F. Combine the bread crumbs and pistachios on a plate; add the tuna, one piece at a time, turning to coat evenly.

*3.* Transfer the tuna to a 9 × 13-inch nonstick baking pan. Bake until the crust is browned and the tuna is cooked through, 6–10 minutes.

Per serving (1 tuna steak): 290 Cal, 13 g Fat, 2.5 g Sat Fat, 145 mg Chol, 160 mg Sod, 14 g Carb, 2 g Fib, 30 g Prot, 64 mg Calc. ***POINTS: 6.***

———◆———

*Chef's Tip:* Instead of cutting the tuna into steaks, ask your fishmonger for a 2-pound piece of the loin. Prepare the recipe as directed, except roast the tuna in a 350°F oven about 20 minutes and slice it at the table. If the tuna is fully cooked after roasting but the crust did not brown, simply broil the steaks 5 inches from the heat until crisp.

*Pistachio-Crusted Tuna, Grilled Vidalia Onions, and Garlic-Rosemary Potatoes*

# Grilled Vidalia Onions

**MAKES 8 SERVINGS**

Super-sweet, juicy Vidalia onions, which hail from Georgia, are at their peak from May through June—perfect timing for our Father's Day feast. In fact, these onions are often readily available at the supermarket, so here's an excellent opportunity to experience their unique flavor.

8 **small Vidalia onions**

2 **teaspoons chopped**
  **fresh rosemary**

2 **teaspoons chopped**
  **fresh thyme**

½ **teaspoon salt**

**Freshly ground pepper, to taste**

¼ **cup balsamic vinegar**

*1.* Prepare the grill for indirect heating (by heating only one side of the grill). Cut 16 (12-inch) squares of foil; set aside.

*2.* Peel the onions; trim a thin slice from the root end so the onions can stand upright, but leave the root intact. Place 1 onion, root end-down, on a cutting board. Make 3 or 4 horizontal cuts across the onion, but do not cut all the way through. Stack 2 squares of foil; transfer the onion to the center. Repeat with the remaining onions and foil.

*3.* Combine the rosemary, thyme, salt, and pepper in a cup; sprinkle evenly over the onions. Press the foil up against the side of each onion to form a pouch, leaving the top of the onions exposed. Pour 1½ teaspoons of the vinegar into each pouch.

*4.* Place the onions over the indirect heat section (the unheated side) of the grill. Grill the onions until very tender, about 1 hour. Remove the foil from each onion, reserving the juice from each pouch. Arrange the onions on a plate, and drizzle with the juices.

Per serving (1 onion): 35 Cal, 0 g Fat, 0 g Sat Fat, 0 mg Chol, 150 mg Sod, 8 g Carb, 2 g Fib, 1 g Prot, 22 mg Calc. ***POINTS: 0.***

———◆———

*Chef's Tip:* Leaving the root end of the onions intact helps hold them together as they grill. If you want a jump start, prepare the onions as directed through Step 3; place on a baking sheet and let stand at room temperature for up to 12 hours.

# Garlic-Rosemary Potatoes

**MAKES 8 SERVINGS**

New potatoes are young potatoes of any variety. These tubers retain their shape beautifully when cooked, so they're ideal for this simple pan roast. New potatoes are in season from spring to early summer, so take advantage of the contrasting colors available. Red Bliss, Yukon Gold, blue, even purple are some of the delicious choices.

8 **small red new potatoes**
1 **tablespoon olive oil**
2 **teaspoons fresh lemon juice**
1 **garlic clove, minced**
1 **teaspoon chopped**
 **fresh rosemary**
¼ **teaspoon salt**
**Freshly ground pepper, to taste**

*1.* Preheat the oven to 400°F. Spray an 8-inch square baking dish with nonstick spray.

*2.* Bring the potatoes and enough cold water to cover to a boil in a medium saucepan. Reduce the heat and simmer until partially cooked, 10–12 minutes.

*3.* Drain the potatoes; transfer to the baking dish. Drizzle with the oil and lemon juice. Sprinkle with the garlic, rosemary, salt, and pepper. Roast, turning occasionally, until the skins are golden and the potatoes are tender when pierced with a fork, about 20 minutes.

Per serving (1 potato): 90 Cal, 2 g Fat, 0 g Sat Fat, 0 mg Chol, 80 mg Sod, 17 g Carb, 1 g Fib, 2 g Prot, 7 mg Calc. *POINTS: 2.*

———◆———

*Chef's Tip:* To make ahead, partially cook the potatoes as directed in Step 2, then cover and refrigerate overnight. Roast the potatoes up to two hours ahead the next day, then reheat in the oven or enjoy them at room temperature.

# Sautéed Sesame Spinach

MAKES 8 SERVINGS

This quick, iron-rich sauté combines fresh spinach with the nutty taste of toasted sesame seeds. Diced red onion, bell pepper, and tomato provide additional color and crunch.

1 tablespoon olive oil

1 red onion, diced

1 red bell pepper, seeded and diced

2 garlic cloves, minced

2 (10-ounce) bags triple-washed spinach leaves, cleaned

1 tomato, peeled, seeded, and chopped

2 tablespoons sesame seeds, toasted

½ teaspoon salt

Freshly ground pepper, to taste

*1.* Heat a large nonstick skillet over high heat. Swirl in the oil, then add the onion, bell pepper, and garlic. Cook, stirring frequently, until golden brown, 10–12 minutes.

*2.* Add the spinach, a handful or two at a time. Cook, stirring frequently, until the spinach starts to wilt, 4–5 minutes.

*3.* Add the tomato. Cook, stirring frequently, until the tomato is very hot and tender, about 2 minutes longer. Sprinkle with the sesame seeds, salt, and pepper. Serve at once.

Per serving (⅓ cup): 76 Cal, 4 g Fat, 0 g Sat Fat, 0 mg Chol, 54 mg Sod, 7 g Carb, 1 g Fib, 1 g Prot, 46 mg Calc. *POINTS: 2.*

*Chef's Tip:* To toast the sesame seeds, place them in a small dry skillet over medium-low heat. Cook, shaking the pan and stirring constantly, until lightly browned and fragrant, 1 to 2 minutes. Watch them carefully; sesame seeds can burn quickly. Transfer the toasted seeds to a plate to cool.

# Black Pepper Biscuits with Smoked Trout Spread

**MAKES 16 SERVINGS**

Dad will love these peppery mini-biscuits filled with creamy smoked trout spread.
Look for smoked trout in the deli section of the supermarket.

2 cups all-purpose flour
1 tablespoon sugar
2 teaspoons baking powder
½ teaspoon cracked
  black pepper
¼ teaspoon baking soda
¼ teaspoon salt
¼ cup butter, chopped
  and chilled
1¼ cups fat-free buttermilk
½ cup yogurt cheese*
2 tablespoons light sour cream
3 tablespoons flaked
  smoked trout

*1.* Preheat the oven to 400°F. Spray a baking sheet with nonstick spray.

*2.* To make the biscuits, combine the flour, sugar, baking powder, pepper, baking soda, and salt in a large bowl. With a pastry blender or 2 knives, cut the butter into the dry ingredients to form fine crumbs. Make a well in the center; add 1 cup of the buttermilk and mix just until blended.

*3.* Turn the dough onto a lightly floured surface; roll out to ½-inch thickness. With a 2-inch round biscuit cutter, cut out 16 biscuits. Arrange the biscuits on the baking sheet. Lightly brush the tops with 2 tablespoons of the buttermilk. Bake until golden brown, 12–15 minutes. Remove from the baking sheet and cool completely on a rack.

*4.* To make the smoked trout spread, combine the yogurt cheese, sour cream, and the remaining 2 tablespoons buttermilk in a bowl; stir in the trout.

*5.* Split the biscuits. Spread each bottom half with 2 teaspoons of the smoked trout spread; top with the remaining biscuit half.

*To make ½ cup yogurt cheese, spoon 1 cup plain fat-free yogurt into a coffee filter- or cheesecloth-lined strainer; set over a bowl. Refrigerate, covered, at least 24 hours.

Per serving (1 biscuit): 100 Cal, 4 g Fat, 3 g Sat Fat, 10 mg Chol, 120 mg Sod, 15 g Carb, 0 g Fib, 3 g Prot, 42 mg Calc. ***POINTS: 2.***

———◆———

*Chef's Tip:* You can freeze the biscuits in a zip-close plastic bag for up to three weeks. Reheat the frozen biscuits in a 250°F oven, about 10 minutes.

# Chocolate Cream Pie

**MAKES 12 SERVINGS**

This luscious dessert is so rich and satiny smooth, it's positively decadent! The combination of semisweet chocolate and cocoa powder in the filling is the secret to its deep, dark chocolate taste.

**2 cups graham cracker crumbs**
**7 tablespoons sugar**
**2 tablespoons water**
**1 egg white, lightly beaten**
**¾ cup yogurt cheese,\* at room temperature**
**1½ ounces semisweet chocolate, melted and cooled to room temperature**
**4 egg whites**
**¼ cup unsweetened cocoa powder**

*1.* Preheat the oven to 325°F. Spray an 8-inch pie plate with nonstick spray.

*2.* To make the crust, combine the graham cracker crumbs and 2 tablespoons of the sugar in a bowl with a fork. Add the water and the beaten egg white; mix well. Press the crumb mixture evenly into the pie plate. Bake until the crust is set and lightly browned, about 8 minutes. Cool on a rack while preparing the filling.

*3.* To make the filling, combine the yogurt cheese and semisweet chocolate in a bowl until blended; set aside.

*4.* Combine the remaining 4 egg whites and the remaining 5 tablespoons sugar in a mixing bowl; set over a pot of 1 inch of simmering water. Stir until the sugar dissolves and the mixture is warm to the touch (about 110°F). Remove the mixing bowl from the heat. With a hand-held mixer at high speed, beat the mixture until the whites stand in medium, glossy peaks, about 6 minutes.

*5.* Using a large rubber spatula, gently fold half the beaten whites into the chocolate mixture, until almost combined. Repeat with the remaining beaten whites. Sift the cocoa powder over top of the mixture and fold gently until blended. Spoon the filling into the crust. Refrigerate at least 4 hours or overnight.

\*To make ¾ cup yogurt cheese, spoon 1½ cups plain fat-free yogurt into a coffee filter- or cheesecloth-lined strainer; set over a bowl. Refrigerate, covered, at least 24 hours.

Per serving (½2 of pie): 120 Cal, 3 g Fat, 1 g Sat Fat, 0 mg Chol, 65 mg Sod, 23 g Carb, 1 g Fib, 5 g Prot, 71 mg Calc. **POINTS: 2.**

———◆———

*Chef's Tip:* For best results, have all of the filling ingredients at room temperature before assembling.

# A GRADUATION CELEBRATION

*Cheese Straws*
—
*Chilled Corn and Avocado Gazpacho*
—
*Grilled Tuna with Mango-Blueberry Salsa*
—
*Minted Potato and Pea Salad*
—
*Couscous and White Beans with Apricots and Almonds*
—
*Mediterranean Green Beans and Tomatoes*
—
*Lemon Bars*
—
*Blueberry-Filled Cookie Cups*

## Cheese Straws

**MAKES 24 SERVINGS**

Extra-sharp cheddar cheese and flavorful shredded Parmesan make all the difference to these tempting savories, which make the perfect accompaniment to the gazpacho. Store in an airtight container at room temperature for up to two days or in the freezer for up to three months.

1 cup all-purpose flour
½ teaspoon coarsely ground pepper
⅛ teaspoon cayenne
5 tablespoons cold butter, cut into pieces
4 ounces extra-sharp cheddar cheese, shredded (1 cup)
¼ cup shredded Parmesan cheese
3–4 tablespoons cold water

*1.* Preheat the oven to 375°F. Combine the flour, coarsely ground pepper, and cayenne in a food processor. Add the butter and pulse until the mixture forms crumbs. Add the cheddar cheese, Parmesan cheese, and water; pulse until the mixture forms a ball.

*2.* Turn the dough onto a lightly floured surface and roll into a 9-inch square, about ¼-inch thick. Cut into 3 × ½-inch strips, making a total of 48.

*3.* Place the cheese strips on a large ungreased nonstick baking sheet and bake until golden, about 15 minutes. With a wide spatula, transfer the cheese straws to a rack to cool completely.

Per serving (2 cheese straws): 64 Cal, 4 g Fat, 3 g Sat Fat, 12 mg Chol, 65 mg Sod, 4 g Carb, 0 g Fib, 2 g Prot, 81 mg Calc. ***POINTS: 2.***

# Chilled Corn and Avocado Gazpacho

## MAKES 12 SERVINGS

Cool as ice and satisfyingly crunchy, this gazpacho is the perfect antidote for a steamy summer day. Fresh corn kernels (no need to cook them) add a surprising burst of sweetness, and the avocado mellows the spice from the jalapeño. You can make this soup up to three days ahead and store it, covered, in the refrigerator. Prepare the avocado no more than one hour ahead.

4 **ears fresh corn, husks and silks removed**

4 **medium yellow or red tomatoes, chopped**

2 **green bell peppers, seeded and diced**

2 **cucumbers, peeled, seeded, and diced**

1 **large red onion, finely chopped**

6 **cups tomato juice**

4 **cups low-sodium chicken or vegetable broth**

6 **tablespoons balsamic vinegar**

6 **tablespoons chopped fresh cilantro**

2 **garlic cloves, minced**

1 **jalapeño pepper, seeded and minced (wear gloves to prevent irritation)**

2 **avocados, peeled and diced**

2 **teaspoons fresh lime juice**

*1.* Cut the kernels from the corn cobs and place in an extra-large bowl. Add the tomatoes, bell peppers, cucumbers, and onion.

*2.* Combine the tomato juice, broth, vinegar, cilantro, garlic, and jalapeño pepper in a large bowl. Pour over the vegetables. Cover and refrigerate until well chilled, at least 3 hours or up to 3 days.

*3.* Just before serving, toss the avocados with the lime juice; serve alongside the gazpacho.

Per serving (1⅓ cups soup with 2 tablespoons avocado): 128 Cal, 5 g Fat, 1 g Sat Fat, 0 mg Chol, 470 mg Sod, 20 g Carb, 4 g Fib, 4 g Prot, 31 mg Calc. ***POINTS: 2.***

*Chef's Tip:* Pour the chilled soup into a large glass pitcher and set it in a bowl of ice. Have a ladle alongside the pitcher, so guests can scoop some of the vegetables from the bottom. Arrange glass tumblers on a tray to pour the soup into. Serve the avocado in a small glass bowl on the side.

# Grilled Tuna with Mango-Blueberry Salsa

**MAKES 12 SERVINGS**

It's easy to grill tuna for a crowd. Simply marinate the steaks the day before, then quickly sear them on a hot grill the day of the party. They're especially good when cooked medium-rare with a little pink in the center. The mango salsa can be made ahead of time and kept in the refrigerator for up to three days. If you prefer, marinate and grill a variety of seafood, such as tuna steaks, swordfish steaks, salmon fillets, and jumbo shrimp.

2 ripe mangos, peeled and diced
1 pint fresh blueberries, chopped
1 red onion, finely chopped
¼ cup chopped fresh cilantro
4 teaspoons grated lime rind
5 tablespoons fresh lime juice
2 teaspoons salt
½ teaspoon sugar
1 jalapeño pepper, seeded and finely chopped (wear gloves to prevent irritation)
12 (5-ounce) tuna steaks, about ¾-inch thick
1 teaspoon coarsely ground pepper
¾ teaspoon ground coriander

*1.* To prepare the salsa, combine the mangos, blueberries, onion, cilantro, 2 teaspoons of the lime rind, 2 tablespoons of the lime juice, 1 teaspoon of the salt, the sugar, and jalapeño pepper. Cover and refrigerate for at least 20 minutes or up to 3 days.

*2.* Sprinkle the tuna with the remaining 2 teaspoons lime rind, 3 tablespoons lime juice, 1 teaspoon salt, the ground pepper, and coriander. Refrigerate, covered, for at least 20 minutes or up to 24 hours.

*3.* Spray the grill rack with nonstick spray and prepare the grill, or spray a nonstick ridged grill pan with nonstick spray and set over medium-high heat. Grill the tuna, 5 inches from the heat, until browned on the outside but still a little pink in the center, 3–4 minutes on each side. Serve with the salsa.

Per serving (1 tuna steak with ½ cup salsa): 249 Cal, 7 g Fat, 2 g Sat Fat, 54 mg Chol, 447 mg Sod, 11 g Carb, 2 g Fib, 34 g Prot, 23 mg Calc. ***POINTS: 5.***

---

*Chef's Tip:* Serve the tuna steaks on a large Bibb lettuce–lined platter with a mound of salsa in the center.

# Minted Potato and Pea Salad

**MAKES 12 SERVINGS**

To best bring out the flavors of the mint and garlic, serve this potato salad warm or at room temperature.
Choose potatoes that are the same size so they cook evenly, taking care not to overcook them.
To make ahead, prepare the potato salad without the mint and refrigerate, covered, for up to two days.
Before serving, allow the salad to come to room temperature for about two hours, then stir in the mint.

2 **pounds small**
  **red-skinned potatoes**

2 **cups fresh or frozen tiny peas**

2 **tablespoons**
  **white-wine vinegar**

2 **tablespoons dry white wine**

2 **tablespoons extra-virgin**
  **olive oil**

1 **garlic clove, minced**

½ **teaspoon salt**

⅛ **teaspoon freshly**
  **ground pepper**

1 **cup fresh mint leaves,**
  **coarsely chopped**

*1.* With enough water to cover, bring the potatoes to a boil in a large saucepan. Reduce the heat and simmer, covered, until just tender, about 10 minutes, adding the peas during the last 2 minutes of cooking. Drain and let cool slightly. Cut the potatoes in half and place with the peas in a large bowl.

*2.* Meanwhile, combine the vinegar, wine, oil, garlic, salt, and pepper in a small bowl. Pour over the warm potatoes and peas, then toss to coat. Add the mint, toss well, and serve warm.

Per serving (⅔ cup): 106 Cal, 2 g Fat, 0 g Sat Fat, 0 mg Chol, 123 mg Sod, 19 g Carb, 3 g Fib, 3 g Prot, 18 mg Calc. **POINTS: 2.**

# Couscous and White Beans with Apricots and Almonds

### MAKES 12 SERVINGS

Israeli or Mediterranean couscous is larger than the familiar boxed granular couscous. It often comes toasted but can also come in smaller packages, untoasted and with flavoring envelopes. If the latter is all you can find, discard the flavoring envelope. You'll find this salad teeming with its own delicious flavors and lots of crunchy vegetables. To make ahead, prepare the salad without the almonds and refrigerate, covered, for up to three days. Let the salad come to room temperature for about two hours, then sprinkle with the almonds just before serving.

1 cup Israeli couscous

2 cups water

1 (15-ounce) can cannellini beans, rinsed and drained

1 red or yellow bell pepper, seeded and finely chopped

1 small red onion, finely chopped

½ cup minced flat-leaf parsley

6 dried apricot halves, chopped

1½ tablespoons fresh lemon juice

2 teaspoons extra-virgin olive oil

½ teaspoon salt

¼ teaspoon freshly ground pepper

¼ cup sliced almonds, toasted

*1.* Bring the couscous and water to a boil in a medium saucepan. Reduce the heat and simmer, uncovered, until tender, about 8 minutes; drain. Place in a large bowl.

*2.* Add the cannellini beans, bell pepper, onion, parsley, apricots, lemon juice, oil, salt, and ground pepper to the couscous; mix well. Serve while still warm or at room temperature, sprinkled with the almonds.

Per serving (scant ½ cup): 122 Cal, 2 g Fat, 0 g Sat Fat, 0 mg Chol, 151 mg Sod, 20 g Carb, 3 g Fib, 5 g Prot, 27 mg Calc. **POINTS: 2.**

---

*Chef's Tip:* To toast the almonds, place them in a small dry skillet over medium-low heat. Cook, shaking the pan and stirring constantly, until lightly browned and fragrant, 3 to 4 minutes. Watch them carefully when toasting; almonds can burn quickly. Transfer the nuts to a plate to cool.

*Couscous and White Beans with Apricots and Almonds*

# Mediterranean Green Beans and Tomatoes

**MAKES 12 SERVINGS**

Everyday green beans take on a festive air when marinated with this vinaigrette and topped with grape tomatoes, kalamata olives, and goat cheese. Substitute fresh asparagus for the green beans if you prefer. You can prepare this salad ahead of time and refrigerate it, covered, for up to two days, but stir in the tomatoes and goat cheese just before serving.

2 **pounds fresh green beans, trimmed and cut in half**

2 **tablespoons extra-virgin olive oil**

2 **tablespoons balsamic vinegar**

1 **teaspoon salt**

½ **teaspoon coarsely ground pepper**

½ **teaspoon sugar**

1 **small garlic clove, minced**

2 **pints grape or cherry tomatoes, halved**

6 **scallions, sliced**

6 **kalamata olives, pitted and chopped**

2 **ounces goat cheese, crumbled**

*1.* Bring a large pot of water to a boil. Add the green beans, return to a boil, and cook until just crisp-tender, 4–5 minutes. Rinse under cold running water, drain, and place in a large bowl.

*2.* Combine the oil, vinegar, salt, pepper, sugar, and garlic in a small bowl. Pour over the beans. Add the tomatoes, scallions, and olives; toss to coat. Sprinkle with the goat cheese and serve.

Per serving (⅔ cup): 73 Cal, 4 g Fat, 1 g Sat Fat, 4 mg Chol, 250 mg Sod, 8 g Carb, 3 g Fib, 3 g Prot, 63 mg Calc. ***POINTS: 1.***

*Chef's Tip:* To serve green beans with bright green color and crisp texture, cook them for just a few minutes, then run them under cold water to stop the cooking.

# Lemon Bars

A favorite, easy-to-assemble treat, these lemon bars watch the fat and calories while still keeping all the fresh lemony-sweet flavor. You can make them up to three days ahead of time and keep them in the refrigerator in a covered container with plastic wrap between the layers.

1 cup + 5 teaspoons
  all-purpose flour
2 tablespoons
  whole-wheat flour
½ cup confectioners' sugar
½ teaspoon salt
6 tablespoons cold butter,
  cut into pieces
2 large eggs
2 egg whites
⅔ cup granulated sugar
1½ teaspoons grated lemon rind
½ cup fresh lemon juice
3 tablespoons fat-free milk

1. Preheat the oven to 350°F. Spray an 8-inch square baking dish with nonstick spray.

2. Combine 1 cup of the all-purpose flour, the whole-wheat flour, confectioners' sugar, and salt in a food processor. Add the butter and pulse until the mixture forms crumbs. Press the mixture firmly with your fingers into the bottom of the baking dish. Bake until light brown, 16–18 minutes.

3. Meanwhile, whisk the eggs, egg whites, granulated sugar, lemon rind, lemon juice, milk, and the remaining 5 teaspoons all-purpose flour in a bowl until smooth. Pour over the warm crust and bake until a knife inserted in the center comes out clean, about 15 minutes. Cool completely in the pan on a rack. Cut into 24 bars.

Per serving (1 bar): 89 Cal, 3 g Fat, 2 g Sat Fat, 26 mg Chol, 80 mg Sod, 13 g Carb, 0 g Fib, 2 g Prot, 7 mg Calc. **POINTS: 2.**

*Chef's Tip:* For an extra touch of sweetness, sprinkle the cooled lemon bars with sifted confectioners' sugar.

*Blueberry-Filled Cookie Cups and Lemon Bars*

# Blueberry-Filled Cookie Cups

Allow yourself several hours to make these delicate cookie cups. They need to be cooked in batches of four, carefully transferring each warm cookie to drape over a small glass while the dough is still warm. If the cookie firms up before it is draped over the glass, return it to the oven to heat for 45 to 60 seconds. You can make the cookie cups ahead of time and store them in single layers in airtight containers at room temperature for up to two days. The blueberry filling keeps well in the refrigerator for up to three days. Fill the cookie cups just before you're ready to serve them.

¼ cup butter

¼ cup granulated sugar

3 tablespoons light corn syrup

2 egg whites

⅓ cup + 3 tablespoons
   all-purpose flour

Dash salt

4 cups fresh blueberries

¼ cup packed brown sugar

1 tablespoon fresh lemon juice

Confectioners' sugar,
   for sprinkling

*1.* To make the cookie cups, preheat the oven to 350°F. Spray a nonstick baking sheet with nonstick spray.

*2.* Melt the butter in a medium saucepan. Remove from the heat and stir in the granulated sugar and corn syrup. Add the egg whites and stir until well mixed. Stir in ⅓ cup of the flour and the salt until all of the flour is moistened.

*3.* Drop the batter by the tablespoonful, 4 at a time, onto the baking sheet (each tablespoon of batter will spread to a 3–4-inch circle). Bake until light golden, about 7 minutes. Meanwhile, set out 4 small glasses with a 2-inch base or custard cups, turned upside down.

*4.* Let the cookies cool 10–20 seconds, then with a large spatula, lift the cookies off the baking sheet and drape them over the upturned glasses. Let the cookie cups cool completely until they are firm. Repeat with the remaining cookie batter, making a total of 12 cookie cups.

*5.* To make the filling, combine 2 cups of the blueberries, the brown sugar, juice, and the remaining 3 tablespoons flour in a medium saucepan. Cook over medium heat, stirring constantly, until the mixture boils and thickens. Remove from the heat and let cool. Stir in the remaining 2 cups blueberries.

*6.* Spoon a scant ¼ cup of the blueberry filling into each cookie cup, sprinkle with confectioners' sugar, and serve at once.

Per serving (1 filled cookie cup): 131 Cal, 4 g Fat, 2 g Sat Fat, 10 mg Chol, 69 mg Sod, 24 g Carb, 1 g Fib, 2 g Prot, 9 mg Calc. *POINTS: 3.*

# FOURTH OF JULY BARBECUE

*Warm Golden-Potato and Pea Salad*
—
*Mixed Grill of Garden Vegetables with Charmoula*
—
*Grilled Vegetable Pizzas*
—
*Grilled Flank Steak with Chimichurri*

*Citrus Slaw with Avocado and Red Onion*
—
*Tangy Barbecued Chicken with Orange Dipping Sauce*
—
*Cheddar Cheese Corn Sticks with Roasted Corn*
—
*Coconut Angel Food Cake*
—
*Meringue Flags*

## Warm Golden-Potato and Pea Salad

### MAKES 12 SERVINGS

In some parts of the country, tender new peas make their debut just in time for the Fourth of July. We think they are perfect tossed with buttery-tasting Yukon Gold potatoes and zesty mustard vinaigrette.

2  pounds Yukon Gold potatoes
¼ cup white-wine vinegar
3  tablespoons Dijon mustard
3  tablespoons vegetable oil
½ teaspoon salt
Freshly ground pepper, to taste
1  cup fresh green peas, cooked or frozen peas, thawed
½ cup minced scallions (white part only)
2  tablespoons chopped fresh chives

*1.* Bring the potatoes and enough water to cover to a boil in a large saucepan. Reduce the heat and simmer, covered, until tender, 15–20 minutes; drain.

*2.* Meanwhile, to prepare the dressing, whisk together the vinegar, mustard, oil, salt, and pepper in a large bowl.

*3.* When the potatoes are just cool enough to handle, cut into ½-inch slices. Immediately add the potatoes to the dressing and toss gently to coat. Stir in the peas, scallions, and chives; toss gently. Serve at once.

Per serving (½ cup): 113 Cal, 1 g Fat, 0 g Sat Fat, 0 mg Chol, 171 mg Sod, 24 g Carb, 2 g Fib, 2 g Prot, 22 mg Calc. **POINTS: 2.**

# Mixed Grill of Garden Vegetables with Charmoula

**MAKES 12 SERVINGS**

You might call *charmoula* the pesto of Morocco. It's typically served with grilled or baked fish, but we think its exotic taste is fabulous with smoky grilled vegetables.

⅓ cup olive oil

¼ cup fresh lemon juice

3 tablespoons chopped fresh parsley

2 tablespoons chopped fresh cilantro

1 teaspoon minced garlic

¾ teaspoon paprika

½ teaspoon ground cumin

½ teaspoon salt

Freshly ground pepper, to taste

Pinch cayenne

2 dozen baby carrots

2 dozen asparagus spears

1 fennel bulb, quartered

3 red bell peppers

2 dozen fresh white mushrooms

2 zucchini, cut in ½-inch slices

2 sweet onions, cut in ½-inch slices

*1.* To prepare the charmoula, whisk together the oil, lemon juice, parsley, cilantro, garlic, paprika, cumin, salt, ground pepper, and cayenne in a medium bowl. Set aside.

*2.* Put the carrots in a steamer basket; set in a saucepan over 1 inch of boiling water. Cover tightly and steam just until tender, about 5 minutes. Transfer the carrots to a large bowl. Repeat the process, steaming the asparagus, 4 minutes, then the fennel, 4 minutes.

*3.* Spray the grill rack with nonstick spray; prepare the grill.

*4.* Arrange the bell peppers on the grill. Grill 5 inches from the heat, turning occasionally with tongs, until lightly charred, about 8 minutes. Transfer the bell peppers to a bowl; cover the bowl with plastic wrap, and steam 10 minutes. When cool enough to handle, peel, cut in half, and discard the seeds.

*5.* Add the roasted peppers, mushrooms, zucchini, and onions to the vegetables in the bowl. Drizzle the vegetables with ½ cup of charmoula; toss to coat. Marinate at room temperature, 30 minutes.

*6.* Grill the vegetables, in batches, until cooked through, about 3 minutes on each side.

*7.* Transfer the grilled vegetables to a bowl or platter; drizzle with the remaining charmoula.

Per serving (⅓ cup vegetables with 2 tablespoons charmoula): 90 Cal, 1 g Fat, 0 g Sat Fat, 0 mg Chol, 55 mg Sod, 21 g Carb, 6 g Fib, 5 g Prot, 63 mg Calc. **POINTS: 1.**

◆

*Chef's Tip: Charmoula* can be prepared a day ahead and refrigerated in an airtight container. For a different flavor, replace some or all of the lemon juice with red-wine vinegar. The carrots, asparagus, fennel, and roasted pepper can be prepared as directed through Step 4 up to two days ahead. Refrigerate the vegetables separately in zip-close plastic bags or airtight containers.

# Grilled Vegetable Pizzas

**MAKES 12 SERVINGS**

Preparing the grill for indirect heating is critical for the success of this recipe. Here's how to do it: If you have a gas grill, preheat just one side; if you have a charcoal grill, mound the charcoal on one side of the grill. To cut the prep time, we suggest using store-bought pizza dough.

Cornmeal, for sprinkling

4 medium fresh beets

2 (12-ounce) packages fresh pizza dough or frozen pizza dough, thawed

1½ cups part-skim ricotta cheese

4 garlic cloves, minced

4 scallions, minced

1 bunch arugula, cleaned and coarsely chopped

¼ cup grated Parmesan cheese

½ teaspoon salt

Freshly ground pepper, to taste

1 teaspoon minced fresh chives

2 tablespoons olive oil

*1.* Spray the grill rack with nonstick spray; prepare the grill for indirect heating. Lightly sprinkle 2 large baking sheets with the cornmeal.

*2.* Meanwhile, simmer the beets in enough water to cover until they are just tender enough to pierce with a fork, 20–30 minutes. Plunge into a bowl of ice water to stop the cooking. When cool enough to handle, drain, peel, and slice.

*3.* Sprinkle a work surface lightly with flour. Flour your hands and press each package of dough into a 10-inch circle. Or cut each package of dough into 6 pieces and press into 12 (4-inch) circles. Transfer the dough to the prepared baking sheets, gently stretching the dough back into 10-inch or 4-inch crusts. Lightly spray the crusts with nonstick spray.

*4.* Slide the crusts from the baking sheets onto the direct heat section of the grill. Grill the crusts until firm, about 90 seconds. Flip the crusts with a large spatula; grill 1 minute. Transfer the crusts to the indirect heat section of the grill. Top evenly with the ricotta, garlic, scallions, arugula, and beets. Sprinkle with the Parmesan cheese, salt, pepper, and chives; drizzle with the oil.

*5.* Cover the grill. Grill the pizzas, rotating so they cook evenly, until the toppings are very hot and the crust is fully cooked, 5–6 minutes for large pizzas, 2–3 minutes for individual pizzas.

Per serving (⅙ of large pizza or 1 individual pizza): 158 Cal, 2 g Fat, 1 g Sat Fat, 30 mg Chol, 290 mg Sod, 18 g Carb, 3 g Fib, 8 g Prot, 80 mg Calc. ***POINTS: 3.***

◆

*Chef's Tip:* To transfer the crusts more easily to the grill, place them on baking sheets without a rim on at least one side. If you don't have a covered grill, it's easy to improvise by using an inverted large metal bowl or the lid of a wok for a cover.

## Grilling Pizza

Why grill pizza? Because it's delicious! Setting up the grill and fire correctly is crucial for success: If you're using a charcoal grill, arrange the coals on one side of the grill; on a gas grill, light only one side. In either case, allow the grill to thoroughly preheat. Scrub the rack well to remove any carbon or drippings, then rub or spray lightly with a little oil or nonstick spray (do this away from the fire). Set the rack back on the grill and let it get very hot. While the grill is preheating, shape the dough into circles. Sprinkle a little cornmeal on a baking sheet; then transfer the circles to the baking sheet.

*1.* When ready to grill, have everything you need on hand—sauces and toppings, a large spatula, large tongs, cutting board, and knife. Getting the dough onto the grill is the tricky part. Lift the end of the dough closest to you up from the baking sheet and slide onto the hot side of the grill.

*2.* Once the dough is firm and golden on one side, flip it over to cook the other side.

*3.* With tongs, pull the pizza crusts to the cool side of the grill, then add the toppings and a very fine drizzle of olive oil. Cover the grill with a lid or a large metal bowl and finish cooking the pizzas.

# Grilled Flank Steak with Chimichurri

**MAKES 12 SERVINGS**

Argentina is world-famous for its great beef barbecue. *Chimichurri*, a gutsy blend of olive oil, vinegar, parsley, oregano, onion, and plenty of garlic, is the national condiment of that country. It's as popular on steak as ketchup is on burgers here.

  6 **garlic cloves**
  ½ **teaspoon salt**
  ⅓ **cup water**
  ⅓ **cup extra-virgin olive oil**
  ⅓ **cup red-wine vinegar**
  2 **plum tomatoes, peeled, seeded, and chopped**
  ¼ **cup seeded and minced red bell pepper**
  2 **tablespoons minced onion**
  2 **tablespoons minced flat-leaf parsley**
  2 **tablespoons minced fresh oregano**
  2 **tablespoons minced fresh cilantro**
  1 **jalapeño pepper, minced (wear gloves to prevent irritation)**
  2 **(1¼-pound) flank steaks, trimmed of all visible fat**
**Freshly ground pepper, to taste**

*1.* To prepare the chimichurri, mash the garlic with the side of a large knife; chop coarsely. Sprinkle ¼ teaspoon of the salt over the garlic; continue to chop and mash until the mixture forms a paste. Transfer the paste to a bowl; stir in the water, oil, and vinegar until smooth. Add the tomatoes, bell pepper, onion, parsley, oregano, cilantro, and jalapeño. Let the mixture stand about 1 hour for the flavors to blend.

*2.* Spray the grill rack with nonstick spray. Prepare the grill. Pat the steaks dry with paper towels; sprinkle both sides with the remaining ¼ teaspoon salt and the pepper.

*3.* Grill the steaks 5 inches from the heat, about 4 minutes on each side for medium-rare. Transfer the steaks to a cutting board; let stand 5–10 minutes. Thinly slice and serve with the chimichurri.

Per serving (¹⁄₁₂ of steak with 1 tablespoon chimichurri): 229 Cal, 10 g Fat, 3 g Sat Fat, 98 mg Chol, 680 mg Sod, 2 g Carb, 0 g Fib, 32 g Prot, 20 mg Calc. ***POINTS: 5.***

*Grilled Flank Steak with Chimichurri and Mixed Grill of
Garden Vegetables with Charmoula*

# *Citrus Slaw with Avocado and Red Onion*

**MAKES 12 SERVINGS**

With two kinds of cabbage, iron-rich spinach, creamy avocado, and a refreshing grapefruit-honey dressing, this slaw offers a bright respite from the spicier items on the menu. While the salad can be refrigerated up to 12 hours in advance, add the avocado only at the last possible moment so it stays green.

½ cup low-sodium vegetable or
  chicken broth
2 teaspoons cornstarch
2 teaspoons cold water
¼ cup fresh grapefruit juice
½ teaspoon honey
¼ cup vegetable oil
¼ teaspoon salt
Freshly ground pepper, to taste
1 (10-ounce) bag triple-washed
  fresh spinach, shredded
2 cups shredded red cabbage
2 cups shredded Savoy cabbage
1 grapefruit, peeled and cut
  into segments
1 small red onion, thinly sliced
1 avocado, pitted, peeled,
  and sliced
Cracked black peppercorns,
  for garnish

*1.* To prepare the dressing, bring the broth to a boil in a small saucepan. Combine the cornstarch and water in a cup; drizzle the cornstarch mixture into the broth, stirring constantly. Cook, stirring constantly, until the mixture boils and thickens, about 1 minute. Remove the pan from the heat; stir in the grapefruit juice and the honey. Cool completely, then whisk in the oil, salt, and ground pepper.

*2.* Combine the spinach, red cabbage, Savoy cabbage, grapefruit segments, and onion with ½ cup of the dressing in a salad bowl; toss to coat.

*3.* Gently toss the avocado with the remaining dressing in a small bowl. Arrange on top of the cabbage mixture; garnish with the cracked peppercorns.

Per serving (⅓ cup): 85 Cal, 1 g Fat, 0 g Sat Fat, 30 mg Chol, 145 mg Sod, 11 g Carb, 8 g Fib, 6 g Prot, 22 mg Calc. ***POINTS: 1.***

# Tangy Barbecued Chicken with Orange Dipping Sauce

**MAKES 12 SERVINGS**

What's a Fourth of July bash without chicken on the barbecue? To make sure each guest gets a tasty serving, we've grilled chicken-breast strips on skewers and slathered them with a down-home barbecue sauce. The sauce is perfect with pork and beef too, so go on and double the recipe—it can be refrigerated for up to five days, or frozen for up to a month in an airtight container.

½ cup thawed frozen orange juice concentrate

½ cup chili sauce

⅓ cup molasses

¼ cup low-sodium chicken broth

3 tablespoons reduced-sodium soy sauce

2 tablespoons fresh lemon juice

1 tablespoon prepared dark-brown mustard

1 garlic clove, minced

1 teaspoon Worcestershire sauce

1 teaspoon hot pepper sauce

1 jalapeño pepper, minced (wear gloves to prevent irritation) (optional)

¼ teaspoon salt

1¼ pounds skinless boneless chicken breasts, cut into 2-inch strips

Orange swedges, for garnish

*1.* Place 12 (6-inch) bamboo skewers and enough cold water to cover in a shallow pan. Let the skewers soak 1 hour.

*2.* Bring the orange juice concentrate, chili sauce, molasses, broth, soy sauce, lemon juice, mustard, garlic, Worcestershire sauce, hot pepper sauce, jalapeño (if using), and salt to a boil in a small saucepan. Reduce the heat and simmer, stirring occasionally, until slightly thickened, about 10 minutes. Remove the sauce from the heat; transfer about ½ cup of the sauce to a serving bowl. Cover and set aside.

*3.* Spray the grill or broiler rack with nonstick spray; prepare the grill or preheat the broiler.

*4.* Drain the skewers; thread the chicken evenly onto each. Dip each skewer into the barbecue sauce in the saucepan, gently shaking off any excess. Discard any sauce left in the saucepan. Grill or broil the chicken 5 inches from the heat until cooked through, about 2 minutes on each side.

*5.* Transfer the skewers to a platter; garnish with the orange wedges and serve with the reserved ½ cup of sauce.

Per serving (1 skewer with 2 teaspoons sauce): 169 Cal, 3 g Fat, 1 g Sat Fat, 68 mg Chol, 200 mg Sod, 2 g Carb, 0 g Fib, 14 g Prot, 10 mg Calc. **POINTS: 4.**

---

*Chef's Tip:* To make a skewer showpiece, cut a grapefruit in half and place it cut-side down on a platter. Stick the skewers into the grapefruit to make a bouquet.

# Cheddar Cheese Corn Sticks with Roasted Corn

**MAKES 12 SERVINGS**

Making corn sticks on a grill? Absolutely! The smoky taste is fantastic. Plus, there's no hot oven to mess with so you won't break a sweat. Serve the sticks directly from the hot pan so they're moist and tender inside and crispy outside.

| |
|---|
| **3 ears fresh corn, with husks** |
| **1 cup yellow cornmeal** |
| **¾ cup all-purpose flour** |
| **1 tablespoon sugar** |
| **2 teaspoons baking powder** |
| **1 teaspoon salt** |
| **1½ cups fat-free buttermilk** |
| **1 large egg, lightly beaten** |
| **2 egg whites, lightly beaten** |
| **2 tablespoons vegetable oil** |
| **⅓ cup shredded sharp cheddar cheese** |

*1.* Preheat the oven to 375°F. Rinse the corn to dampen the husks and place in a baking pan.

*2.* Roast until the husks are browned and the corn kernels are tender, about 30 minutes. When the corn is cool enough to handle, husk the corn and remove the silks. Cut the kernels from the cob; set aside.

*3.* Meanwhile, prepare the grill for a moderate fire.

*4.* Spray a cast-iron corn-stick pan or a 9-inch round cast-iron skillet with nonstick spray. Heat the pan on the grill while mixing the corn stick batter.

*5.* To prepare the batter, combine the cornmeal, flour, sugar, baking powder, and salt in a large bowl. Combine the buttermilk, egg, egg whites, and oil in a small bowl until blended. With a wooden spoon or rubber spatula, stir the buttermilk mixture into the cornmeal mixture until just evenly moistened. Gently fold in the corn kernels.

*6.* Pour the batter into the prepared pan; sprinkle the top evenly with the cheese. Return the pan to the grill; cover and grill, occasionally repositioning the pan to avoid scorching, until the corn sticks are brown and begin to pull away from the sides of the pan, 30–40 minutes. Cool in the pan 10 minutes before serving.

Per serving (1 corn stick): 140 Cal, 2 g Fat, 0 g Sat Fat, 45 mg Chol, 220 mg Sod, 26 g Carb, less than 1 g Fib, 6 g Prot, 14 mg Calc. ***POINTS: 3.***

———◆———

*Chef's Tip:* To cut down on last-minute measuring and chopping, prepare the recipe as directed through Step 2. Transfer the corn to a zip-close plastic bag. Combine the buttermilk, egg, egg whites, and oil as directed; transfer to a covered jar. Refrigerate the corn and buttermilk mixture for up to two days. Mix and store the dry ingredients in a zip-close plastic bag at room temperature for up to two days.

# Coconut Angel Food Cake

**MAKES 12 SERVINGS**

Mile-high and lighter than air, angel food cake has always been an all-American favorite. Cream of coconut gives this cake a rich, mellow flavor not ordinarily found in the traditional recipe. Look for cream of coconut in the beverage aisle of large supermarkets with other cocktail mixes and blends.

1⅔ cups cake flour

1 teaspoon baking powder

12 egg whites

1 teaspoon cream of tartar

2 cups sifted confectioners' sugar

5 tablespoons cream of coconut

1 teaspoon vanilla extract

1 teaspoon coconut extract

2 tablespoons water

2 tablespoons shredded unsweetened coconut

*1.* Preheat the oven to 375°F. Set a 10 × 4-inch straight-sided tube pan nearby.

*2.* Sift the flour and the baking powder twice into a medium bowl.

*3.* With an electric mixer at low speed, beat the egg whites in a large bowl until frothy, about 2 minutes. Add the cream of tartar. Increase the speed to medium and beat in 1¾ cups of the sifted confectioners' sugar, 1 tablespoon at a time, until shiny, medium peaks form; do not overbeat.

*4.* Sprinkle 4 rounded tablespoons of the flour mixture over the batter and, with large rubber spatula, gently fold in the flour mixture, until almost combined. Repeat with the remaining flour mixture, 4 rounded tablespoons at a time. Gently fold in 3 tablespoons of the cream of coconut, the vanilla extract, and coconut extract, until just blended. Spoon the batter into the pan and spread evenly.

*5.* Bake immediately, until the cake pulls slightly away from the sides of the pan, 35–40 minutes. Invert onto a bottleneck or inverted metal funnel and cool completely, 2–3 hours. To loosen the cake, run a thin-bladed knife around the edges of the pan and center tube. Invert onto a plate or cake rack, then reinvert, right-side up.

*6.* To prepare the glaze, bring the remaining 2 tablespoons cream of coconut and the water to a boil in a small saucepan. Remove from the heat; stir in the remaining ¼ cup sifted confectioners' sugar until smooth. Pour the glaze evenly over the cake; sprinkle the coconut over the top. Let the cake stand until the glaze is set, about 1 hour. Cut into 12 slices.

Per serving (1⁄12 of cake): 141 Cal, 2 g Fat, 1 g Sat Fat, 6 mg Chol, 95 mg Sod, 25 g Carb, 0 g Fib, 5 g Prot, 20 mg Calc. **POINTS: 3.**

# Meringue Flags

**MAKES 12 SERVINGS**

Three cheers for the red (raspberry), white (whipped topping), and blue (blueberry) topping! You can make the meringue shells ahead and store them in an airtight container in a cool, dry place for up to a month. Just avoid baking meringues on a humid day—they need dry air to dry out completely after baking.

6 egg whites
½ teaspoon cream of tartar
1 cup sugar
12 tablespoons light non-dairy
  whipped topping
2 pints fresh raspberries
1 pint fresh blueberries

1. Preheat the oven to 225°F. Line 2 large baking sheets with foil.
2. With an electric mixer at medium speed, beat the egg whites and the cream of tartar in a large bowl until just frothy. Gradually sprinkle in the sugar, 2 tablespoons at a time, until the sugar completely dissolves and the whites stand in stiff, glossy peaks, about 10 minutes.
3. Spoon the egg white mixture onto the baking sheets, making 12 (3 × 5-inch) rectangles. Spread the mixture with the back of a spoon or a small metal spatula, leaving about ½ inch between each meringue.
4. Bake the meringues until they feel crisp to the touch, about 2 hours. Turn the oven off and leave the meringues in the oven until they are crisp and dry to the touch, about 1 hour longer.
5. Cool the meringues on the baking sheets on racks 10 minutes. Carefully loosen and transfer the meringues with a metal spatula to the racks to cool completely.
6. Spread 1 tablespoon of the whipped topping onto each meringue; decorate with the raspberries and blueberries in the design of an American flag.

Per serving (1 meringue): 116 Cal, 1 g Fat, 0 g Sat Fat, 0 mg Chol, 32 mg Sod, 26 g Carb, 3 g Fib, 2 g Prot, 15 mg Calc. **POINTS: 2.**

# BASTILLE DAY DINNER

*Radish Salad with Pears*
—
*Pissaladière*
—
*Leg of Lamb with Flageolets*
—
*Braised Leeks*
—
*Warm Potato Salad*
—
*Broiled Radicchio Salad with Shaved Fennel and Oranges*
—
*Celeriac and Tart Apple Salad*
—
*Cherry Clafouti*

## Radish Salad with Pears

**MAKES 6 SERVINGS**

You can make this refreshing and unusual salad the morning of your dinner party. Store, covered, in the refrigerator, but allow it to come up to room temperature for about 30 minutes before serving.

1 (16-ounce) bag radishes, cut into very thin slices

2 pears, cored and cut into very thin slices

¼ cup white-wine vinegar

2 tablespoons olive oil

1 teaspoon sugar

½ teaspoon salt

Freshly ground pepper, to taste

3 tablespoons plain low-fat yogurt

*1.* Combine the sliced radishes and pears in a large bowl.

*2.* To make the dressing, whisk together the vinegar, oil, sugar, salt, and pepper in a small bowl. Whisk in the yogurt, then drizzle over the radishes and pears; toss to coat. Cover and refrigerate at least 1 hour or up to 12 hours before serving.

Per serving (½ cup): 90 Cal, 2 g Fat, 0 g Sat Fat, 0 mg Chol, 210 mg Sod, 18 g Carb, 1 g Fib, 1 g Prot, 28 mg Calc. *POINTS: 2.*

*Pissaladière*

# Pissaladière

**MAKES 12 SERVINGS**

This tomato and olive pizza, popular in southern France, makes a good start to the evening. You can buy fresh or frozen pizza dough from your favorite pizza shop, bakery, or supermarket. Allow frozen dough to thaw in the refrigerator at least 24 hours before using. When time is an issue, you can defrost the dough in the microwave on the defrost setting for 8 to 10 minutes. In either case, for easier handling, let the dough come to room temperature before stretching and rolling it. Look for salt-packed anchovies in gourmet shops or delicatessens. Soak them in enough cold water to cover for 24 hours, changing the water every 8 hours to remove the excess salt.

3–4 **plum tomatoes, sliced**
1 **garlic clove, minced**
1 **(12-ounce) ball fresh or thawed frozen pizza dough**
½ **cup roasted red bell pepper strips**
4 **salt-packed anchovy fillets, soaked, drained, and cut into strips**
12 **pitted ripe black olives, slivered**
¼ **cup grated Parmesan cheese**
**Chopped fresh herbs such as: rosemary, parsley, oregano, basil, chives**

*1.* Preheat the oven to 375°F. Spray a baking sheet with olive-oil nonstick spray.

*2.* Spread the tomato slices on the baking sheet, sprinkle with the garlic and spray lightly with olive-oil nonstick spray. Roast until the tomatoes begin to dry and the juices brown, 60–75 minutes. Let stand 15 minutes to cool slightly.

*3.* Increase the oven temperature to 450°F. Spray a deep 12-inch tart pan or pie plate with nonstick spray.

*4.* On a lightly floured surface, roll and stretch out the dough ¼-inch thick. Line the tart pan with the dough. Arrange the tomatoes evenly over the dough. Make a latticework pattern with the roasted bell peppers and anchovies on top of the tomatoes. Top with the olives, then sprinkle with the Parmesan cheese and herbs. Bake until the crust is golden brown, 20–30 minutes. Cut into wedges and serve at once, or let cool 10 minutes.

Per serving (¹⁄₁₂ of pissaladière): 158 Cal, 2 g Fat, 1 g Sat Fat, 30 mg Chol, 290 mg Sod, 18 g Carb, 3 g Fib, 8 g Prot, 80 mg Calc. ***POINTS: 3.***

◆

*Chef's Tip:* Enjoy any leftover *pissaladière* as a quick lunch or appetizer the next day. Or, wrap tightly and freeze. Unwrap and reheat the *pissaladière* directly from the freezer in a 400°F oven until hot, about 12 minutes.

# Leg of Lamb with Flageolets

**MAKES 8 SERVINGS**

Flageolets are pale green beans, usually available dried in gourmet shops. If using dried beans, pick over about one cup, then rinse in cool water and drain. Bring the beans and enough cold water to cover to a boil. Reduce the heat and simmer until barely tender, about 45 minutes.

1 (2¼-pound) boneless leg of lamb, butterflied and trimmed of all visible fat

3 tablespoons Dijon mustard

½ cup dry white wine

3 garlic cloves, minced

1 tablespoon minced fresh tarragon, or 1 teaspoon dried

½ teaspoon salt

Freshly ground pepper, to taste

1 onion, minced

¾ cup diced tomatoes

2 cups cooked or canned flageolets or navy beans, rinsed and drained

1 cup low-sodium chicken or beef broth

*1.* Open the lamb out flat and remove any cartilage, sinew, and excess fat. Combine the mustard, 2 tablespoons of the wine, the garlic, tarragon, salt, and pepper in a zip-close plastic bag; add the lamb. Squeeze out the air and seal the bag; turn to coat the lamb. Refrigerate, turning the bag occasionally, for at least 8 hours or up to 24 hours.

*2.* Preheat the oven to 400°F. Spray the rack of a roasting pan with nonstick spray and place in the roasting pan.

*3.* Remove the lamb from the marinade; discard the marinade. Roll the lamb and secure with twine or skewers. Set the lamb on the roasting rack and roast until an instant-read thermometer, inserted in the center, registers 160°F for medium, about 55 minutes.

*4.* Remove the lamb from the oven, cover loosely with foil, and let stand 10–15 minutes before removing the twine and slicing.

*5.* While the lamb is resting, pour or spoon off any fat in the roasting pan, leaving behind as much of the juice from the roast as possible. Heat the roasting pan over high heat. Add the onion and tomatoes and cook, stirring constantly, until golden brown, about 10 minutes. Add the remaining wine to the roasting pan and cook, scraping up the browned bits from the bottom of the pan, until the wine is cooked away, about 8 minutes. Add the flageolets and broth; bring to a boil. Reduce the heat and simmer until the bean sauce is reduced to about 3 cups, about 15 minutes. Slice the lamb and serve with the bean sauce.

Per serving (⅛ of lamb with generous ⅓ cup bean sauce): 226 Cal, 7 g Fat, 2 g Sat Fat, 72 mg Chol, 350 mg Sod, 12 g Carb, 4 g Fib, 28 g Prot, 56 mg Calc. *POINTS: 4.*

# *Braised Leeks*

Braised dishes of all types improve as they mellow overnight. Prepare the leeks ahead of time by braising them until tender, then refrigerate, covered, for up to two days. When you are ready to serve them, reheat the leeks, covered, in a 350°F oven for 10 minutes. Then uncover, add the crumb topping, and bake until a crisp brown crust forms, about 15 minutes.

3 **large leeks, cleaned and**
   **quartered lengthwise**
¾ **cup low-sodium vegetable or**
   **chicken broth**
**Juice of ½ lemon**
¼ **teaspoon salt**
**Freshly ground pepper, to taste**
1 **slice white bread, made into**
   **coarse crumbs**
1 **tablespoon minced sun-dried**
   **tomatoes**
1 **tablespoon minced**
   **fresh parsley**
2 **teaspoons minced**
   **fresh chives**
1 **teaspoon butter, melted**
2 **tablespoons shredded or**
   **grated Parmesan cheese**

*1.* Preheat the oven to 350°F. Spray an 8-inch square baking dish with nonstick spray.

*2.* Lay the leeks in the dish; drizzle with the broth, lemon juice, salt, and pepper. Cover tightly and braise in the oven until half way tender, about 20 minutes. Remove the cover and cook until the leeks are very tender and the broth is reduced slightly, 20–30 minutes.

*3.* Preheat the broiler. Combine the bread crumbs, sun-dried tomatoes, parsley, chives, and butter; sprinkle over the leeks. Sprinkle with the Parmesan cheese. Broil until the topping is brown and a crisp crust forms, 2–3 minutes.

Per serving (⅙ of casserole): 92 Cal, 2 g Fat, 1 g Sat Fat, 4 mg Chol, 218 mg Sod, 16 g Carb, 2 g Fib, 3 g Prot, 93 mg Calc. *POINTS: 2.*

◆

*Chef's Tip:* Leeks often contain sand in between their layers. Here's how to clean them: Trim away most of the dark green tops and the roots, leaving the root end intact to hold the layers together. Slice the leek lengthwise to within a half inch of the root end. Hold the leek by the root end, fan open the layers, and rinse thoroughly under cold running water.

# *Warm Potato Salad*

**MAKES 6 SERVINGS**

Although this salad is typically served warm, it can be made in advance, refrigerated for up to 24 hours, then brought to room temperature before serving. Allow at least 30 minutes at room temperature to let the flavors meld before serving.

  1 **pound Yukon Gold potatoes**
1¼ **teaspoons salt**
  2 **teaspoons vegetable oil**
  1 **lean turkey bacon strip, minced**
  1 **onion, minced**
1½ **cups low-sodium chicken broth**
  ¼ **cup cider or white-wine vinegar**
  ½ **teaspoon sugar**
  2 **tablespoons minced fresh chives**
    **Freshly ground pepper, to taste**

*1.* Place the potatoes, enough water to cover, and 1 teaspoon of the salt in a large saucepan; bring to a boil. Reduce the heat and simmer, covered, until tender, 25–30 minutes; drain. When the potatoes are cool enough to handle, peel them and cut into ½-inch slices; place in a medium bowl.

*2.* Heat a small nonstick skillet over medium heat. Swirl in the oil, then add the bacon. Cook until crisp, 3–5 minutes. With a slotted spoon, remove the bacon bits and add to the potatoes. Add the onion to the skillet and cook, stirring occasionally, until golden, about 8 minutes. Add the broth, vinegar, sugar, and the remaining ¼ teaspoon salt; cook, scraping up the browned bits from the bottom of the skillet, until slightly reduced, about 5 minutes. Stir in the chives and pepper; pour over the potatoes, then toss to coat. Serve warm or let cool to room temperature before serving.

Per serving (⅓ cup): 100 Cal, 2 g Fat, 1 g Sat Fat, 3 mg Chol, 112 mg Sod, 17 g Carb, 2 g Fib, 3 g Prot, 17 mg Calc. ***POINTS: 2.***

# Broiled Radicchio Salad with Shaved Fennel and Oranges

**MAKES 6 SERVINGS**

This recipe calls for broiling the radicchio. However, if you have the grill hot at any point up to two days before your party, try grilling the radicchio instead for an intense, smoky flavor.

2 heads radicchio, quartered

2 tablespoons olive oil

¾ teaspoon salt

Freshly ground pepper, to taste

3 oranges, peeled and cut into segments

1 fennel bulb, trimmed and shaved or very thinly sliced

3 tablespoons minced fresh chives

2 tablespoons thawed frozen orange juice concentrate

1 tablespoon water

Juice of 1 lemon

½ teaspoon crushed red pepper

*1.* Spray the broiler rack with nonstick spray; preheat the broiler.
*2.* Toss the radicchio with 1 tablespoon of the oil, ½ teaspoon of the salt, and the ground pepper. Broil, 5 inches from the heat, until the radicchio is lightly browned and the leaves wilt, about 2 minutes on each side. Let cool. Cut out and discard the cores, then slice the radicchio into fine shreds. Place the radicchio, oranges, and fennel in a salad bowl.
*3.* To make the dressing, whisk the chives, orange juice concentrate, water, lemon juice, crushed red pepper, and the remaining 1 tablespoon olive oil and ¼ teaspoon salt in a small bowl. Drizzle over the radicchio mixture; toss gently to coat. Serve at room temperature.

Per serving (½ cup): 100 Cal, 4 g Fat, 1 g Sat Fat, 0 mg Chol, 310 mg Sod, 14 g Carb, 3 g Fib, 1 g Prot, 51 mg Calc. ***POINTS: 2.***

———◆———

*Chef's Tip:* To make a pretty composed salad for a first course, mound the radicchio mixture onto the center of individual serving plates and garnish with additional crushed red pepper, fennel leaves, and slivered black olives.

# Celeriac and Tart Apple Salad

**MAKES 6 SERVINGS**

A salad of this kind is typically made with crème fraîche and mayonnaise, but we've substituted tangy buttermilk and light sour cream—with refreshing results. Celeriac, or celery root, tastes like a cross between celery and parsley and is available in larger supermarkets year-round. Choose small to medium roots with no soft or dark brown spots. Substitute jicama if celeriac is unavailable. Jicama does not need to be cooked for this salad. You can assemble the salad a day ahead and keep it covered in the refrigerator.

2 tablespoons fresh lemon juice
¾ teaspoon salt
1 celeriac, peeled and diced or julienned
¼ cup fat-free buttermilk
3 tablespoons light sour cream
2 tablespoons Dijon mustard
1 teaspoon sugar
2 Granny Smith apples, cored and diced or julienned

*1.* Bring a large pot half-filled with water, 1 tablespoon of the lemon juice, and the salt to a boil. Add the celeriac and cook until tender, about 8 minutes. With a slotted spoon, transfer the celeriac to a large bowl of ice water. Cool 1 minute, then drain on layers of paper towels. Place the celeriac in a salad bowl.

*2.* To make the dressing, whisk together the buttermilk, sour cream, mustard, sugar, and the remaining 1 tablespoon lemon juice in a small bowl. Drizzle over the celeriac; add the apples and toss gently to coat. Cover and refrigerate for at least 1 hour or up to 12 hours before serving.

Per serving (⅓ cup): 85 Cal, 1 g Fat, 0 g Sat Fat, 30 mg Chol, 145 mg Sod, 11 g Carb, 8 g Fib, 6 g Prot, 22 mg Calc. ***POINTS: 1.***

———◆———

*Chef's Tip:* Both apples and celeriac discolor quickly once cut. To prevent discoloring, put the pieces in water mixed with a little apple cider vinegar (1 tablespoon vinegar to 1 quart water). Chefs refer to this as acidulated water. Apples and celeriac can be kept this way up to four hours. Drain them and blot on paper towels before using.

# Cherry Clafouti

**MAKES 6 SERVINGS**

*Clafouti* originated in Alsace, a region of France noted for its cherries. You can easily substitute other fruits, such as apples or pears, when they are in season. If you replace the cherries with apples, replace the kirsch with an apple brandy or Calvados. If using pears, substitute pear brandy or any other colorless brandy distilled from a fermented fruit.

4 cups pitted fresh sour cherries
2 tablespoons kirsch
3 large eggs
6 tablespoons sugar
1¾ cups fat-free milk
1 tablespoon dark rum
½ teaspoon vanilla extract
⅛ teaspoon salt
1½ cups sifted all-purpose flour
Confectioners' sugar

*1.* Preheat the oven to 350°F. Spray a 2-quart baking dish with nonstick spray.

*2.* Marinate the cherries and kirsch in a bowl at room temperature for at least 5 minutes or up to 1 hour.

*3.* With an electric mixer at medium speed, beat the eggs and sugar until foamy. Mix in the milk, rum, vanilla, and salt. With the mixer at low speed, stir in the flour until all the flour is just moistened. Spread one-third of the batter in the baking dish. Scatter the cherries evenly over the batter. Spread the remaining batter over the cherries, covering them evenly. Bake until a toothpick inserted near the center comes out clean, about 30 minutes.

*4.* Dust with confectioners' sugar. Serve hot, warm, or at room temperature.

Per serving (1/6 of clafouti): 180 Cal, 6 g Fat, 4 g Sat Fat, 32 mg Chol, 142 mg Sod, 40 g Carb, 3 g Fib, 2 g Prot, 42 mg Calc. ***POINTS: 4.***

*Chef's Tip:* You can present this rustic dish directly from a ceramic gratin or baking dish at the dinner table. Accompany it with a rich French-roast coffee served in demitasse cups.

# A CLASSIC CLAMBAKE

*Iced Tea Infusions*
—
*Warm Salad of White Beans with Tomatoes and Arugula*
—
*New England Shore Dinner*
—
*Trio of Dipping Sauces: Roasted Garlic and Mustard Dipping Sauce;*
*Buttermilk and Dill Dipping Sauce; Tomato Dipping Sauce*
—
*Tomato Salad*
—
*Baked Ricotta Cheese*
—
*Watermelon, Watercress, and Red Onion Salad*
—
*Peach Cobbler*

## *Iced Tea Infusions*

**MAKES 18 SERVINGS (6 OF EACH FLAVOR)**

An infusion is the flavor that is extracted from one thing—in this case lemon, mint, and strawberry—to give flavor to another—iced tea here. Prepare the iced tea using freshly boiled water. Steep the tea bags slightly longer than you normally would, since the syrup infusions will dilute the tea slightly.

**Grated rind and juice of 2 lemons**
**10 sprigs fresh mint**
**1 cup sliced fresh strawberries**
**or whole raspberries**
**2 cups water**
**1½ cups sugar**
**1 gallon (16 cups) unsweetened**
**iced tea**

*1.* Combine the lemon rind and juice in a medium bowl. Put the mint in a second bowl and bruise it by pressing it against the bowl with the back of a wooden spoon. Put the berries in a third bowl and mash with the back of a spoon or a potato masher.

*2.* Bring the water and sugar to a boil in a medium saucepan. Remove from the heat and pour equal amounts (about 1 cup) into each of the three bowls. Let the mixtures cool to room temperature, then strain into 3 clean jars or bottles. Cap or cover tightly and refrigerate up to 1 week.

*3.* To prepare each glass of iced tea infusion, fill a large glass with ice, add ¾ cup iced tea, then stir in 3 tablespoons of any one of the flavored syrup mixtures.

Per serving (1 cup): 68 Cal, 0 g Fat, 0 g Sat Fat, 0 mg Chol, 1 mg Sod, 17 g Carb, 0 g Fib, 0 g Prot, 3 mg Calc. ***POINTS: 1.***

# Warm Salad of White Beans with Tomatoes and Arugula

**MAKES 6 SERVINGS**

Whether piping hot right from the skillet or at room temperature, afer the flavors have softened and mellowed, this classic combination of "beans and greens" is a sure-fire winner. Serving this at room temperature conveniently allows you to assemble it up to two hours in advance of the clambake.

1 tablespoon olive oil
1 small onion, chopped
2 garlic cloves, minced
1 teaspoon crushed red pepper
½ teaspoon chopped fresh
   rosemary, or pinch dried
¼ teaspoon salt
Freshly ground pepper, to taste
½ cup low-sodium vegetable or
   chicken broth
½ cup balsamic vinegar
2 tomatoes, seeded and cut
   into eighths
2 cups cooked or canned
   white navy beans,
   rinsed and drained
2 bunches arugula, cleaned and
   coarsely chopped

*1.* Heat a nonstick skillet over medium heat. Swirl in the oil, then add the onion. Cook, stirring occasionally, until golden brown, about 8 minutes. Add the garlic, crushed red pepper, rosemary, salt, and ground pepper. Cook, stirring frequently, until fragrant, 2–3 minutes.

*2.* Add the broth and vinegar to the skillet; bring to a boil over high heat. Add the tomatoes and beans; stir them gently over high heat long enough to fully heat them, 3–4 minutes. Remove the pan from the heat and gently fold in the arugula to barely wilt the leaves. Serve at once or let cool to room temperature.

Per serving (½ cup): 160 Cal, 10 g Fat, 1 g Sat Fat, 0 mg Chol, 207 mg Sod, 17 g Carb, 5 g Fib, 6 g Prot, 62 mg Calc. **POINTS: 3.**

# New England Shore Dinner

**MAKES 6 SERVINGS**

A traditional shore dinner is cooked in a rock-lined pit dug in the sand at the beach. After a roaring fire has burned out and heated the stones, they are covered with seaweed. Then fish, shellfish, and vegetables are layered with more seaweed. The pit is covered with a tarp and the shore dinner left to steam, while you collect seashells or play in the surf. Here though, for the landlocked, we call for a clam steamer. Serve the dinner with one or two of the dipping sauces in this menu.

1 teaspoon vegetable oil

1 small onion, minced

1 garlic clove, minced

1½ cups low-sodium chicken or vegetable broth

1 bay leaf

1 sprig fresh thyme

3–4 whole black peppercorns

3 ears fresh corn, shucked and halved

6 small Red Bliss potatoes, parboiled

12 (about 1-inch) boiling onions, parboiled

3 (5-ounce) lobster tails, split lengthwise

6 (2-ounce) pieces of scrod fillet

2 dozen mussels, scrubbed and debearded

*1.* Heat a steamer pan or large pot over medium heat. Swirl in the oil, then add the onion and garlic. Cook, stirring occasionally, until the onion is translucent, 3–5 minutes. Add the broth, bay leaf, thyme, and peppercorns; bring to a simmer.

*2.* Arrange the corn, potatoes, boiling onions, and lobster tails in the first tier of a tiered steamer or as the first layer in a deep steaming basket. Arrange the scrod and mussels in the second tier or as the top layer. Cover the steamer tightly, place over the simmering broth, and steam until all of the vegetables are tender and the fish is opaque in the center, 30–35 minutes. Remove the cover, discard the bay leaf, and serve the vegetables, fish, and shellfish with a cup of the flavorful broth on the side and a selection of dipping sauces [recipes follow].

Per serving (⅙ of dinner): 300 Cal, 6 g Fat, 2 g Sat Fat, 95 mg Chol, 710 mg Sod, 26 g Carb, 3 g Fib, 37 g Prot, 88 mg Calc. *POINTS: 6.*

———◆———

*Chef's Tip:* To parboil the potatoes and boiling onions, place them in a saucepan with enough water to cover; bring to a boil. Reduce the heat and simmer, covered, until partially cooked, 5 to 8 minutes; drain. You can keep the parboiled vegetables, covered, in the refrigerator for up to two days.

*New England Shore Dinner with Dipping Sauces*

# Roasted Garlic and Mustard Dipping Sauce

The garlic for this dipping sauce can be roasted anytime the oven is already on.
An exact temperature or cooking time is not important, as long as the garlic develops a rich,
brown color and the flesh becomes soft enough to mash easily. The dipping sauce may
be stored in the refrigerator for up to three days.

½ cup low-sodium vegetable or
   chicken broth
2 teaspoons cold water
2 teaspoons cornstarch
¼ cup malt vinegar
4 cloves of roasted garlic,
   mashed to a paste
2 tablespoons Dijon mustard
½ teaspoon honey
2 tablespoons peanut oil
¼ teaspoon salt
Freshly ground pepper, to taste

*1.* Bring the broth to a boil in a saucepan. Stir the water into the cornstarch in a small bowl and drizzle it into the simmering broth, stirring constantly until the mixture boils and thickens, about 1 minute.

*2.* Remove the pan from the heat, then add the vinegar, garlic, mustard, and honey. Let the mixture cool completely, then drizzle in the oil, salt, and pepper, whisking constantly. Serve in small cups with the shore dinner.

Per serving (about 3 tablespoons): 58 Cal, 5 g Fat, 1 g Sat Fat, 0 mg Chol, 136 mg Sod, 3 g Carb, 0 g Fib, 1 g Prot, 12 mg Calc. *POINTS: 2.*

———◆———

*Chef's Tip:* To reserve any unused roasted garlic, peel the cloves and place them in a small jar. Cover with a good quality cooking or salad oil, then cover the jar and refrigerate for up to four days. Use the oil in other sautéed dishes that would benefit from a subtle roasted-garlic aroma.

# Buttermilk and Dill Dipping Sauce

### MAKES 6 SERVINGS

Rich, thick yogurt cheese adds texture and tang to this light sauce. It can also
add zip to other sauces or salad dressings. So you might want to make the whole cup
of yogurt cheese, as directed below, to have some on hand. It will keep in an
airtight container in the refrigerator for up to four days.

½ **cup fat-free buttermilk**

2 **tablespoons yogurt cheese***

2 **tablespoons fat-free cream
  cheese, at room temperature**

2 **tablespoons minced fresh dill**

2 **teaspoons minced shallot
  or scallion**

2 **teaspoons fresh lemon juice**

1 **teaspoon white-wine vinegar**

¼ **teaspoon salt**

**Freshly ground pepper, to taste**

Combine the buttermilk, yogurt cheese, cream cheese, dill, shallot,
lemon juice, vinegar, salt, and pepper in a small bowl; mix until
smooth. Refrigerate, covered, at least 1 hour before serving to let
the flavors meld. Serve in small cups with the shore dinner.

Per serving (about 3 tablespoons): 17 Cal, 0 g Fat, 0 g Sat Fat, 1 mg Chol,
150 mg Sod, 2 g Carb, 0 g Fib, 2 g Prot, 46 mg Calc. ***POINTS: 0.***

*To make 1 cup yogurt cheese, spoon 2 cups plain nonfat yogurt
into a coffee filter- or cheesecloth-lined strainer; place over a bowl.
Refrigerate, covered, for 24 hours. Transfer the finished cheese to
an airtight container and refrigerate.

# Tomato Dipping Sauce

Though low in fat, this dipping sauce has rich flavor and substantial texture. Double or triple the recipe so you have some on hand to pair with steamed vegetables, use as a vinaigrette, or dress a dish of steamed or broiled fish. Keep the sauce refrigerated in a tightly sealed container for up to five days.

**2 teaspoons olive oil**

**2 teaspoons minced shallots**

**1 garlic clove, minced**

**2 tablespoons tomato paste**

**2 cups chopped tomatoes (fresh or canned)**

**2 tablespoons chopped flat-leaf parsley**

**1 tablespoon balsamic vinegar**

**Freshly ground pepper, to taste**

*1.* Heat a nonstick skillet over medium heat. Swirl in the oil, then add the shallots and garlic. Cook, stirring frequently, until translucent, 3–4 minutes. Add the tomato paste and cook, stirring constantly, until fragrant, 3–4 minutes. Add the chopped tomatoes and cook over medium heat until slightly thickened, about 10 minutes. Remove from the heat and cool slightly.

*2.* Puree the tomato mixture in a blender. Add the parsley, vinegar, and pepper; pulse until the mixture is an even texture. Serve in small cups with the shore dinner.

Per serving (about 3 tablespoons): 34 Cal, 2 g Fat, 0 g Sat Fat, 0 mg Chol, 12 mg Sod, 5 g Carb, 1 g Fib, 0 g Prot, 9 mg Calc. ***POINTS: 1.***

# Tomato Salad

MAKES 6 SERVINGS

When a selection of tomatoes is available at your favorite market or farm stand,
try this salad with a combination of yellow and red tomatoes of different sizes and shapes.
Make the vinaigrette up to two days in advance, but if possible, combine the tomatoes
with the vinaigrette no more than an hour before serving.

**2 tablespoons red-wine vinegar**
**1 tablespoon sherry vinegar**
**1 tablespoon minced shallots**
**¼ teaspoon salt**
**Freshly ground pepper, to taste**
**1 sprig fresh basil**
**1 tablespoon olive oil**
**1 pound tomatoes, halved,
   sliced, or cut into wedges**
**Chopped or finely shredded
   fresh basil leaves**

1. To make the dressing, whisk together the red-wine and sherry vinegars, the shallots, salt, pepper, and basil in a small bowl. Bruise the basil with the back of a wooden spoon. Let the mixture stand at room temperature for 20 minutes. Discard the basil sprig. Whisk in the oil.

2. Place the tomatoes in a salad bowl. Drizzle with the dressing and scatter with the chopped or shredded basil, tossing gently to coat. Let the salad rest at room temperature at least 30 minutes or up to 1 hour before serving.

Per serving (⅙ of salad): 40 Cal, 3 g Fat, 0 g Sat Fat, 0 mg Chol, 104 mg Sod, 5 g Carb, 0 g Fib, 1 g Prot, 5 mg Calc. *POINTS: 1.*

# Baked Ricotta Cheese

**MAKES 6 SERVINGS**

Ricotta cheese, simply seasoned, then baked until browned, is warm and comforting in
a way that takes us back to childhood. It makes a perfect foil—contrasting in flavor, color,
and texture—for the tomato salad.

¾ **cup part-skim ricotta cheese**
½ **teaspoon salt**
2 **teaspoons extra-virgin olive oil**
**Freshly ground pepper, to taste**

*1.* Preheat the oven to 375°F. Combine the ricotta cheese and salt;
spoon into a small baking dish.
*2.* Drizzle the cheese with the oil and sprinkle with pepper. Bake
until browned and the cheese bubbles around the edges of the
dish, about 20 minutes.
*3.* Remove the cheese from the oven and let it set for about
10 minutes before serving.

Per serving (2 tablespoons): 80 Cal, 5 g Fat, 3 g Sat Fat, 15 mg Chol, 220 mg Sod,
3 g Carb, 0 g Fib, 6 g Prot, 155 mg Calc. ***POINTS: 2.***

———◆———

*Chef's Tip:* Baked ricotta cheese makes an excellent stuffing for cherry tomatoes and mushroom
caps for hors d'oeuvres. You can flavor the ricotta with minced fresh herbs or roasted garlic before
baking. Then spoon or pipe the mixture into hollowed cherry tomatoes or small mushroom
caps and broil just until browned, about 5 minutes.

# Watermelon, Watercress, and Red Onion Salad

MAKES 6 SERVINGS

Invigorate your palate with this unusual, yet delicious combination. When you soak the red onion up to eight hours ahead of time, you improve its flavor and color *and* you cut down on last-minute work. Choose seedless watermelon, if it's available.

½ **medium red onion, thinly sliced and separated into rings**

3 **cups watermelon, cubed and seeded**

1 **bunch watercress, trimmed, rinsed, and dried**

2 **tablespoons white-wine vinegar**

1 **tablespoon vegetable oil**

¼ **teaspoon salt**

**Freshly ground pepper, to taste**

1 **tablespoon toasted pine nuts**

*1.* Put the onion in a small bowl, cover with cold water, and refrigerate for at least 4 or up to 8 hours. This will crisp and sweeten the onion.

*2.* Combine the watermelon and watercress in a salad bowl.

*3.* To make the dressing, whisk together the vinegar, oil, salt, and pepper in a small bowl. Drizzle over the watermelon and watercress, tossing gently to coat. Top with the onion rings and pine nuts, just before serving.

Per serving (¾ cup): 58 Cal, 3 g Fat, 0 g Sat Fat, 0 mg Chol, 136 mg Sod, 9 g Carb, 1 g Fib, 1 g Prot, 19 mg Calc. ***POINTS: 1.***

———◆———

*Chef's Tip:* To toast the pine nuts, place them in a small dry skillet over medium-low heat. Cook, shaking the pan and stirring constantly, until lightly browned and fragrant, 3 to 4 minutes. Watch them carefully when toasting; pine nuts can burn quickly. Transfer the nuts to a plate to cool.

# Peach Cobbler

**MAKES 6 SERVINGS**

Cobblers are a classic American dessert, but there is no nationwide consensus on what constitutes a true cobbler crust. This rendition features a tender, cake-like topping. Bake the cobbler just before leaving for the shore (or backyard!). Wrap it up in clean tea towels to stay warm until you are ready to serve it.

1½ cups all-purpose flour
¾ cup sugar
1 teaspoon baking powder
⅛ teaspoon cinnamon
Pinch ground nutmeg
1 cup fat-free milk
1 large egg
1 egg white
½ teaspoon vanilla extract
½ teaspoon grated lemon rind
3 cups sliced fresh or thawed frozen peaches

*1.* Preheat the oven to 375°F. Spray an 8-inch square baking dish with nonstick spray.

*2.* Combine the flour, ½ cup of the sugar, the baking powder, cinnamon, and nutmeg in one bowl. Combine the milk, egg, egg white, vanilla, and lemon rind in another bowl. Add the egg mixture to the flour mixture; stir until just blended.

*3.* Layer the peaches in the baking dish. Sprinkle with the remaining sugar. Spoon the flour mixture over the peaches. Bake until the topping is brown and springs back when touched, 45–60 minutes. Serve hot.

Per serving (⅙ of cobbler): 140 Cal, 1 g Fat, 0 g Sat Fat, 18 mg Chol, 40 mg Sod, 30 g Carb, 1 g Fib, 7 g Prot, 32 mg Calc. *POINTS: 3.*

———◆———

*Chef's Tip:* Fruits have different levels of sweetness. Their flavors also change with the season. Taste the fruit before you add the sugar, and use only enough to bring out the flavor—not mask it. For a wonderful caramel or maple flavor, substitute dark brown sugar or maple syrup.

# FAMILY REUNION BARBECUE

*Barbecued Sliced Potatoes with Parmesan*
—
*Big Ranch Salad with Jumbo Croutons*
—
*Grilled Flank Steak with Homemade Barbecue Sauce*
—
*Cheddar and Pickle–Studded Turkey Burgers*
—
*Minted Zucchini Salad*
—
*Grilled Corn on the Cob with Lemon-Thyme Butter*
—
*Chocolate Chip Cookies*
—
*Raspberry-Peach Crumble Pie*

## Barbecued Sliced Potatoes with Parmesan

**MAKES 12 SERVINGS**

Simple and delicious, these spuds kick off a hearty yet festive family-style menu. To save last-minute preparation time, slice and season the potatoes one to two hours before you're ready to grill them. Though the potatoes are great hot, they are also good served at room temperature, which means you can make them before the gathering gets going.

**6** (8-ounce) russet potatoes, scrubbed
**3** tablespoons olive oil
**1** teaspoon salt
**½** teaspoon freshly ground pepper
**5** tablespoons grated Parmesan cheese
**1** teaspoon crushed red pepper

*1.* Slice each potato lengthwise into 6 (¼-inch thick) slices. Combine the potatoes, oil, salt, and pepper in a large bowl; toss to coat.

*2.* Spray the grill rack with nonstick spray; prepare the grill. Grill the potatoes in a single layer (in batches if necessary), 5 inches from the heat, covered, about 6 minutes. Turn the potatoes and sprinkle with the Parmesan cheese. Grill, covered, until tender, about 6 minutes longer. Transfer the potatoes to a serving platter and sprinkle with the crushed red pepper.

Per serving (3 slices): 141 Cal, 4 g Fat, 1 g Sat Fat, 2 mg Chol, 250 mg Sod, 23 g Carb, 2 g Fib, 3 g Prot, 46 mg Calc. **POINTS: 3.**

# Big Ranch Salad with Jumbo Croutons

**MAKES 12 SERVINGS**

You can't go wrong with this basic salad of lettuce, tomatoes, and cucumber, made
hearty and more appealing with chunky croutons. To save time on the day of the reunion,
make the dressing and refrigerate for up to two days (the flavors will develop); and
bake the croutons, let them cool, then store in a zip-close plastic bag for up to two days.
If you prefer, substitute three cups of packaged fat-free croutons.

 8 **ounces semolina Italian bread,**
   **cut into ½-inch cubes**
 2 **medium heads romaine**
   **lettuce, cleaned and torn**
   **into bite-size pieces**
   **(about 18 cups)**
 2 **cucumbers, peeled and cut**
   **into ¼-inch thick slices**
 4 **beefsteak tomatoes, each**
   **cored and cut into 6 wedges**
 1 **medium red onion,**
   **thinly sliced**
 1 **cup fat-free buttermilk**
10 **whole fresh basil leaves**
 3 **tablespoons light sour cream**
 2 **tablespoons low-fat**
   **mayonnaise**
 1 **tablespoon fresh lemon juice**
 2 **teaspoons sugar**
 1 **teaspoon garlic powder**
 ½ **teaspoon salt**
 ¼ **teaspoon freshly**
   **ground pepper**

*1.* Preheat the oven to 375°F. Arrange the bread cubes in single
layers on 2 baking sheets; bake until golden and crisp,
7–9 minutes. Remove from the oven and set aside to cool.
*2.* Combine the lettuce, cucumbers, tomatoes, onion, and
croutons in a large bowl. Toss well to mix.
*3.* Combine the buttermilk, basil, sour cream, mayonnaise, lemon
juice, sugar, garlic powder, salt, and pepper in a blender; puree
1 minute. Pour the dressing over the lettuce mixture and toss well
to coat. Serve at once.

Per serving (2 cups): 103 Cal, 2 g Fat, 1 g Sat Fat, 2 mg Chol, 265 mg Sod,
18 g Carb, 3 g Fib, 4 g Prot, 76 mg Calc. *POINTS: 2.*

# Grilled Flank Steak with Homemade Barbecue Sauce

**MAKES 12 SERVINGS**

This flank steak gets flavor from a dry spice rub—a great way to add robust taste to any meat, poultry, or fish. The barbecue sauce provides extra zip for those who want it.

3 tablespoons packed dark brown sugar
1 tablespoon paprika
1 tablespoon chili powder
1 tablespoon ground cumin
2 teaspoons onion powder
1½ teaspoons garlic powder
¾ teaspoon salt
2 pounds flank steak, trimmed of all visible fat
1½ cups ketchup
3 tablespoons molasses
¼ teaspoon ground ginger

*1.* To make the dry rub, combine 1 tablespoon of the brown sugar, the paprika, 2 teaspoons of the chili powder, 2 teaspoons of the cumin, the onion powder, 1 teaspoon of the garlic powder, and the salt in a small bowl. Sprinkle over both sides of the flank steak.

*2.* Spray the grill rack with nonstick spray; prepare the grill. Grill the steak 5 inches from the heat until an instant-read thermometer, inserted in the center of the steak, registers 145°F for medium-rare, 7–9 minutes on each side. Transfer to a cutting board and let stand, covered loosely with foil, about 10 minutes. Thinly slice the steak on a sharp angle.

*3.* Meanwhile, to prepare the barbecue sauce, combine the ketchup, molasses, and ginger with the remaining 2 tablespoons brown sugar, 1 teaspoon chili powder, 1 teaspoon cumin, and ½ teaspoon garlic powder in a medium saucepan; bring to a boil. Reduce the heat and simmer, covered, stirring occasionally, about 5 minutes. Serve with the steak.

Per serving (¹⁄₁₂ of steak with 2 tablespoons barbecue sauce): 183 Cal, 6 g Fat, 2 g Sat Fat, 43 mg Chol, 551 mg Sod, 16 g Carb, 1 g Fib, 17 g Prot, 33 mg Calc. ***POINTS: 4.***

*Chef's Tip:* You can make the dry rub up to a month ahead and store it in a zip-close plastic bag in a cool dark place. While you're at it, double the recipe for the rub to have some on hand for another barbecue in the season. You can prepare the barbecue sauce up to a week ahead, store it in the refrigerator, then reheat it in a saucepan when needed.

# Cheddar and Pickle—Studded Turkey Burgers

### MAKES 12 SERVINGS

Cheese and pickles in the burgers not only add juicy flavor but also offer a topic for conversation. You can mix and shape the burgers up to 24 hours ahead and keep them in an airtight container in the refrigerator; put them on the grill about 15 minutes before mealtime. Serve with additional ketchup if you like.

3 pounds ground skinless turkey breasts

6 ounces reduced-fat sharp cheddar cheese, cut into ¼-inch cubes

1 cup plain dry bread crumbs

½ cup dill pickle slices, drained and chopped

½ cup ketchup

1 teaspoon salt

½ teaspoon freshly ground pepper

12 hamburger buns

12 romaine lettuce leaves

3 medium tomatoes, each cut into 4 slices

*1.* Combine the ground turkey, cheese, bread crumbs, pickles, ketchup, salt, and pepper in a large bowl. Form the mixture into 12 (¾-inch thick) burgers.

*2.* Spray the grill rack with nonstick spray; prepare the grill. Grill the burgers 5 inches from the heat until an instant-read thermometer, inserted in the center of the burgers, registers 165°F, 7–8 minutes on each side.

*3.* Place the burgers in the buns with the lettuce and tomato.

Per serving (1 burger): 363 Cal, 9 g Fat, 3 g Sat Fat, 75 mg Chol, 854 mg Sod, 33 g Carb, 2 g Fib, 36 g Prot, 208 mg Calc. *POINTS: 8.*

—◆—

*Chef's Tip:* Place the burgers in the buns in a napkin-lined basket, and serve bowls of the lettuce, tomatoes, and ketchup on the side so guests can help themselves. For a Greek twist, add 1½ teaspoons of dried oregano to the burger mixture and substitute 6 ounces of reduced-fat feta cheese for the cheddar.

*Cheddar and Pickle–Studded Turkey Burgers, Big Ranch Salad with Jumbo Croutons, and Grilled Corn on the Cob with Lemon-Thyme Butter*

# Minted Zucchini Salad

**MAKES 12 SERVINGS**

If it's convenient to make this salad last minute, do so—it's great served warm. Otherwise, prepare it two to three hours ahead and serve it at room temperature. Or prepare it up to two days ahead and refrigerate, then bring to room temperature before serving. To take this recipe south of the border, substitute lime juice and lime rind for the lemon and replace the mint with chopped fresh cilantro. For a touch of heat, stir in some chopped, seeded jalapeño peppers.

| | |
|---|---|
| 1 | tablespoon extra-virgin olive oil |
| 6 | garlic cloves, sliced |
| 2 | red bell peppers, seeded and cut into ½-inch pieces |
| 3 | pounds zucchini (about 5), trimmed and cut into ¼-inch thick half moons |
| 3 | tablespoons chopped fresh mint |
| 2 | teaspoons grated lemon rind |
| 2 | tablespoons fresh lemon juice |
| 1½ | teaspoons salt |
| ½ | teaspoon freshly ground pepper |

*1.* Heat a large nonstick skillet over medium-high heat. Swirl in 1½ teaspoons of the oil, then add 3 of the garlic cloves. Cook, stirring frequently, until fragrant, about 30 seconds. Add 1 of the bell peppers and cook, stirring frequently, about 1 minute. Add half of the zucchini and cook, stirring occasionally, until crisp-tender, 3–5 minutes. Transfer to a large bowl.

*2.* Repeat cooking the vegetables with the remaining 1½ teaspoons oil, 3 garlic cloves, 1 bell pepper, and the remaining half of zucchini. Add to the zucchini mixture and let cool about 5 minutes.

*3.* Add the mint, lemon rind, lemon juice, salt, and pepper to the zucchini mixture; toss well. Serve at once or at room temperature.

Per serving (⅔ cup): 32 Cal, 1 g Fat, 0 g Sat Fat, 0 mg Chol, 295 mg Sod, 5 g Carb, 2 g Fib, 1 g Prot, 22 mg Calc. ***POINTS: 0.***

———◆———

*Chef's Tip:* If you're using zucchini from your own garden, or if you have access to zucchini blossoms, don't let these sweet little edibles go to waste; garnish the salad with one or two of them.

# Grilled Corn on the Cob with Lemon-Thyme Butter

**MAKES 12 SERVINGS**

Served in their earth-scented husks, freshly grilled corn on the cob are perfect party food. To help keep the corn husks from charring, soak the corn in a large bowl of water for 10 to 15 minutes before grilling.

6 tablespoons salted light butter, softened

2 tablespoons grated lemon rind

1 teaspoon chopped fresh thyme, or ½ teaspoon dried

¼ teaspoon salt

¼ teaspoon freshly ground pepper

12 fresh corn on the cob, in the husk

*1.* Combine the butter, lemon rind, thyme, salt, and pepper in a small bowl.

*2.* Peel back the husk leaves from the corn and, without removing them, remove and discard the corn silk. Fold the husks back up around the corn.

*3.* Spray the grill rack with nonstick spray; prepare the grill. Grill the corn 5 inches from the heat, turning several times, until tender and lightly charred, 7–9 minutes. Serve the corn in the husks with the lemon-thyme butter in a small dish on the side.

Per serving (1 corn on the cob with about 1½ teaspoons butter): 118 Cal, 5 g Fat, 3 g Sat Fat, 10 mg Chol, 88 mg Sod, 20 g Carb, 2 g Fib, 3 g Prot, 3 mg Calc. *POINTS: 2.*

*Chocolate Chip Cookies*

# Chocolate Chip Cookies

**MAKES 36 SERVINGS**

You'll keep the kids *and* the adults happy if you serve these all-around-favorite cookies at your family gathering. Be sure not to overbake them—they should have a slightly chewy texture when cool. You can make them, wrap them well, and freeze them for up to three months.

1¼ cups all-purpose flour
½ teaspoon baking soda
½ cup salted light butter, softened
½ cup packed light brown sugar
¼ cup granulated sugar
1 large egg
½ teaspoon vanilla extract
⅓ cup reduced-fat semisweet chocolate chips

*1.* Preheat the oven to 350°F. Spray 2 baking sheets with nonstick spray.

*2.* Combine the flour and baking soda in a small bowl; set aside.

*3.* With an electric mixer at high speed, beat the butter, brown sugar, and granulated sugar until light and fluffy. Add the egg and vanilla; beat well. With the mixer at low speed, stir in the flour mixture until all of the flour is just moistened. Stir in the chocolate chips.

*4.* Drop the dough by slightly rounded teaspoons, 1½ inches apart, onto the baking sheets. Bake until almost set and lightly golden, 11–13 minutes. Cool on the baking sheets on racks until firm, 2–3 minutes. Remove the cookies from the baking sheets and cool completely on racks.

Per serving (1 cookie): 55 Cal, 2 g Fat, 1 g Sat Fat, 10 mg Chol, 32 mg Sod, 9 g Carb, 0 g Fib, 1 g Prot, 5 mg Calc. ***POINTS: 1.***

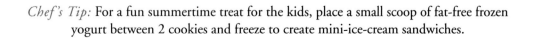

*Chef's Tip:* For a fun summertime treat for the kids, place a small scoop of fat-free frozen yogurt between 2 cookies and freeze to create mini-ice-cream sandwiches.

# Raspberry-Peach Crumble Pie

**MAKES 16 SERVINGS**

You can make this pie early in the day, let it sit on a rack until dessert time, then serve
it at room temperature. Or reheat it in a 350°F oven until warm, about 20 minutes.
For a quick alternative, substitute 8 cups of thawed frozen peaches for the fresh peaches
and 1 cup frozen raspberries for the fresh raspberries.

1 (7½-ounce) package
    refrigerated pie dough
3 pounds fresh peaches, pitted
    and sliced
¾ cup + ⅓ cup packed light
    brown sugar
¼ cup cornstarch
1 teaspoon cinnamon
½ teaspoon ground ginger
¼ teaspoon ground cardamom
½ pint fresh raspberries
⅓ cup rolled oats
¼ cup all-purpose flour
4 teaspoons salted light butter,
    melted

*1.* Preheat the oven to 425°F. Line a 9-inch pie plate with the
dough. Crimp the edges to form a fluted rim; refrigerate.
*2.* Combine the peaches, ¾ cup of the sugar, the cornstarch,
cinnamon, ginger, and cardamom in a medium bowl. Gently fold
in the raspberries, then pour into the dough-lined pie plate.
*3.* Combine the remaining ⅓ cup sugar, the oats, flour, and melted
butter in medium bowl; mix until the mixture holds together in
clumps when squeezed. Sprinkle over the peach mixture. Stand the
pie on a foil-lined baking sheet and bake 20 minutes. Cover the
pie loosely with foil and bake until the filling is bubbly and thick,
50–60 minutes longer. Cool on a rack 30 minutes. Serve warm,
or let cool to room temperature.

Per serving (⅟₁₆ of pie): 184 Cal, 5 g Fat, 2 g Sat Fat, 2 mg Chol, 97 mg Sod,
34 g Carb, 2 g Fib, 2 g Prot, 22 mg Calc. ***POINTS: 4.***

———◆———

*Chef's Tip:* Sprinkle the pie with a light dusting of confectioners' sugar and garnish with a fresh mint sprig.

# AN OPERA PICNIC

*Peach Royale*
—
*Portobellos with Tuscan Bean Salad*
—
*White Gazpacho with Green Grapes*
—
*Burgundy-Peppercorn Beef Bruschetta*
—
*Poached Salmon Fillets in Rice Paper*
—
*Squash Darioles*
—
*Grilled New Potatoes with Mustard Seed Dipping Sauce*
—
*American Bounty Cobbler*

## Peach Royale

**MAKES 4 SERVINGS**

Peaches form the bookends for this elegant picnic, with this upscale cocktail on one side and a down-home peach cobbler on the other. If you prefer, substitute crème de cassis for the peach liqueur. Pop the champagne and assemble this drink at the picnic site.

**2 tablespoons peach-flavored brandy or liqueur**

**1½ cups chilled champagne**

Divide the peach brandy evenly between 4 champagne flutes. Pour in the champagne, adding it in two stages. With a tall slender spoon, gently swirl the drink to blend.

Per serving (1 drink): 73 Cal, 0 g Fat, 0 g Sat Fat, 0 mg Chol, 0 mg Sod, 3 g Car, 0 g Fib, 0 g Prot, 7 mg Calc. ***POINTS: 1.***

*Chef's Tip:* Try the two-stage pour to keep the champagne from bubbling over: For the first stage, slowly pour in just enough champagne to fill each glass halfway. After you've poured the fourth half-glass, return to the first glass you poured and complete the second stage, filling each glass with bubbly.

*Portobellos with Tuscan Bean Salad*

# *Portobellos with Tuscan Bean Salad*

**MAKES 4 SERVINGS**

Tuscan dishes are vibrant with the strong flavors of fresh vegetables and herbs. Savor the interplay of sharp, subtle, earthy ingredients. Celery juice is available in most larger markets or health food stores, but if you have difficulty finding it, make your own by pureeing chopped fresh celery with a little water. Strain the puree and use the juice here, or anytime you want to add a hint of celery to a soup or rice dish.

¼ cup celery juice, or low-sodium vegetable or chicken broth

¼ teaspoon cornstarch

1 teaspoon water

2 tablespoons champagne vinegar

2 tablespoons extra-virgin olive oil

½ cup rinsed and drained canned cannellini beans

¼ cup minced carrot

¼ cup minced celery

¼ cup minced red bell pepper

¼ cup minced yellow bell pepper

2 tablespoons minced scallions

¼ teaspoon salt

Freshly ground pepper, to taste

8 small (2-inch) portobello mushrooms caps, cleaned

1 tablespoon minced fresh chives

2 teaspoons chopped fresh cilantro

*1.* Bring the celery juice to a boil in a small saucepan. Dissolve the cornstarch in the water and whisk into the boiling broth. Transfer to a medium bowl and allow to cool. Add the vinegar, then slowly whisk in the oil. Add the beans, carrot, celery, red and yellow bell peppers, scallions, salt, and pepper; toss gently to coat. Cover and let stand at room temperature about 1 hour (refrigerate the salad if holding longer than 1 hour).

*2.* Preheat the oven to 350°F. Spray a baking sheet with nonstick spray. Place the mushroom caps on the baking sheet and spray lightly with olive-oil nonstick spray. Cover with foil and bake until tender, 15–20 minutes. Transfer to a platter to cool.

*3.* Spoon the bean salad onto the mushroom caps, then sprinkle with the chives and cilantro.

Per serving (2 mushroom caps): 130 Cal, 7 g Fat, 1 g Sat Fat, trace Chol, 330 mg Sod, 12 g Carb, 3 g Fib, 4 g Prot, 40 mg Calc. ***POINTS: 3.***

*Chef's Tip:* Portobello mushrooms have a wonderful, meaty texture that pairs well with substantial fillings. Before roasting them, cut away the stems and gently scrape out the gills. You can save the stems to add to a pot of broth at another time.

# White Gazpacho with Green Grapes

**MAKES 6 SERVINGS**

This unusual white gazpacho is derived from the Andalusian tradition of thickening a refreshing, cold vegetable soup with bread and almonds. For a sweeter version, substitute melon for some or all of the cucumber. A thermos would be perfect for transporting this soup to the picnic site.

¾ cup low-sodium
    vegetable broth
1½ teaspoons cornstarch
½ teaspoon water
3 tablespoons sherry vinegar
1 tablespoon extra-virgin
    olive oil
3 cups crustless cubed firm
    white bread (½ of a
    French loaf)
¼ cup chopped blanched
    almonds
1 teaspoon minced garlic
3 cups diced cucumbers (peel
    and seed before dicing)
½ teaspoon salt
 Freshly ground pepper, to taste
1½ cups halved green
    seedless grapes
¼ cup chopped flat-leaf parsley

*1.* Bring the broth to a boil. Dissolve the cornstarch in the water and whisk into the boiling broth. Remove from the heat and allow to cool. Add the vinegar and then slowly whisk in the oil; set aside.
*2.* Soak the bread cubes in just enough cold water to barely cover them, until evenly moistened, about 30 minutes; then squeeze the water out of the bread. Transfer half of the soaked bread to a food processor. Add the almonds and garlic; puree. Add the cucumbers, salt, and pepper; pulse until the soup is a relatively smooth puree. Transfer the soup to a container. Puree the remaining bread with the thickened broth mixture; stir into the rest of the soup. Cover and refrigerate until very cold.
*3.* Pour the chilled soup into individual serving bowls. Garnish with the grapes and parsley.

Per serving (½ cup): 150 Cal, 7 g Fat, 1 g Sat Fat, 0 mg Chol, 310 mg Sod, 19 g Carb, 2 g Fib, 4 g Prot, 45 mg Calc. **POINTS: 3.**

---

*Chef's Tip:* If you're not toting this gazpacho to a picnic site, try serving it in cucumber cups. Select firm cucumbers that are at least 2 inches in diameter. Cut them into 4-inch sections, leaving the peel on. Use a melon baller or a grapefruit spoon to scoop out the seeds and some of the flesh, leaving enough flesh at the bottom of each section to form a cup.

# Burgundy-Peppercorn Beef Bruschetta

**MAKES 4 SERVINGS**

To keep this dish simple, use lean roast beef from the deli. For a deluxe version, roast a small piece of beef tenderloin and slice it yourself. Tenderloin has a smooth, melting texture that brings this simple, open-face sandwich to another level. Make the Burgundy-peppercorn sauce up to three days ahead, but assemble the sandwiches just before you pack up the picnic basket.

½ teaspoon vegetable oil
2 teaspoons minced shallots
½ cup Burgundy or similar dry red wine
2 teaspoons cracked black pepper
8 thin slices French bread
1 garlic clove, peeled and cut in half
4 thin slices roasted beef sirloin (about 4 ounces)

*1.* Heat a large saucepan over medium heat. Swirl in the oil, then add the shallots and cook, stirring constantly, until the shallots are tender and translucent, about 2 minutes. Add the wine and pepper and simmer until the mixture is reduced to about 2 tablespoons, about 10 minutes.

*2.* Preheat the broiler. Spray a nonstick baking sheet with nonstick spray. Arrange the bread on the baking sheet and spray with olive-oil nonstick spray. Rub lightly with the halved garlic clove, then broil until browned on both sides, about 1 minute on each side.

*3.* To assemble the bruschettas, cut the beef slices in half. Drape one half on each toasted bread slice. Spoon about ¾ teaspoon of the Burgundy-peppercorn sauce over each.

Per serving (2 bruschettas): 120 Cal, 4 g Fat, 1 g Fat, 25 mg Chol, 380 mg Sod, 7 g Carb, 0 g Fib, 10 g Prot, 18 mg Calc. *POINTS: 3.*

# Poached Salmon Fillets in Rice Paper

**MAKES 4 SERVINGS**

Cooked salmon bundled in rice paper makes the perfect package to take to a picnic. Rice paper is available at Asian markets and comes in various sizes and shapes—small to large, round or square. We use small rounds for this dish. Made from rice flour, these edible delicate wrappers only need to be soaked briefly before using. You can make these bundles up to four hours ahead and keep them in the refrigerator, covered with dampened paper towels and plastic wrap.

1½ cups semi-dry white wine

3 cups low-sodium chicken broth

4 fresh parsley sprigs

3 fresh dill sprigs

1 fresh thyme sprig

2–3 whole black peppercorns

½ teaspoon salt

4 (4-ounce) salmon fillet pieces

1 cup thinly sliced seedless cucumber

¼ cup thinly sliced red onion

1 tablespoon olive oil

2 tablespoons white-wine vinegar

2 tablespoons minced fresh basil

1 tablespoon minced fresh parsley

Freshly ground pepper, to taste

4 small round rice paper wrappers

1 cup shredded Boston lettuce

Whole parsley leaves

*1.* Bring the wine and broth to a simmer in a wide, shallow pot. Add the parsley, dill, thyme, peppercorns, and ¼ teaspoon of the salt; continue to simmer until the broth is flavorful, about 5 minutes. With a slotted spoon or spatula, lower the salmon into the simmering broth. Reduce the heat and poach the salmon until it is just opaque in the center, about 10 minutes. Transfer the salmon to a dish then moisten with a spoonful or two of the broth. Cover and refrigerate until well chilled.

*2.* Toss the cucumber and onion with the oil, vinegar, basil, and parsley in a small bowl. Season with the remaining ¼ teaspoon salt and the pepper.

*3.* To assemble the packets, soak the rice paper in enough warm water to cover until pliable, about 45 seconds. Remove the wrappers from the water and lay on a work surface. Top each with ¼ cup shredded lettuce, ¼ cup of the cucumber salad, then a salmon fillet; top each fillet with a single whole parsley leaf. Fold the wrapper around the salmon, completely enclosing it. Place, seam-side down, on a platter. Cover and refrigerate until ready to transport to the picnic.

Per serving (1 packet): 290 Cal, 16 g Fat, 3 g Fat, 65 mg Chol, 90 mg Sod, 9 g Carb, 0 g Fib, 24 g Prot, 27 mg Calc. ***POINTS: 7.***

———◆———

*Chef's Tip:* If desired, tie the rice paper packets with scallion or leek leaf ribbons. Use long thin strips cut from the green part of the scallion or leek.

# Squash Darioles

This wonderful chilled, molded vegetable dish is easy to vary, according to which vegetables are available in your market. Substitute eggplant for the zucchini and broccoli florets for the carrots, if you prefer. A dariole is a special type of mold, but feel free to use any mold you like, including small teacups or custard cups. To make it easy to transport the darioles, you might choose to use a muffin tin.

2 **medium plum tomatoes, cored and cut into ½ inch slices**

2 **teaspoons minced garlic**

½ **teaspoon salt**

**Freshly ground pepper, to taste**

1 **medium zucchini, cut into ⅛–inch slices**

1 **medium yellow squash, cut into ⅛–inch slices**

1 **large carrot, cut into ⅛–inch slices**

2 **teaspoons extra-virgin olive oil**

**Balsamic vinegar**

*1.* Preheat the oven to 325°F. Place the tomato slices on a rack on a foil-lined baking sheet. Spray the tomatoes with olive-oil nonstick spray. Sprinkle with the garlic, salt, and pepper. Roast until the slices have dried and browned, 1–1½ hours.

*2.* Put the zucchini and yellow squash in a steamer basket; set in a saucepan over 1 inch of boiling water. Cover tightly and steam until tender and translucent, about 4 minutes. Transfer the zucchini and squash to a bowl; let cool. Put the carrot in the steamer basket and steam until tender, about 6 minutes.

*3.* Spray 4 dariole molds or 4-ounce custard cups lightly with cooking spray. Fill the molds in the following sequence: First, a layer of roasted tomato, followed by zucchini, then carrots, then yellow squash, ending with another layer of tomato. Press them down to ensure that the vegetables are compact. Cover with foil and refrigerate for up to 12 hours.

*4.* To serve, unmold onto a platter (or into a shallow container, ready to transport to the picnic). Drizzle each dariole with ½ teaspoon of the olive oil and several drops of balsamic vinegar.

Per serving (1 dariole): 60 Cal, 2 g Fat, 0 g Fat, 0 mg Chol, 300 mg Sod, 8 g Carb, 3 g Fib, 2 g Prot, 27 mg Calc. *POINTS: 1.*

---

*Chef's Tip:* Instead of steaming the zucchini and yellow squash, cut it into thin slices lengthwise and grill them. You can wrap them around the inside of the dariole mold to give the dish a very different look and a very different flavor.

# Grilled New Potatoes with Mustard Seed Dipping Sauce

**MAKES 4 SERVINGS**

These smoky potatoes are grilled on skewers and paired with a pungent dipping sauce for a do-it-yourself potato salad. If you're pressed for time, you can simply steam the potatoes until tender and skip the grill altogether. Use any small potato for this dish, such as fingerling or blue potatoes. Parcook the potatoes and make the dipping sauce up to two days ahead, but grill the potatoes no more than three hours before you plan to serve them.

6 **new potatoes (about 1½ inches in diameter)**
¾ **teaspoon salt**
½ **cup low-sodium vegetable or chicken broth**
2 **teaspoons cornstarch**
2 **teaspoons cold water**
¼ **cup cider vinegar**
1 **tablespoon Dijon mustard**
1 **tablespoon whole-grain mustard**
1 **teaspoon mustard seeds**
½ **teaspoon honey**
2 **tablespoons vegetable oil**
**Freshly ground pepper, to taste**

*1.* Place the potatoes, ½ teaspoon of the salt, and enough water to cover in a large saucepan; bring to a boil. Reduce the heat and simmer, covered, until partially cooked, 10–12 minutes; drain. When the potatoes are cool enough to handle, cut them in half and thread them on 8 (6-inch) skewers, with the cut sides facing in the same direction.

*2.* Preheat the grill. Spray the potatoes with nonstick spray and grill, turning from time to time, until the potatoes are very tender and browned, about 8 minutes.

*3.* To make the dipping sauce, bring the broth to a boil in a saucepan. Mix the cornstarch and water in a small bowl. Drizzle it into the simmering broth, stirring constantly until thickened, about 1 minute. Transfer to a bowl, then add the vinegar, mustard, mustard seeds, honey, the remaining ¼ teaspoon salt, and the pepper. When completely cool, drizzle in the oil, whisking constantly. Serve the potatoes with the dipping sauce.

Per serving (1 skewer with ¼ cup dipping sauce): 90 Cal, 4 g Fat, 0 g Sat Fat, 0 mg Chol, 425 mg Sod, 12 g Carb, 1 g Fib, 2 g Prot, 16 mg Calc. ***POINTS: 2.***

# American Bounty Cobbler

**MAKES 6 SERVINGS**

Cobblers are a traditional American dessert, and like any traditional dish, their interpretation varies from region to region. Biscuit toppings over the fruit are popular in some areas, pie crusts in others. We've opted to adorn our fruit with a moist, delicious cake batter. Bake the cobbler early in the day of your picnic and serve it at room temperature.

3 cups peeled, pitted, and sliced fresh peaches (about 4 peaches)
½ cup sugar
⅛ teaspoon ground nutmeg
¾ cup all-purpose flour
1 teaspoon baking powder
½ cup fat-free milk
1 large egg
1 teaspoon vanilla extract
1 teaspoon grated lemon rind

1. Preheat the oven to 350°F. Spray an 8-inch square baking dish with nonstick spray.
2. Combine the peaches with ¼ cup of the sugar and the nutmeg in a medium bowl; toss until evenly coated. Let the peaches sit for at least 20 minutes while preparing the batter topping.
3. In a large bowl, stir together the flour, baking powder, and remaining ¼ cup sugar. In a medium bowl, blend the milk, egg, vanilla, and lemon rind. Stir the milk mixture into the flour mixture until the dry ingredients are evenly moistened and the batter is smooth.
4. Transfer the fruit to the baking dish. Spread the batter over the fruit. Bake until the topping is brown and springs back when touched, about 30 minutes. Let the cobbler rest 30 minutes. Serve warm or at room temperature.

Per serving (⅙ of cobbler): 98 Cal, 1 g Fat, 0 g Sat Fat, 52 mg Chol, 158 mg Sod, 21 g Carb, 2 g Fib, 2 g Prot, 78 mg Calc. ***POINTS: 2.***

———◆———

*Chef's Tip:* Enjoy any leftovers of this tasty cobbler for brunch or breakfast the next day, topped with a small scoop of fat-free vanilla yogurt.

# *fall*

## Corn Pudding with Cranberries and Sage

### MAKES 8 SERVINGS

Sweet-tart dried cranberries and chopped fresh sage give this wonderfully satisfying corn pudding its intense flavor. Although the dish can be made ahead, serve it fresh from the oven for the lightest texture.

¼ cup fresh bread crumbs

1 cup fat-free evaporated milk

¼ cup dried cranberries

2 cups frozen corn kernels, thawed

1 cup canned cream-style corn

2 large eggs

3 egg whites

2 scallions, minced

3 fresh sage leaves, minced, or ½ teaspoon dried

¾ teaspoon salt

Freshly ground pepper, to taste

*1.* Preheat the oven to 325°F. Spray a 1½-quart baking dish with nonstick spray. Coat the bottom and sides with the bread crumbs.

*2.* Bring the evaporated milk and cranberries to a simmer in a small saucepan. Meanwhile, combine the corn, cream-style corn, eggs, egg whites, scallions, sage, salt, and pepper in a large bowl. Gradually whisk in the hot milk mixture; pour into the baking dish.

*3.* Bake until the pudding is set, the top puffs, and the edges are browned, about 1 hour. Let stand 10 minutes before serving.

Per serving (⅓ cup): 88 Cal, 1 g Fat, 0 g Sat Fat, 27 mg Chol, 244 mg Sod, 15 g Carb, 1 g Fib, 5 g Prot, 93 mg Calc. *POINTS: 2.*

# Pumpkin-Apple Bisque

## MAKES 8 SERVINGS

Bisque is a thick, smooth soup that usually consists of pureed vegetables or fish, and cream. We achieve a bisque's typical creamy texture in this luscious concoction by replacing the cream with pureed fresh pumpkin and potatoes. Apple cider and freshly grated nutmeg add a subtle sweetness; sautéed fresh apples and pumpkin seeds, a delightful crunch.

1 apple, cored and finely diced

3 tablespoons hulled, unsalted pumpkin seeds

2 teaspoons unsalted butter, melted

1 teaspoon minced fresh thyme

Pinch freshly grated nutmeg

1 tablespoon vegetable oil

1 small onion, finely diced

2 teaspoons minced garlic

3 cups apple cider

3 cups low-sodium chicken broth

3 cups diced fresh pumpkin

2 baking potatoes, peeled and diced

1 bay leaf

½ teaspoon salt

Freshly ground pepper, to taste

*1.* Preheat the oven to 350°F. Combine the apple, pumpkin seeds, butter, thyme, and nutmeg in a bowl. Transfer to a baking sheet and bake until the apple and pumpkin seeds are golden, 20–30 minutes. Transfer to a plate and set aside.

*2.* Heat a heavy saucepan over medium heat. Swirl in the oil, then add the onion. Cook until translucent, about 3 minutes. Add the garlic; cook until fragrant, about 30 seconds. Add the cider, broth, pumpkin, potatoes, bay leaf, salt, and pepper; bring to a boil. Reduce the heat and simmer, until the pumpkin and potatoes are soft enough to mash easily, about 30 minutes.

*3.* Remove the saucepan from the heat; let the soup cool for a few minutes. Transfer the soup in batches to a blender or food processor and puree. Return the soup to the saucepan and bring to a simmer. Garnish with the apple and pumpkin seeds and serve.

Per serving (¾ cup soup with 1 tablespoon garnish): 103 Cal, 3 g Fat, 1 g Sat Fat, 3 mg Chol, 228 mg Sod, 17 g Carb, 2 g Fib, 2 g Prot, 19 mg Calc. *POINTS: 2.*

*Chef's Tip:* Carve miniature pumpkins to make individual bowls for the bisque, or make a tureen by carving a large pumpkin. If you prefer, substitute 2 tablespoons of slivered almonds for the pumpkin seeds. The soup can be refrigerated up to three days ahead, or frozen in zip-close plastic bags or airtight freezer containers for up to two months.

# Southwest Chicken Salad Wraps

**MAKES 8 SERVINGS**

These do-ahead zesty wraps, spiked with jalapeño and lime, make great party fare. For richer flavor, substitute smoked chicken or turkey breast for the regular chicken.

1 **cup minced cooked chicken breast**

¼ **cup diced tomato**

1 **tablespoon fresh lime juice**

1 **tablespoon minced roasted bell pepper**

1 **tablespoon minced scallion (white portion only)**

1 **tablespoon chopped fresh cilantro**

1 **teaspoon minced fresh chives**

½ **teaspoon salt**

¼ **teaspoon minced garlic**

¼ **teaspoon minced jalapeño pepper (wear gloves to prevent irritation)**

**Freshly ground pepper, to taste**

4 **(8-inch) fat-free flour tortillas**

*1.* Combine the chicken, tomato, lime juice, roasted bell pepper, scallion, cilantro, chives, salt, garlic, jalapeño, and pepper in a bowl. Cover and refrigerate at least 2 hours or up to 2 days.

*2.* Divide the chicken mixture between the tortillas and roll up. Refrigerate, tightly wrapped, at least 20 minutes or up to 2 hours. Cut each sandwich in half before serving.

Per serving (½ sandwich): 164 Cal, 4 g Fat, 1 g Sat Fat, 36 mg Chol, 337 mg Sod, 19 g Carb, 1 g Fib, 14 g Prot, 37 mg Calc. **POINTS: 3.**

# Green Chile Rice

A trio of fresh basil, cilantro, and chiles gives this rice its terrific flavor and color.
Poblano chiles are definitely worth seeking out here—you simply won't get the same
fabulously rich, earthy flavor using ordinary green bell peppers. Poblanos
can be found in specialty markets and in most large supermarkets.

4 **fresh poblano chiles (about**
   **1 pound)**
½ **cup chopped fresh basil**
½ **cup chopped fresh cilantro**
¾ **teaspoon salt**
3½ **cups water**
2 **tablespoons vegetable oil**
2 **garlic cloves, minced**
2 **cups long-grain white rice**

*1.* Preheat the broiler. Line a baking sheet with foil; place the chiles
on the baking sheet. Broil 5 inches from the heat, turning
frequently with tongs, until lightly charred, about 10 minutes.
Wrap the chiles in the foil and let steam for 10 minutes. When
cool enough to handle, peel and discard the seeds.

*2.* Puree the chiles, basil, cilantro, and salt with 1 cup of the water
in a blender or food processor.

*3.* Heat a large saucepan over medium heat. Swirl in the oil, then
add the garlic. Cook, stirring frequently, until fragrant, about
30 seconds. Add the rice and cook, stirring, until lightly toasted,
2–3 minutes. Add the chile mixture and the remaining 2½ cups
water; bring to a boil. Reduce the heat and simmer, covered,
until the rice is tender, 16–18 minutes. Fluff the rice with a fork
and serve at once.

Per serving (⅔ cup): 208 Cal, 4 g Fat, 2 g Sat Fat, 9 mg Chol, 300 mg Sod,
39 g Carb, 1 g Fib, 4 g Prot, 21 mg Calc. ***POINTS: 4.***

*Chef's Tip:* To make the rice ahead, prepare as directed except, as soon as the rice is barely tender,
spread it on a baking sheet to cool. Transfer to a large zip-close plastic bag; refrigerate up to two days.
To reheat, combine the rice and 1 tablespoon water in a microwavable bowl. Cover with wax paper
and microwave on High until hot, about 3 minutes. Stir, then cover and let stand about 5 minutes.

*Enchiladas Verdes*

# Enchiladas Verdes

Here's a welcome switch from enchiladas swimming in red sauce. We add iron-rich spinach to the cheese filling, then prepare our own zesty salsa verde using fresh tomatillos (Mexican green tomatoes). The salsa whips up in a flash, thanks to the food processor.

| | |
|---|---|
| **2 teaspoons vegetable oil** | *1.* Heat a large nonstick skillet over high heat. Swirl in the oil, then add the onion, almonds, and garlic. Cook, stirring, until the onion and almonds are golden, about 8 minutes. Transfer to a plate to cool. |
| **1 onion, chopped** | |
| **3 tablespoons sliced almonds** | |
| **1 garlic clove, minced** | |

**2 teaspoons vegetable oil**
**1 onion, chopped**
**3 tablespoons sliced almonds**
**1 garlic clove, minced**
**1 cup fat-free cottage cheese**
**⅓ cup light sour cream**
**1 (10-ounce) box frozen chopped spinach, thawed and squeezed dry**
**8 medium tomatillos, quartered (remove papery husks and rinse before cutting)**
**1 cup sliced scallions**
**⅔ cup chopped fresh cilantro**
**1 jalapeño pepper, roasted, peeled, seeded, and chopped (wear gloves to prevent irritation)**
**2 tablespoons chopped fresh mint**
**½ teaspoon ground cumin**
**½ teaspoon ground coriander**
**12 (6-inch) corn tortillas**
**¾ cup shredded Monterey Jack cheese**

*1.* Heat a large nonstick skillet over high heat. Swirl in the oil, then add the onion, almonds, and garlic. Cook, stirring, until the onion and almonds are golden, about 8 minutes. Transfer to a plate to cool.

*2.* Puree the cottage cheese in a food processor or blender. With the machine running, add the sour cream. Transfer mixture to a large bowl; stir in the spinach and the reserved onion and almonds.

*3.* In a clean processor bowl; puree the tomatillos, scallions, cilantro, jalapeño, mint, cumin, and coriander. Transfer the sauce to a shallow bowl.

*4.* Preheat the oven to 350°F. Spray a large baking dish with nonstick spray.

*5.* Heat a cast iron or heavy-bottomed skillet over medium heat. Add a tortilla and toast until pliable, about 15 seconds on each side. Dip the tortilla into the sauce to coat it very lightly on both sides.

*6.* Transfer the tortilla to a work surface. Place a spoonful of the filling slightly to one side of the center of the tortilla and roll up. Transfer the roll to the baking dish. Repeat with the remaining tortillas, sauce, and filling to make 12 enchiladas. Spoon the remaining sauce over the enchiladas, then sprinkle the cheese over the top. Cover the dish with foil and bake until the enchiladas are hot and the cheese melts, 25–35 minutes.

Per serving (1 enchilada): 160 Cal, 7 g Fat, 3 g Sat Fat, 15 mg Chol, 105 mg Sod, 17 g Carb, 4 g Fib, 9 g Prot, 112 mg Calc. ***POINTS: 3.***

———◆———

*Chef's Tip:* The spinach filling can be prepared in advance and kept covered in the refrigerator for up to two days. For best flavor and texture, however, it is best to toast and fill the tortillas no more than two hours before baking them. Leftover tortillas reheat in the microwave, covered with wax paper (1 to 2 minutes on High for one tortilla).

# Buttermilk Sherbet

Yes, buttermilk is tangy, but we add just enough sweeteners and a whole vanilla bean to make this frosty treat taste truly delicious. Real vanilla beans are expensive, but worth it. They supply true flavor and a speckled look that announces the presence of real vanilla.

1 **quart low-fat buttermilk**

1½ **cups light corn syrup**

½ **cup sugar**

1 **vanilla bean, split lengthwise**
**or 2 teaspoons vanilla extract**

½ **cup fresh lemon juice**

*1.* Combine the buttermilk, corn syrup, sugar, and vanilla bean in a medium saucepan. Heat over low heat, stirring frequently, just until the sugar melts. Pour the mixture into a 9 × 13-inch baking pan and refrigerate until very cold, about 2 hours. Remove the vanilla bean and scrape the seeds from the bean back into the mixture. Add the vanilla extract (if using) and lemon juice; freeze until firm, at least 8 hours.

*2.* Let the mixture soften at room temperature, 5 minutes. Transfer to a food processor or blender and pulse until smooth and creamy. Pour the mixture into plastic freezer containers and freeze until firm, at least 8 hours. (Or, freeze in an ice cream maker according to the manufacturer's directions.) Keep frozen until ready to serve.

Per serving (¼ cup): 76 Cal, 0 g Fat, 0 g Sat Fat, 20 mg Chol, 55 mg Sod, 18 g Carb, 0 g Fib, 1 g Prot, 37 mg Calc. ***POINTS: 2.***

*Chef's Tip:* If you make the sherbet ahead of time (it will keep for up to six weeks), use the same technique ice-cream manufacturers use: Cut a piece of plastic wrap and press it directly onto the sherbet's surface. Then seal the container with an airtight lid.

# Macerated Strawberries

Serve these sweet, syrupy strawberries with the Buttermilk Sherbet and Fudge Brownies. Or present them on their own as a simple dessert, spoon them over angel food cake, or drizzle them over waffles or pancakes.

2 **pints fresh strawberries, hulled and sliced**

2 **tablespoons sugar**

½ **teaspoon vanilla extract**

½ **teaspoon finely grated orange rind**

Place the strawberries in a large bowl. Sprinkle with the sugar, vanilla, and orange rind; toss to coat. Macerate the strawberries at room temperature at least 1 hour or cover and refrigerate for up to 1 day. Serve the berries with their juices.

Per serving (3 tablespoons): 29 Cal, 0 g Fat, 0 g Sat Fat, 0 mg Chol, 1 mg Sod, 7 g Carb, 1 g Fib, 0 g Prot, 8 mg Calc. *POINTS: 0.*

◆

*Chef's Tip:* Macerate means to soak fruit in wine, liquor, or syrup to infuse the fruit with the flavor of the soaking liquid. When meat, fish, or vegetables are similarly soaked, the term used is marinate. Try this same macerating technique with other juicy seasonal fruits, such as fresh peaches, nectarines, cherries, or plums.

# Fudge Brownies

MAKES 16 SERVINGS

These cocoa squares are just dandy on their own, but for a special treat, serve them with the Buttermilk Sherbet and Macerated Strawberries to make ice cream sundaes. The brownies get their south-of-the-border taste from cinnamon and coffee. Plus, to cut the fat, we add prune puree to replace some of the butter, which intensifies the chocolate flavor and enhances the fudgy texture.

1 cup all-purpose flour

½ cup unsweetened cocoa powder

½ teaspoon baking powder

½ teaspoon cinnamon

½ teaspoon salt

½ cup unsalted butter, melted

½ cup prune puree

¾ cup sugar

1 large egg, lightly beaten

2 egg whites

¼ cup brewed espresso or strong coffee

1 teaspoon vanilla extract

*1.* Preheat the oven to 350°F. Spray a 9 × 13-inch pan with nonstick spray.

*2.* Combine the flour, cocoa, baking powder, cinnamon, and salt in a medium bowl.

*3.* Beat the butter, prune puree, sugar, egg, egg whites, coffee, and vanilla in a large bowl until well mixed. Stir in the flour mixture until just moistened. Scrape the batter into the pan. Bake until a toothpick inserted in the center comes out clean, about 35 minutes. Cool completely in the pan on a rack. Cut into 16 brownies.

Per serving (1 brownie): 110 Cal, 7 g Fat, 4 g Sat Fat, 39 mg Chol, 15 mg Sod, 11 g Carb, 1 g Fib, 2 g Prot, 9 mg Calc. *POINTS: 3.*

———————◆———————

*Chef's Tip:* For a nifty presentation, bake the brownies as directed, except scrape the batter into a jelly-roll pan and reduce the baking time to 25 minutes. Cut the brownies into 32 "fingers." Press 2 "fingers" into each scoop of Buttermilk Sherbet, then spoon the Macerated Strawberries around the sherbet.

*Fudge Brownies*

# CHILDREN'S HALLOWEEN PARTY

*Vegetable Sticks with Ranch Dip*

—

*Spiced Eyeball Cider*

—

*Pepperoni Pizza*

—

*Chicken Nuggets with Blood-Red Salsa Dip*

—

*Peanut Spaghetti*

—

*Fruit with Creamy Marshmallow Dip*

—

*Halloween Cookies*

—

*Trick-or-Treat Caramel Sundaes*

## *Vegetable Sticks with Ranch Dip*

**MAKES 8 SERVINGS**

Familiar-tasting and creamy, ranch dressing makes eating vegetables, much more palatable to kids. Use any fresh vegetables that you know are their favorites, such as celery sticks or sweet grape tomatoes. Or use this as an opportunity to introduce them to a new vegetable, such as crunchy jicama or sweet fresh fennel, cut into sticks.

½ cup fat-free ranch dressing

2 tablespoons grated carrot

2½ teaspoons finely chopped flat-leaf parsley

16 carrot sticks

16 cucumber sticks

Combine the dressing, carrot, and parsley in a medium bowl. Serve as a dip for the vegetables.

Per serving (4 veggie sticks with 1 tablespoon dip): 25 Cal, 0 g Fat, 0 g Sat Fat, 0 mg Chol, 144 mg Sod, 6 g Carb, 0 g Fib, 0 g Prot, 14 mg Calc. ***POINTS: 1.***

———◆———

*Chef's Tip:* Make the dip a day ahead and keep it covered in the refrigerator until party time. The vegetables can be cut and kept in zip-close plastic bags in the refrigerator for up to two days.

# Spiced Eyeball Cider

For kid appeal, float the marshmallow "eyeballs" on top of the cider just before serving. Serve the cider hot or refrigerate, after straining, for up to five days and serve cold. Take a tip from food-safety experts and always buy cider that has been pasteurized.

8 cups apple cider
2 tablespoons packed dark
   brown sugar
2 cinnamon sticks, broken
   in half
8 whole cloves
24 mini-marshmallows

1. Combine the cider, sugar, cinnamon, and cloves in a large saucepan; bring to a boil. Reduce the heat and simmer, covered, about 30 minutes.

2. Pour the cider through a strainer into a punch bowl. Add the marshmallows and ladle into mugs.

Per serving (1 cup): 136 Cal, 0 g Fat, 0 g Sat Fat, 0 mg Chol, 10 mg Sod, 34 g Carb, 0 g Fib, 0 g Prot, 20 mg Calc. *POINTS: 3.*

*Chef's Tip:* To avoid burns, let the cider cool for about ten minutes before serving.

# Pepperoni Pizza

Ready-to-eat, thinly sliced turkey pepperoni gives lots of flavor and goes a long way. You get about 16 slices from just an ounce, making it perfect for keeping the **POINTS** low and the flavor high in this all-time favorite pizza. To make things easier, the pizza can be assembled and loosely covered with plastic wrap for up to an hour ahead.

1 **cup prepared tomato sauce**
1 **(10-ounce) package thin pizza crust**
1 **ounce (from a 6-ounce package) ready-to-eat thinly sliced turkey pepperoni**
1 **cup shredded part-skim mozzarella cheese**

*1.* Preheat the oven to 450°F.
*2.* Leaving a 1¼-inch margin around the edge, spread the tomato sauce over the crust. Distribute the pepperoni evenly over the tomato sauce, then sprinkle with the cheese. Bake until heated through and the cheese is melted, about 10 minutes.

Per serving (⅛ of pizza): 182 Cal, 6 g Fat, 2 g Sat Fat, 20 mg Chol, 614 mg Sod, 20 g Carb, 1 g Fib, 10 g Prot, 115 mg Calc. **POINTS: 4.**

*Chef's Tip:* Whenever children are involved, the tried-and-true adage, "Keep it simple," applies. So opt for bottled tomato sauce and packaged preshredded cheese.

# Chicken Nuggets with Blood-Red Salsa Dip

**MAKES 8 SERVINGS**

Kid-pleasing chicken nuggets are a cinch to make. You can coat them, arrange on the baking sheet, cover loosely with plastic wrap, and refrigerate for up to an hour before you're ready to bake them. If the chicken is coated too far ahead, the coating may get soggy. The salsa dip can be made a day ahead, covered, and refrigerated.

½ cup mild salsa
1 plum tomato, diced
1 pound skinless boneless
  chicken breasts, cut in
  24 chunks
⅓ cup low-fat buttermilk
6 tablespoons seasoned chicken
  coating mix

1. Combine the salsa and tomato in a small serving bowl; cover and refrigerate.
2. Combine the chicken and buttermilk in a medium bowl. Cover and marinate in the refrigerator 30 minutes. Drain the chicken and discard the buttermilk.
3. Preheat the oven to 400°F. Spray a baking sheet with nonstick spray.
4. Place 2 tablespoons of the coating mix in a zip-close plastic bag; add 8 pieces of the chicken, then shake the bag to coat. Arrange the chicken on the baking sheet. Repeat with the remaining coating mix and chicken. Bake the chicken until cooked through and golden, about 15 minutes. Serve with salsa.
5. Spear each chicken nugget with a toothpick if the children are old enough to handle them with care.

Per serving (3 nuggets with 1½ tablespoons salsa dip): 99 Cal, 2 g Fat, 1 g Sat Fat, 31 mg Chol, 220 mg Sod, 6 g Carb, 0 g Fib, 13 g Prot, 26 mg Calc. *POINTS: 2.*

# Peanut Spaghetti

**MAKES 8 SERVINGS**

Peanut butter, spaghetti, and kids…need we say more? Breaking the spaghetti in thirds makes it easier to mix with the other ingredients and easier for children to eat. The recipe can be prepared ahead of time, leaving out the scallions and peanuts, and kept at room temperature for up to two hours. Sprinkle with the scallions and peanuts just before serving.

8 ounces spaghetti, broken in thirds

¼ pound fresh snow peas, trimmed and cut diagonally in thirds

1 teaspoon Asian (dark) sesame oil

¼ cup water

1 tablespoon sugar

2 tablespoons reduced-sodium soy sauce

2 tablespoons smooth peanut butter

2 teaspoons rice vinegar

¼ teaspoon freshly ground pepper

⅓ cup thinly sliced scallions

3 tablespoons chopped dry-roasted peanuts

*1.* Cook the spaghetti according to package directions, but about 1 minute before the end of the cooking time, add the snow peas to the pot. Drain the spaghetti and snow peas into a colander, cool under cold running water, and drain well. Transfer the spaghetti and snow peas to a large bowl; add the sesame oil and toss to coat.

*2.* Puree the water, sugar, soy sauce, peanut butter, vinegar, and pepper in a blender. Pour the puree over the spaghetti. Add the scallions and peanuts and toss to coat. Serve at room temperature.

Per serving (½ cup): 175 Cal, 5 g Fat, 1 g Sat Fat, 0 mg Chol, 297 mg Sod, 27 g Carb, 2 g Fib, 6 g Prot, 20 mg Calc. ***POINTS: 4.***

*Chef's Tip:* Put the scallions and peanuts in small bowls for kids to sprinkle (or not) on their portion of spaghetti themselves.

# Fruit with Creamy Marshmallow Dip

This smooth, creamy dip is good with the fruit suggested in this recipe, but any bite-size chunks of fresh fruit, such as pineapple or mango, can be substituted. You can make the dip and cut up the fruit the day before, then store separately in the refrigerator until serving time.

¾ cup low-fat strawberry yogurt

⅓ cup light cream cheese
   or Neufchâtel

¼ cup marshmallow fluff

16 fresh strawberries

½ cantaloupe, peeled and cut
   into 16 (1-inch) chunks

½ honeydew melon,
   peeled and cut into
   16 (1½-inch) chunks

32 seedless grapes

With an electric mixer at medium speed, beat the yogurt, cream cheese, and marshmallow fluff until blended. Cover and refrigerate until chilled, at least three hours or up to overnight. Serve the marshmallow dip in a bowl, surrounded by the fruit.

Per serving (10 pieces fruit with 2 tablespoons dip): 129 Cal, 2 g Fat, 1 g Sat Fat, 4 mg Chol, 84 mg Sod, 26 g Carb, 2 g Fib, 3 g Prot, 66 mg Calc. *POINTS: 2.*

*Chef's Tip:* If your children are old enough to handle toothpicks responsibly, and to facilitate dipping and eating, be sure to provide plenty of colorful toothpicks.

*Halloween Cookies*

# Halloween Cookies

Cat, bat, ghost, and pumpkin cookies help create the Halloween party spirit, but if you don't have Halloween cookie cutters, you can use a 2 to 2½-inch round cookie cutter. If you're up for it, let the kids have fun doing their own decorating. The undecorated cookies will keep in airtight containers at room temperature for up to three weeks.

⅓ cup granulated sugar
¼ cup sliced blanched almonds
¼ cup butter, softened
½ teaspoon vanilla extract
1 egg yolk
1 cup cake flour (not self-rising)
2 tablespoons confectioners' sugar
⅛ teaspoon salt

ICING

2 cups confectioners' sugar
1½ tablespoons pasteurized powdered egg whites
3 tablespoons water
Black food coloring paste
Red, green, and yellow food coloring

1. Pulse the granulated sugar and almonds in a food processor until finely ground. Add the butter and vanilla extract; process, scraping the bowl once, until lightly fluffy, 1 minute. Add the egg yolk and pulse to combine. Add the flour, confectioners' sugar, and salt; pulse until a dough just forms. Wrap the dough in plastic wrap and refrigerate until firm, about 2 hours.

2. Preheat the oven to 350°F. Line 2 large baking sheets with parchment paper. Divide the dough in half. On a lightly floured surface, roll out each piece ⅛-inch thick. Using Halloween cookie cutters or any 2–2½-inch cookie cutter, cut out shapes, re-rolling the scraps of dough to make a total of 24 cookies. With a spatula, place 1 inch apart on the baking sheets. Bake 1 sheet at a time, until the cookies are still light on top and golden on the bottom, 8–9 minutes. Remove the cookies from the baking sheets and cool completely on racks.

3. To make the icing, combine the confectioners' sugar, powdered egg whites, and water in a medium bowl and beat with a wooden spoon until blended. Divide the icing among 4 or 5 small bowls. Leave 1 bowl white. Add black food coloring paste to another bowl, until the icing is black. Tint another bowl with red and yellow food coloring, a drop at a time, until the icing is orange. Create brown with black and yellow coloring. Place a sheet of wax paper underneath the rack of cookies to catch the drips, then decorate the cookies. Let dry completely.

Per serving (1 cookie): 96 Cal, 3 g Fat, 1 g Sat Fat, 14 mg Chol, 30 mg Sod, 17 g Carb, 0 g Fib, 1 g Prot, 6 mg Calc. *POINTS: 2.*

# Trick-or-Treat Caramel Sundaes

**MAKES 8 SERVINGS**

Any small candy pieces from the trick or treat bag can be used in place of the mini
M & M candies. Instead of decorating the ice cream in the kitchen, put the candies in small
bowls and let your little witches and goblins conjure up their own sundaes.

2⅔ cups low-fat vanilla ice cream
  or frozen yogurt

8 tablespoons fat-free
  caramel syrup

8 teaspoons mini M & M candies

2 teaspoons confetti sprinkles

Place a ⅓-cup scoop of ice cream in each of 8 small bowls. Drizzle
the caramel syrup over the ice cream and sprinkle with the
M & Ms and confetti sprinkles.

Per serving (⅓ cup ice cream with ⅛ of toppings): 158 Cal, 5 g Fat, 3 g Sat Fat,
14 mg Chol, 114 mg Sod, 29 g Carb, 0 g Fib, 2 g Prot, 78 mg Calc. *POINTS: 4.*

# HARVEST DINNER

*Butternut Squash Soup*
—
*Corn Crêpes with Zucchini-Mushroom Filling*
—
*Curried Lentil–Stuffed Eggplant*
—
*Paella with Roasted Vegetables*
—
*Sweet Potatoes with Pineapple*
—
*Cherry Tomatoes, Stuffed with Barley Salad*
—
*Potato, Carrot, Apple, and Pea Salad*
—
*Applesauce-Poppy Seed Cake*

## Butternut Squash Soup

**MAKES 8 SERVINGS**

The essence of fall, butternut squash (spiked with fresh ginger and lime) makes a delightful soup.

2 tablespoons butter
1 small onion, minced
1 celery stalk, diced
1 small carrot, diced
2 garlic cloves, minced
2 teaspoons minced peeled
    fresh ginger
4 cups cubed butternut squash
5 cups low-sodium
    chicken broth
½ cup dry white wine
1 small cinnamon stick
¼ teaspoon ground nutmeg
¼ teaspoon salt
Freshly ground pepper, to taste
½ cup fat-free evaporated milk
2 teaspoons fresh lime juice

*1.* Melt the butter in a large nonstick pot or Dutch oven over medium heat, then add the onion, celery, and carrot. Cook, stirring frequently, until the vegetables are tender, about 5 minutes. Add the garlic and 1 teaspoon of the ginger; cook until fragrant, about 30 seconds. Stir in the squash, broth, wine, cinnamon, nutmeg, salt, and pepper; bring to a boil. Reduce the heat and simmer, stirring often, until the squash is soft enough to mash easily, about 30 minutes.

*2.* Remove the pot from the heat; let the mixture cool for a few minutes. Transfer the mixture in batches to a blender and puree. Return the soup to the pot. Stir in the evaporated milk, lime juice, and remaining 1 teaspoon ginger; return to a simmer.

Per serving (¾ cup): 112 Cal, 3 g Fat, 2 g Sat Fat, 8 mg Chol, 138 mg Sod, 13 g Carb, 3 g Fib, 6 g Prot, 106 mg Calc. *POINTS: 2.*

# *Corn Crêpes with Zucchini-Mushroom Filling*

**MAKES 8 SERVINGS**

Mashed potatoes and corn make these simple crêpes extra special. The dish also features a hearty, exotic mushroom filling, which can be prepared with any variety of seasonal mushrooms.

**ZUCCHINI-MUSHROOM FILLING:**

- 1 teaspoon olive oil
- 1 garlic clove, minced
- 1 cup minced assorted mushrooms
- 1 cup minced zucchini
- 1 plum tomato, peeled, seeded, and chopped
- ½ teaspoon dried tarragon
- 2 scallions, thinly sliced on the diagonal
- 3 tablespoons crumbled feta cheese
- ¼ teaspoon freshly ground pepper
- Fresh lemon juice, to taste

**CORN CRÊPES:**

- 2 medium potatoes, peeled and quartered
- ½ cup canned cream-style corn
- ¼ cup all-purpose flour
- ¼ teaspoon salt
- ⅛ teaspoon freshly ground white pepper
- Pinch freshly grated nutmeg
- 1 large egg, lightly beaten
- 1 egg white, lightly beaten
- ½ cup fat-free evaporated milk

*1.* To make the filling, heat a large nonstick skillet over medium heat. Swirl in the oil, then add the garlic. Cook, stirring constantly, until fragrant, about 30 seconds. Add the mushrooms and cook until the liquid evaporates, about 5 minutes. Add the zucchini, tomato, and tarragon, cook until the mixture is dry, about 10 minutes longer. Transfer the filling to a bowl. Stir in the scallions, feta, ground pepper, and lemon juice; set aside.

*2.* To make the crêpes, simmer the potatoes in enough water to cover, until the potatoes are tender, 15–20 minutes. Drain the potatoes in a colander. and cool to room temperature. Transfer to a mixing bowl and mash together with the corn, flour, salt, white pepper, and nutmeg. Stir in the egg, egg white, and evaporated milk.

*3.* Lightly spray a small nonstick skillet or crêpe pan with nonstick spray and set over medium heat until a drop of water sizzles. Pour the batter by a ⅓-cup measure into the skillet, spreading it with the back of a spoon to form a 5-inch crêpe. Cook until the underside is set, 2–3 minutes. Flip and cook until lightly browned, about 2 minutes. Slide the crêpe onto wax paper. Repeat with additional nonstick spray and the remaining batter to make 8 crêpes.

*4.* Preheat the oven to 350°F. Spray a 9 × 13-inch baking dish with nonstick spray. Spoon about 2 tablespoons of the filling on each crêpe and roll up. Place the crêpes, seam-side down, in the baking dish; bake until very hot, about 10 minutes.

Per Serving (1 crêpe): 90 Cal, 2 g Fat, 1 g Sat Fat, 30 g Chol, 270 mg Sod, 14 g Carb, 1 g Fib, 4 g Prot, 74 mg Calc. ***POINTS: 2.***

# Curried Lentil–Stuffed Eggplant

**MAKES 8 SERVINGS**

Italian (or baby) eggplant, prized for its delicate skin and flesh, is a miniature version of the common purple variety. It's the perfect size for this hearty and nutritious recipe, which |can be served solo as a vegetarian entrée. Look for Italian eggplants in the produce section of the supermarket or at your local farm stand.

½ cup green or brown lentils, picked over and rinsed

2 cups low-sodium vegetable broth or water

4 baby Italian eggplants

1 teaspoon olive oil

1 small onion, minced

1 garlic clove, minced

½ teaspoon grated peeled fresh ginger

½ cup minced white mushrooms

½ teaspoon salt

½ teaspoon grated lemon rind

½ teaspoon curry powder

¼ teaspoon cinnamon

¼ teaspoon ground turmeric

Freshly ground pepper, to taste

*1.* Bring the lentils and broth to a boil in a saucepan. Reduce the heat and simmer, until barely tender, 25–30 minutes; set aside.

*2.* Preheat the oven to 350°F. Spray a 9 × 13-inch baking dish with nonstick spray. Halve the eggplants lengthwise and scoop out some of the flesh. Mince the scooped flesh and set aside. Place the eggplant halves in the baking pan.

*3.* Heat a large nonstick skillet over medium heat. Swirl in the oil, then add the onion, garlic, and ginger. Cook, stirring occasionally, until golden, 6–8 minutes. Add the minced eggplant, mushrooms, salt, lemon rind, curry powder, cinnamon, turmeric, and pepper. Cook, stirring occasionally, until the mushrooms begin to release some moisture, about 5 minutes.

*4.* Drain the lentils, reserving about 1 cup of the cooking liquid. Add the lentils to the eggplant and mushroom mixture, then enough of the reserved cooking liquid to moisten the mixture well. Simmer until the liquid is reduced, about 10 minutes.

*5.* Fill each eggplant half with ¼ cup of the lentil mixture. Cover the baking dish with foil and bake until the eggplants are tender and cooked through, 35–40 minutes. Serve at once.

Per serving (½ eggplant): 120 Cal, 3 g Fat, 0 g Sat Fat, 5 g Chol, 420 mg Sod, 17 g Carb, 5 g Fib, 8 g Prot, 23 mg Calc. *POINTS: 2.*

———◆———

*Chef's Tip:* If you can't find Italian eggplants, substitute two of the larger common variety. Prepare the recipe as directed, except cut each eggplant in half and fill each portion with one-quarter of the filling. Bake as directed, then cut each half crosswise into two pieces.

*Paella with Roasted Vegetables*

# Paella with Roasted Vegetables

**MAKES 8 SERVINGS**

While paella can sport a wide range of ingredients, what's critical to making truly great paella is using the proper variety of short-grain white rice. Look for Spanish rice from Valencia or Italian Arborio rice, both available in most supermarkets.

4 fresh beets (about 1 pound)
1 teaspoon fresh lemon juice
4 plum tomatoes, halved
  or sliced
2 carrots, diced
1 small rutabaga, diced
1 zucchini, sliced
1 parsnip, diced
2 tablespoons minced garlic
1 teaspoon salt
Pinch cayenne
½ cup roasted red or green bell
  pepper strips
1 tablespoon sherry vinegar
1½ cups low-sodium
  vegetable broth
½ teaspoon crushed saffron
  threads (optional)
2 teaspoons vegetable oil
½ cup diced onion
1 garlic clove, minced
1 cup short-grain white rice
1 bay leaf
1 cup small broccoli florets
1 cup small cauliflower florets
½ cup frozen green peas,
  thawed

1. Preheat the oven to 425°F.

2. Place the beets in a small baking pan. Roast until they are tender enough to pierce with a fork, about 1½ hours. When cool enough to handle, peel and dice. Transfer to a microwavable bowl, drizzle with the lemon juice and set aside.

3. Meanwhile, combine the tomatoes, carrots, rutabaga, zucchini, and parsnip in a large bowl; lightly spray with olive-oil nonstick spray. Spread the vegetables in a large nonstick baking pan. Sprinkle with the garlic, salt, and cayenne. Roast, stirring occasionally, until the vegetables are tender and browned, about 40 minutes. Transfer to a large bowl and add the roasted bell pepper, and vinegar; toss to coat.

4. Bring the broth to a boil in a saucepan; add the saffron (if using). Reduce the heat and keep at a simmer.

5. Heat a large nonstick deep skillet or paella pan over medium heat. Swirl in the oil, then add the onion and garlic. Cook until softened, 2–3 minutes. Add the rice and cook, stirring frequently, until lightly toasted, 2–3 minutes. Add the broth mixture; bring to a simmer. Add the bay leaf and the roasted vegetable mixture. Reduce the heat and simmer, covered, until the rice is barely tender to the bite, about 10 minutes. Add the broccoli, cauliflower, and peas. Cover and cook until the rice is very tender and the vegetables are cooked, 15–20 minutes.

6. Remove the paella from the heat and let stand, covered, 5 minutes. To serve, discard the bay leaf. Microwave the beets, covered, on High until very hot, about 90 seconds. Fluff the paella with a fork and top with the beets.

Per serving (1½ cups): 360 Cal, 6 g Fat, 0 g Sat Fat, 0 mg Chol, 510 mg Sod, 68 g Carb, 8 g Fib, 13 g Prot, 176 mg Calc. **POINTS: 7.**

# Sweet Potatoes with Pineapple

**MAKES 8 SERVINGS**

It's official: Those cloying, sugary, sweet-potato casseroles are a thing of the past! These tubers have a bright orange flesh that cooks up moist and sweet, so they need little embellishment. We simply cook these beauties with a touch of honey, fresh pineapple, and lemon juice until their natural sugars turn into a luscious syrupy glaze.

2 **pounds sweet potatoes,
peeled and cut into chunks**
½ **cup cubed pineapple (fresh or
canned in juice)**
2 **tablespoons honey**
2 **teaspoons fresh lemon juice**
¼ **teaspoon cinnamon**
¼ **teaspoon salt**
**Freshly ground pepper, to taste**

*1.* Bring the potatoes and enough water to barely cover to a boil in a large saucepan. Reduce the heat and simmer, covered, until the potatoes are tender, 12–15 minutes. Drain the potatoes, reserving ⅓ cup of the cooking liquid.

*2.* Return the potatoes to the same pan. Add the pineapple, honey, lemon juice, cinnamon, salt, and pepper. Continue to cook over low heat until the potatoes are coated and glazed, about 3 minutes. If necessary, add a little of the reserved cooking liquid to prevent the potatoes from becoming too dry.

Per serving (⅓ cup): 82 Cal, 0 g Fat, 0 g Sat Fat, 0 mg Chol, 96 mg Sod, 21 g Carb, 2 g Fib, 1 g Prot, 12 mg Calc. ***POINTS: 1.***

# Cherry Tomatoes Stuffed with Barley Salad

**MAKES 8 SERVINGS**

Tomatoes are particularly sweet at harvest time, and cherry tomatoes are no exception. The versatile grain filling in this dish can easily be doubled. Reserve half and refrigerate up to two days for another meal, as an accompaniment to grilled or broiled salmon, for example. (The cherry tomatoes can be stuffed and refrigerated up to six hours before serving.)

½ cup pearl barley
⅓ cup chopped flat-leaf parsley
¼ cup diced tomato
¼ cup diced cucumber
2 tablespoons chopped fresh mint
1 tablespoon thinly sliced scallions, white portion only
2 teaspoons extra-virgin olive oil
1 teaspoon fresh lemon juice
¼ teaspoon salt
Freshly ground pepper, to taste
16 cherry tomatoes

*1.* Combine the barley and enough cold water to cover in a bowl; let soak 30 minutes, then drain well.

*2.* Transfer the barley to a small saucepan, add enough water to cover and bring to a boil. Reduce the heat and simmer, uncovered, until tender, about 40 minutes. Drain the barley through a sieve, then lower the sieve into a bowl of ice water and let the barley cool for 1 minute. Set the sieve over a bowl and let the barley drain.

*3.* Combine the drained barley, parsley, diced tomato, cucumber, mint, and scallions in a large bowl. Stir in the oil, lemon juice, salt, and pepper.

*4.* Cut the cores from the cherry tomatoes, then make a crisscross cut into the top of each tomato and open it up like a flower. Stuff each with some of the salad.

Per serving (2 stuffed tomatoes): 60 Cal, 2 g Fat, 0 g Sat Fat, 0 mg Chol, 40 mg Sod, 9 g Carb, 5 g Fib, 3 g Prot, 10 mg Calc. ***POINTS: 1.***

# Potato, Carrot, Apple, and Pea Salad

**MAKES 8 SERVINGS**

Mixing vegetables with fruit may seem a bit unconventional, but this salad is really nothing more than a variation on an all-time favorite—the Waldorf salad.

1 large potato, peeled and diced

2 carrots, peeled and diced

½ cup frozen small green peas

Juice of 1 lemon

Juice of 1 orange

2 tablespoons chopped
  flat-leaf parsley

¼ teaspoon salt

Freshly ground pepper, to taste

1 tablespoon olive oil

1 apple, chopped

¼ cup crumbled reduced-fat
  feta cheese

2 teaspoons capers, drained

*1.* Bring the potato and enough water to cover to a boil in a medium saucepan. Reduce the heat and simmer, uncovered, until tender, 8–10 minutes; drain.

*2.* Bring another saucepan of water to a boil. Add the carrots and cook until tender, about 6 minutes. Transfer with a slotted spoon to a bowl of ice water to stop the cooking. Lift the carrots from the water and drain in a colander or sieve. Return the water to a boil; repeat the process with the peas, cooking until tender, about 3 minutes. Cool and drain in the colander with the carrots.

*3.* To make the dressing, whisk the lemon juice, orange juice, parsley, salt, and pepper in a bowl; gradually whisk in the oil until blended.

*4.* Combine the apple, potato, carrots, and peas in a large bowl. Drizzle the dressing over the vegetable mixture and toss to coat. Fold in the feta cheese and capers. Refrigerate the salad for 30 minutes before serving.

Per serving (⅓ cup): 83 Cal, 2 g Fat, 1 g Sat Fat, 1 mg Chol, 157 mg Sod, 14 g Carb, 3 g Fib, 2 g Prot, 17 mg Calc. ***POINTS: 1.***

# Applesauce-Poppy Seed Cake

**MAKES 12 SERVINGS**

This rich, flavorful cake uses applesauce—a traditional ingredient that dates back to the American settlers' time, when butter was scarce but pureed fruits (or fruit butters) were preserved at harvest time to last through the winter. Today, using fruit purees like applesauce is a great way to reduce calories in baked goods. This also increases complex carbohydrates and dietary fiber and helps retain moisture.

2½ **cups all-purpose flour**
2 **tablespoons poppy seeds**
2 **teaspoons baking powder**
¼ **teaspoon salt**
3 **large eggs, lightly beaten**
2 **cups applesauce**
¾ **cup sugar**
½ **teaspoon grated lemon rind**
½ **teaspoon lemon extract**

*1.* Preheat the oven to 350°F. Spray a 10-inch Bundt pan with nonstick spray.

*2.* Combine the flour, poppy seeds, baking powder, and salt in a bowl.

*3.* With an electric mixer at medium speed, beat the eggs and applesauce in a large bowl until smooth. Add the sugar, lemon rind, and lemon extract; beat until smooth and light. With the mixer at low speed, stir in the flour mixture until the flour is just moistened.

*4.* Scrape the batter into the pan. Bake until a toothpick inserted in the center comes out clean, about 35 minutes.

*5.* Cool the cake in the pan on a rack 10 minutes. Remove the cake from the pan and cool completely on the rack. Cut into 12 slices.

Per serving (¹⁄₁₂ of cake): 187 Cal, 2 g Fat, 0 g Sat Fat, 53 mg Chol, 180 mg Sod, 38 g Carb, 2 g Fib, 5 g Prot, 33 mg Calc. ***POINTS: 4.***

◆

*Chef's Tip:* Try any leftover cake toasted and served with fat-free cream cheese for breakfast.

# THANKSGIVING FEAST

*Artichokes in Herb Sauce*
—
*Red Pepper Mousse in Endive*
—
*Roast Turkey with Pan Gravy*
—
*Apple-Sage Dressing*
—
*Spinach and Mustard Green Salad with Peanut Dressing*
—
*Maple-Glazed Brussels Sprouts with Chestnuts*
—
*Glazed Root Vegetables*
—
*Succotash*
—
*Pumpkin Cheesecake*

## Artichokes in Herb Sauce

**MAKES 12 SERVINGS**

Eating an artichoke is a leisurely event that can take the edge off your appetite well before you are overwhelmed by the classic Thanksgiving "groaning board."

12 artichokes, leaves trimmed
3 garlic cloves, peeled and left whole
1 lemon, cut in half
½ cup fresh white bread crumbs
¼ cup chopped fresh basil
¼ cup chopped fresh parsley
2 tablespoons grated Parmesan cheese
2 tablespoons olive oil
Freshly ground pepper, to taste

*1.* Preheat the oven to 375°F.

*2.* Simmer the artichokes, garlic, and lemon in enough water to cover in a large pot until the artichoke stems are tender enough to pierce easily with a knife, about 20 minutes. Drain and transfer to a platter. When cool enough to handle, spread the leaves apart and, with a spoon, scoop out and discard the choke.

*3.* Combine the bread crumbs, basil, parsley, and cheese in a bowl. Pack the mixture into the center of each artichoke then place in a 9 × 13-inch baking dish sprayed with nonstick spray; drizzle with the oil and sprinkle with the pepper. Bake until the artichokes are hot and the bread crumbs are lightly browned, 10–12 minutes.

Per serving (1 artichoke): 70 Cal, 3 g Fat, 0 g Sat Fat, 0 mg Chol, 120 mg Sod, 13 g Carb, 6 g Fib, 00 g Prot, 159 mg Calc. ***POINTS: 1.***

# Red Pepper Mousse in Endive

**MAKES 12 SERVINGS**

Working with gelatin requires a little attention, but the reward for your effort is a delicate mousse that melts in your mouth as soon as you take a bite. You'll need to pipe the mousse onto the endive spears before the mousse has completely set. But once the spears are filled, they can be kept in the refrigerator, loosely covered with plastic wrap, for up to 24 hours.

1 teaspoon olive oil
¼ cup minced onion
1 teaspoon minced garlic
3 red bell peppers, seeded and finely chopped
1 cup low-sodium chicken or vegetable broth
1 tablespoon tomato paste
¾ teaspoon salt
Freshly ground pepper, to taste
Pinch saffron threads, crushed
1 envelope unflavored gelatin
¼ cup dry white wine, chilled
¼ cup heavy cream
30 endive spears (2–3 heads)
¼ cup thin red bell pepper strips, for garnish

*1.* Heat a medium nonstick skillet over medium heat. Swirl in the oil, then add the onion and garlic. Cook until softened, about 3 minutes. Add the chopped bell peppers, broth, tomato paste, salt, pepper, and saffron; bring to a simmer. Cook until the vegetables are tender and the liquid is reduced by half, 20–30 minutes.

*2.* Remove the bell pepper mixture from the heat and cool slightly. Pour the mixture, in batches, into a food processor or blender, filling the container no more than half full; puree. Transfer to a large bowl.

*3.* Sprinkle the gelatin over the wine in a small microwavable bowl and let stand until softened, about 5 minutes. Microwave the mixture on High until the gelatin completely dissolves, 30–40 seconds.

*4.* Stir the dissolved gelatin into the bell pepper puree. Refrigerate the mixture until it mounds when dropped from a spoon, about 20 minutes. Meanwhile, with an electric mixer on medium-high speed, beat the cream until medium peaks form.

*5.* Fold the whipped cream into the bell pepper puree. Spoon the mixture into a pastry bag fitted with a ⅜-inch star tip. Pipe about 1½ tablespoons mousse onto each endive spear and garnish with a strip of red bell pepper.

Per serving (2 pieces): 41 Cal, 3 g Fat, 1 g Sat Fat, 7 mg Chol, 14 mg Sod, 3 g Carb, 1 g Fib, 1 g Prot, 12 mg Calc. ***POINTS: 1.***

◆

*Chef's Tip:* If you want to skip piping the mousse, no problem. Use a spoon to top the endive with the mousse for a more casual appearance.

# Roast Turkey with Pan Gravy

**MAKES 12 SERVINGS, PLUS LEFTOVERS**

Want a moist, succulent bird this Thanksgiving? Then consider baking the dressing separately. The reason? By the time the dressing inside a bird is hot, the turkey, especially the breast meat, will be overcooked. If you like, present the turkey with the dressing spilling from it.

1 (15-pound) fresh or frozen
  turkey, thawed
1 apple
1 bay leaf
1 large sprig fresh thyme
½ bunch flat-leaf parsley
½ lemon
1 teaspoon salt
Freshly ground pepper, to taste
5 cups low-sodium
  chicken broth
⅓ cup cornstarch

*1.* Preheat the oven to 450°F. Spray the rack of a roasting pan with nonstick spray and place in the pan; set aside.

*2.* Remove the neck and giblets from the body and neck cavities of the turkey. Rinse the turkey and drain; pat dry with paper towels. Fill the body cavity with the apple, bay leaf, thyme, and parsley. Tie the legs together with kitchen string. Squeeze the juice from the lemon over the entire bird and season with salt and pepper.

*3.* Place the turkey, breast-side up, on the rack in the pan. Transfer the turkey to the oven and immediately reduce the oven temperature to 350°F. Roast until an instant-read thermometer inserted at least 2 inches into the inner thigh registers 180°F, about 3½ hours (or about 20 minutes per pound).

*4.* Transfer the turkey to a serving platter; discard the apple, bay leaf, thyme, and parsley. Tent with foil and let stand 30 minutes.

*5.* To make the gravy, scrape the drippings from the roasting pan and transfer to a glass measure. Let stand 5 minutes, until the fat rises to the top. Skim off the fat and discard. Combine the remaining skimmed pan drippings and 4 cups of the broth in a saucepan. Dissolve the cornstarch in the remaining 1 cup broth in a bowl. Bring the broth and drippings mixture to a boil. Add the cornstarch mixture, whisking constantly, and simmer until the gravy is thickened, about 5 minutes. Strain through a sieve into a saucepan or gravy boat and keep warm.

*6.* Carve the turkey and serve with the gravy.

Per serving (2 {1½- ounce} slices skinless breast meat with ¼ cup gravy): 172 Cal, 5 g Fat, 2 g Sat Fat, 66 mg Chol, 299 mg Sod, 4 g Carb, 0 g Fib, 26 g Prot, 28 mg Calc. *POINTS: 4.*

## Carving a Turkey

Carving a turkey at the table is one of the great traditions of holiday family gatherings. To make it a fuss-free event, start by arranging a carving station at the head of the table. Have on hand a sharp carving knife, fork, and, for the true performer, a steel to hone the knife. Warm plates should be stacked nearby, and one of the guests, appointed carver's assistant, to pass the turkey-filled plates to the guests.

*1.* Use the fork to hold the turkey steady as you work. To carve the breast meat into slices, first make a horizontal cut at the base of the breast, cutting from the outside in, until you meet the rib bones. Then carve the breast into even slices.

*2.* Cut the legs completely away from the bird. Cut between the thigh and the drumstick at the joint. Cut slices of meat away from the thigh, and reserve the drumsticks for guests who aren't counting ***POINTS*** or to use in soups later on.

*3.* If you're having your guests help themselves to turkey, arrange a layer of breast slices along one side of a serving platter and a layer of dark thigh slices along the other side.

*Roast Turkey with Pan Gravy, Apple-Sage Dressing, and
Maple-Glazed Brussels Sprouts with Chestnuts*

# Apple-Sage Dressing

**MAKES 12 SERVINGS**

When is a stuffing called dressing? When you bake it outside of the bird, according to some folks in some regions of the United States. Sage and apples are a delicious combination and often paired together, but if you're not a sage fan, try oregano or marjoram instead.

| |
|---|
| 2 tablespoons unsalted butter |
| 1 medium onion, chopped |
| 1 cup chopped celery |
| 2½ cups low-sodium chicken broth |
| 2 medium Red Delicious apples |
| 2 teaspoons chopped fresh sage |
| 1 teaspoon chopped fresh thyme |
| ½ teaspoon salt |
| Freshly ground pepper, to taste |
| 6 cups cubed stale bread, about 1 pound |
| ¼ cup flat-leaf parsley, chopped |
| 1 egg white, lightly beaten |

*1.* Preheat the oven to 400°F. Spray a 9 × 13-inch baking dish or large casserole with nonstick spray.

*2.* Melt the butter in a large nonstick skillet over medium heat; add the onion and celery, and cook until softened, about 5 minutes. Add the broth, apples, sage, thyme, salt, and pepper; bring to a boil. Remove from the heat and cool briefly.

*3.* Combine the bread cubes, vegetable mixture, parsley, and egg white in a large bowl. Spoon into the baking dish. Bake until golden brown on top, about 45 minutes.

Per serving (⅓ cup): 88 Cal, 2 g Fat, 1 g Sat Fat, 3 mg Chol, 183 mg Sod, 14 g Carb, 1 g Fib, 3 g Prot, 32 mg Calc. ***POINTS: 2.***

———◆———

*Chef's Tip:* If you only have fresh bread on hand, cut into cubes and spread on a baking sheet. Bake the bread cubes in a 350°F oven until dry, 15 to 20 minutes. Cool completely and proceed with the recipe as directed.

# Spinach and Mustard Green Salad with Peanut Dressing

**MAKES 12 SERVINGS**

Salads can seem like an afterthought on many Thanksgiving menus, but not if you serve this one! It's the combination of gutsy, flavorful greens, strawberries, and an unusual peanut dressing that sets this salad apart. If you can't find baby spinach and mustard green leaves, substitute a good mesclun mix—it's often sold in bulk at the supermarket.

½ cup low-sodium vegetable or chicken broth
1 teaspoon cornstarch
½ teaspoon water
¼ cup malt vinegar
1 tablespoon peanut butter
2½ teaspoons packed dark brown sugar
2 teaspoons chopped fresh chives
½ teaspoon freshly ground pepper
½ teaspoon minced garlic
½ teaspoon mustard powder
2 tablespoons peanut oil
4 cups baby spinach leaves
2 cups mustard greens
½ cup shredded jicama
1 cup sliced ripe strawberries
½ cup sliced red onion

*1.* Bring the broth to a boil in a saucepan. Combine the cornstarch and water in a small bowl, then drizzle into the simmering broth, stirring constantly until thickened, about 1 minute. Remove the pan from the heat and add the vinegar, peanut butter, brown sugar, chives, pepper, garlic, and mustard. When completely cool, drizzle in the oil, whisking constantly.

*2.* Combine the spinach, mustard greens, jicama, strawberries, and onion in a large bowl. Add the dressing and toss to coat. Serve at once on chilled plates.

Per serving (½ cup): 45 Cal, 3 g Fat, 1 g Sat Fat, 0 mg Chol, 73 mg Sod, 4 g Carb, 1 g Fib, 1 g Prot, 21 mg Calc. ***POINTS: 1.***

◆

*Chef's Tip:* Any leftover small endive spears from the Red Pepper Mousse in Endive can be shredded and added to the salad for additional crunch.

# *Maple-Glazed Brussels Sprouts with Chestnuts*

**MAKES 12 SERVINGS**

Brussels sprouts and chestnuts are a time-honored combination during the holidays. This is good news, because Brussels sprouts (a cruciferous vegetable) are a good source of iron and vitamins A and C.

**4 (10-ounce) containers fresh
Brussels sprouts, trimmed**

**1 teaspoon salt**

**⅓ cup maple syrup**

**1 tablespoon butter**

**Freshly ground pepper, to taste**

**¾ cup canned chestnuts, drained**

*1.* Bring a large pot of water to a boil; add the Brussels sprouts and salt. Cook until tender enough to pierce easily with a knife, 5–7 minutes. Drain. Transfer sprouts to a large bowl of ice water; cool 1 minute. Drain on paper towels. Cut the sprouts in half.
*2.* Bring the maple syrup, butter, and pepper to a boil in a large skillet. Add the Brussels sprouts and chestnuts. Cook, stirring frequently, until very hot, about 3 minutes.

Per serving (⅓ cup): 59 Cal, 1 g Fat, 1 g Sat Fat, 3 mg Chol, 254 mg Sod, 12 g Carb, 2 g Fib, 2 g Prot, 30 mg Calc. *POINTS: 1.*

◆

*Chef's Tip:* If loose or bulk Brussels sprouts are available in your supermarket or local farm stand, choose tiny sprouts of approximately the same size—smaller sprouts are more tender. If you buy the 10-ounce containers, separate the sprouts so that you can add the larger sprouts to the boiling water first. Cutting an X in the stem of large sprouts helps them cook evenly.

# Glazed Root Vegetables

**MAKES 12 SERVINGS**

The glaze in this satisfying side dish is simply broth, allowed to cook down until syrupy. There is no added sugar in this recipe beyond that contained in the vegetables themselves.

2 **cups low-sodium chicken broth**
1½ **cups cubed carrots**
1½ **cups cubed rutabagas**
1½ **cups cubed parsnips**
1½ **cups cubed turnips**
1 **tablespoon chopped flat-leaf parsley**
½ **teaspoon salt**
**Freshly ground pepper, to taste**

*1.* Bring the broth to a boil in a large saucepan. Add the carrots and rutabagas. Reduce the heat and simmer 5 minutes. Add the parsnips and turnips and cook until the vegetables are tender, 4–5 minutes. Transfer the vegetables with a slotted spoon to a serving dish; cover and keep warm.

*2.* Increase the heat to high and bring the broth to a boil. Boil, uncovered, until reduced to about one-third of its original volume. Remove from the heat and add the parsley, salt, and pepper. Pour the glaze over the vegetables and serve at once.

Per serving (⅓ cup): 35 Cal, 0 g Fat, 0 g Sat Fat, 0 mg Chol, 149 mg Sod, 8 g Carb, 2 g Fib, 1 g Prot, 28 mg Calc. ***POINTS: 0.***

◆

*Chef's Tip:* If you have homemade chicken or turkey broth, use it for this dish. You may need to increase the amount of salt to compensate for the higher levels of sodium in prepared broth, even for those labeled low-sodium.

# Succotash

The Narragansett Indian word *msickquatash,* meaning "boiled whole kernels of corn," is the origin of the word *succotash*. Most cooks agree that to make a great succotash, you need tender, tasty lima beans and corn. Since both are available frozen, this dish is a snap to put together. Some regional versions call for the addition of bell peppers; others add a bit of minced bacon, as we do here.

1 strip lean turkey bacon, minced
1 tablespoon vegetable oil
1 small onion, minced
1 garlic clove, mashed
2½ cups fresh or thawed frozen corn kernels
1½ cups frozen lima beans or cranberry beans
1 cup low-sodium chicken broth
½ teaspoon salt
Freshly ground pepper, to taste
2 tablespoons chopped flat-leaf parsley

*1.* Heat a medium heavy-bottomed skillet over medium heat. Add the bacon and cook until brown, but not too crisp. Swirl in the oil, then add the onion and cook until softened, 3–5 minutes. Add the garlic and cook 30 seconds.

*2.* Stir in the corn, lima beans, and broth; bring to a boil. Boil until the beans are tender, about 3 minutes. Season with the salt and pepper. Transfer to a serving dish, then sprinkle with the parsley and bacon.

Per serving (⅓ cup): 86 Cal, 1 g Fat, 0 g Sat Fat, 2 mg Chol, 132 mg Sod, 16 g Carb, 4 g Fib, 5 g Prot, 17 mg Calc. *POINTS: 1.*

# Pumpkin Cheesecake

## MAKES 24 SERVINGS

Pumpkin pie may be the sine qua non for some Thanksgiving purists, but this delicate and creamy cheesecake could easily change their minds. The cheesecake can be made and refrigerated up to two days ahead, but we do not recommend freezing it.

1⅓ cups graham cracker crumbs
2 tablespoons granulated sugar
2 tablespoons unsalted butter, melted
2 egg whites, lightly beaten
1½ pounds light cream cheese (Neufchâtel), at room temperature
½ cup packed light brown sugar
1¾ cups pumpkin puree
¾ teaspoon cinnamon
½ teaspoon ground ginger
½ teaspoon ground mace
¼ teaspoon salt
1 cup light sour cream
1 large egg, lightly beaten

1. Preheat the oven to 325°F. Spray a 10-inch round cake pan with nonstick spray; line the bottom with a circle of wax paper.

2. To make the crust, combine the graham cracker crumbs and the granulated sugar with a fork in a bowl. Add the butter and 1 tablespoon of the beaten egg white; mix well. Press the graham mixture into the cake pan using a flat-bottomed glass to form an even crust. Bake until the crust is lightly toasted and set, about 8 minutes. Remove from the oven and let the crust cool slightly.

3. With a mixer on medium speed, beat the cream cheese and brown sugar until very smooth. Add the pumpkin puree, cinnamon, ginger, mace, and salt; beat 3–4 minutes. Add the sour cream and beat 2–3 minutes. Add the remaining egg whites and the egg, beat 2–3 minutes longer, scraping the bowl as necessary. Pour the filling over the crust. Bake until the center of the cake is lightly set, about 1 hour. Cool completely in the pan on a rack, then refrigerate at least 8 hours before unmolding and slicing.

Per serving (¹⁄₂₄ of cake): 110 Cal, 4 g Fat, 2 g Sat Fat, 20 mg Chol, 160 mg Sod, 14 g Carb, 1 g Fib, 4 g Prot, 40 mg Calc. *POINTS: 2.*

---

*Chef's Tip:* To unmold the cake, run a knife around the inside of the pan. Invert the pan onto a plate; lift off the pan and remove the wax paper. Invert again onto a serving plate so that the crust is on the bottom. To slice the cake neatly, dip a sharp knife with a long, thin blade into very hot water. Wipe the blade dry before making each cut.

*Pumpkin Cheesecake*

*Tomato Consommé*
—
*Rosemary Breadsticks*
—
*Chicken-Waldorf Salad*
—
*Green Salad with Citrus Dressing*
—
*Focaccia with Herbs*
—
*Sorbet Sundaes with Melon*
—
*Chocolate Fudge Cookies*
—
*Fruit Juice Spritzers*

## *Tomato Consommé*

**MAKES 4 SERVINGS**

Light and delicately flavored, consommé makes an elegant beginning to any meal. You can make it up to three days ahead and keep it refrigerated. You'll find the flavor is even better after reheating.

1 (14½-ounce) can
  diced tomatoes
1 (14½-ounce) can low-sodium
  beef broth
1 cup water
1 leek, cleaned and thinly sliced
1 celery stalk, diced
1 bay leaf
6 whole black peppercorns
5 whole cloves

*1.* Bring the tomatoes, broth, water, leek, celery, bay leaf, peppercorns, and cloves to a boil in a medium saucepan. Reduce heat and simmer, covered, about 35 minutes. Let cool 10 minutes.

*2.* Pour the broth through a large sieve into a large bowl, pressing down on the vegetables with the back of a large spoon to extract the juices. Discard the vegetables and return the soup to the saucepan. Cover and heat thoroughly.

Per serving (¾ cup): 26 Cal, 0 g Fat, 0 g Sat Fat, 0 mg Chol, 192 mg Sod, 4 g Carb, 0 g Fib, 2 g Prot, 15 mg Calc. **POINTS: 1.**

◆

*Chef's Tip:* Leeks often pick up sand between their layers as they grow. To clean a leek, trim away the dark green tops (reserve the tops for flavoring soups or stews) and the roots, leaving the root end intact to hold the layers together. Slice the leek lengthwise almost through to the root end, then fan open the layers and rinse thoroughly under cold running water.

# Rosemary Breadsticks

**MAKES 12 SERVINGS**

A tube of breadstick dough, found in the dairy case of your supermarket, makes these savory treats a snap to prepare. To make ahead, assemble on the baking sheet as directed, cover with plastic wrap, and refrigerate for up to two hours; then bake as directed. They make a great go-along for the consommé. Leftovers breadsticks freeze well, then reheat easily in a moderate oven for about ten minutes.

1 (11-ounce) tube refrigerated breadstick dough
1 tablespoon extra-virgin olive oil
½ teaspoon dried crushed rosemary

*1.* Preheat the oven to 375°F. Separate the dough to make 12 breadsticks and arrange them on an ungreased baking sheet.
*2.* Combine the oil and rosemary in a small bowl. Brush the dough with the oil mixture. Twist each breadstick several times, and press the ends firmly onto the baking sheet. Bake until golden brown, about 13 minutes. Transfer to a napkin-lined basket and serve hot.

Per serving (1 breadstick): 80 Cal, 2 g Fat, 0 g Sat Fat, 0 mg Chol, 185 mg Sod, 12 g Carb, 0 g Fib, 2 g Prot, 1 mg Calc. *POINTS: 2.*

*Chef's Tip:* For a flavor boost, add two minced garlic cloves to the oil-and-rosemary mixture.

# Chicken-Waldorf Salad

**MAKES 4 SERVINGS**

The original Waldorf salad, created more than a hundred years ago by Oscar Tschirky, maître d'hôtel at the Waldorf Astoria Hotel in New York, was made with apple, celery, and mayonnaise. Walnuts were a later addition. In this version, chicken is added to make a delicious main-dish salad. The salad can be made and refrigerated up to a day ahead, then spooned onto the lettuce just before serving.

⅓ cup fat-free mayonnaise
¼ cup fat-free sour cream
1 tablespoon fresh lemon juice
¼ teaspoon salt
⅛ teaspoon freshly
 ground pepper
2 cups diced cooked skinless
 chicken breast
2 red apples, cored and cut in
 bite-size chunks
1 celery stalk, diced
2 tablespoons chopped
 toasted walnuts
1 tablespoon finely chopped
 flat-leaf parsley
4 lettuce leaves

*1.* Combine the mayonnaise, sour cream, lemon juice, salt, and pepper in a small bowl.

*2.* Combine the chicken, apples, celery, and walnuts in a large bowl. Add the mayonnaise dressing and parsley; toss to combine. Arrange on the lettuce leaves and serve at once.

Per serving (generous 1 cup): 204 Cal, 5 g Fat, 1 g Sat Fat, 52 mg Chol, 358 mg Sod, 17 g Carb, 2 g Fib, 22 g Prot, 62 mg Calc. ***POINTS: 4.***

———— ◆ ————

*Chef's Tip:* To toast the walnuts, place them in a small dry skillet over medium-low heat. Cook, shaking the pan and stirring constantly, until lightly browned and fragrant, 3 to 4 minutes. Watch them carefully when toasting; nuts can burn quickly. Transfer the nuts to a plate to cool.

*Tomato Consommé and Chicken-Waldorf Salad*

# Green Salad with Citrus Dressing

**MAKES 4 SERVINGS**

You can make the dressing a day ahead and keep it refrigerated. While you're at it, make double and use half on another salad later in the week. To save time, buy bagged, prewashed mesclun. Or put together your own mesclun, using a bunch of arugula, some frisee, and a head of radicchio—enough to make six cups torn mixed greens.

6 cups mesclun

2 tablespoons thinly sliced
  fresh basil leaves

1 tablespoon fresh lemon juice

1 tablespoon orange juice

2 teaspoons extra-virgin
  olive oil

½ teaspoon sugar

⅛ teaspoon salt

⅛ teaspoon freshly
  ground pepper

*1.* Combine the mesclun and basil in a large bowl.

*2.* Combine the lemon juice, orange juice, oil, sugar, salt, and pepper in a small bowl; stir with a whisk. Pour the dressing over the salad; toss to combine. Serve at once.

Per serving (1 cup): 38 Cal, 2 g Fat, 0 g Sat Fat, 0 mg Chol, 98 mg Sod, 3 g Carb, 2 g Fib, 2 g Prot, 48 mg Calc. **POINTS: 1.**

# Focaccia with Herbs

**MAKES 6 SERVINGS**

Focaccia, the Italian flatbread that has become so popular, can be made
in advance, wrapped in heavy-duty foil, and frozen. To reheat, thaw the bread,
then bake in a 350°F oven until warm, about 10 minutes.

½ cup warm (105-115°F) water
½ teaspoon sugar
1⅛ teaspoons active dry yeast
1⅓ cups all-purpose flour
½ teaspoon salt
½ teaspoon dried rubbed sage
½ teaspoon dried thyme
1½ teaspoons extra-virgin
   olive oil

*1.* Combine the water and sugar in a small bowl. Sprinkle in the yeast and let stand until foamy, about 5 minutes.

*2.* Combine the flour, salt, sage, and thyme in a food processor. With the machine running, scrape the yeast mixture through the feed tube; pulse about 1 minute, until dough forms a smooth ball.

*3.* Spray a medium bowl with nonstick spray; put the dough in the bowl. Cover lightly with plastic wrap and let the dough rise in a warm spot until it doubles in size, about 35 minutes.

*4.* Spray a baking sheet with nonstick spray. Punch down the dough. Sprinkle a work surface lightly with flour. Turn the dough onto the surface, knead lightly; with a lightly floured rolling pin, roll into a 8 × 9-inch rectangle. Transfer to the baking sheet. Cover the dough loosely with plastic wrap and let rise in a warm spot until it doubles in size, about 35 minutes.

*5.* Preheat the oven to 425°F. Uncover the dough and, with a wooden spoon handle, make indentations at 1-inch intervals on the top. Gently brush the dough with the oil and bake until the bread sounds hollow when tapped, about 20 minutes. Cool on the baking sheet on a rack about 5 minutes. To serve, slide the focaccia onto a cutting board, then cut into 6 rectangles and serve warm.

Per serving (1 rectangle): 115 Cal, 1 g Fat, 0 g Sat Fat, 0 mg Chol, 195 mg Sod, 22 g Carb, 1 g Fib, 3 g Prot, 7 mg Calc. ***POINTS: 2.***

*Chef's Tip:* To make focaccia by hand, combine the water, sugar, and yeast in a large bowl; set aside until foamy. Stir in the flour, salt, sage, and thyme until the dough starts to gather around the spoon. Turn out the dough on a lightly floured surface; knead until the dough is smooth and elastic, about 10 minutes. For a crispier crust use a baking or pizza stone and preheat it in the oven for 20 minutes.

# *Sorbet Sundaes with Melon*

**MAKES 4 SERVINGS**

The fruit for this refreshing dessert can be prepared a day ahead, covered, and refrigerated. Other fresh fruits, such as blueberries, mango, grapes, or kiwi fruit, can be substituted for the melon. Any flavor sorbet can be used, but lemon works particularly well with most fruit combinations.

½ cup diced cantaloupe
½ cup diced honeydew melon
3 tablespoons orange juice
1½ teaspoons fresh lime juice
1⅓ cups lemon sorbet
4 fresh mint sprigs
4 teaspoons flaked
    sweetened coconut

*1.* Combine the cantaloupe, honeydew, orange juice, and lime juice in a medium bowl; cover and refrigerate.

*2.* To serve, place a ⅓-cup scoop of sorbet in each of 4 sundae glasses. Top with the melon mixture, mint, and coconut.

Per serving (1 sundae): 100 Cal, 1 g Fat, 0 g Sat Fat, 0 mg Chol, 21 mg Sod, 24 g Carb, 0 g Fib, 1 g Prot, 7 mg Calc. ***POINTS: 2.***

*Chef's Tip:* For an elegant touch, serve in stemmed glasses, such as martini glasses. Then set the glasses on individual plates and place a Chocolate Fudge Cookie on each plate.

# Chocolate Fudge Cookies

**MAKES 16 SERVINGS**

Like most cookies, these can be made weeks ahead, packed in airtight
containers, and frozen. Take the number of cookies you need out of the freezer
about an hour before lunch and serve with the Sorbet Sundaes.

½ cup all-purpose flour
⅛ teaspoon baking soda
2 tablespoons butter, softened
¼ cup granulated sugar
3 tablespoons packed dark
  brown sugar
1 egg white
½ teaspoon vanilla extract
3 tablespoons unsweetened
  cocoa powder

*1.* Preheat the oven to 350°F. Spray a nonstick baking sheet with
nonstick spray.

*2.* Combine the flour and baking soda in a medium bowl; set aside.

*3.* With an electric mixer at medium speed, beat the butter,
granulated sugar, brown sugar, egg white, vanilla, and cocoa until
well blended. With the mixer at low speed, stir in the flour mixture
until all the flour is just moistened.

*4.* Drop the batter by rounded teaspoons, 1½ inches apart, onto
the baking sheet and bake, 10–12 minutes. Cool on the baking
sheet on a rack, about 2 minutes. Remove from the baking sheet
and cool completely on the rack.

Per serving (1 cookie): 52 Cal, 2 g Fat, 1 g Sat Fat, 4 mg Chol, 24 mg Sod, 9 g Carb,
0 g Fib, 1 g Prot, 5 mg Calc. ***POINTS: 1.***

# Fruit Juice Spritzers

The tropical and perfumy flavor of guava and passion fruit juice lends an exotic touch to these drinks. If you like, you can substitute any combination of the myriad juices that are available. Try cranberry and grapefruit or raspberry and orange. To get a head start on the drinks, combine the fruit juices in a pitcher and refrigerate until you are ready to mix the spritzers.

1 cup cran-raspberry juice

1 cup guava and passion
  fruit juice

Ice cubes

2 cups seltzer water

4 lime wedges

Combine the fruit juices in a pitcher. Pour the juices into 4 tall glasses filled with ice cubes, add the seltzer, and stir to combine. Squeeze the lime wedges into each drink and add the wedges to the glasses.

Per serving (1 cup): 74 Cal, 0 g Fat, 0 g Sat Fat, 0 mg Chol, 3 mg Sod, 19 g Carb, 1 g Fib, 0 g Prot, 12 mg Calc. *POINTS: 1.*

———◆———

*Chef's Tip:* If the season is right and you have impatiens in your garden, try floating a petal or two in each glass. The petals are edible and quite sweet.

# A COZY AFTERNOON TEA

*Smoked-Salmon-and-Cucumber Canapés*
—
*Egg-and-Tomato Pinwheel Sandwiches*
—
*Cheese Scones*
—
*Bran Tea Bread*
—
*Chelsea Buns*
—
*Dundee Cake*
—
*Maids of Honour*
—
*Ginger-Meringue Creams*

## Smoked-Salmon-and-Cucumber Canapés

**MAKES 6 SERVINGS**

It just wouldn't be an English afternoon tea without cucumber sandwiches or smoked salmon. These canapés incorporate both. They are best made just before you're ready to serve them, but they can be kept covered with plastic wrap in the refrigerator for up to two hours.

**6** slices brioche or challah, toasted

**2** ounces light cream cheese or Neufchâtel

**¼** large seedless cucumber, thinly sliced

**6** thin slices (about 4 ounces) smoked salmon, halved then rolled up

**12** sprigs flat-leaf parsley

*1.* Using a 2½-inch cookie cutter, cut 2 rounds from each slice of brioche. (Save the trimmings to make into fresh bread crumbs for later use.)

*2.* Spread 1 teaspoon of the cream cheese on one slice of brioche. Add a few overlapping cucumber slices, then top with one piece of salmon and a parsley sprig. Repeat with the remaining brioche, cream cheese, cucumber, salmon, and parsley, making a total of 12 canapés.

Per serving (2 canapés): 95 Cal, 4 g Fat, 2 g Sat Fat, 18 mg Chol, 215 mg Sod, 9 g Carb, 0 g Fib, 6 g Prot, 24 mg Calc. ***POINTS: 2.***

# Egg-and-Tomato Pinwheel Sandwiches

**MAKES 6 SERVINGS**

Dainty egg-and-tomato sandwiches are a long-time favorite throughout the British Isles. If you prefer not to fuss making pinwheels, simply sandwich the filling between two slices of bread and cut into triangles. They are best made just before you're ready to serve, but they can be kept covered with plastic wrap in the refrigerator up to two hours. If you like, make the egg-and-tomato filling ahead of time and refrigerate it covered for up to two days.

2 **hard-cooked eggs, finely chopped**

1 **small plum tomato, finely chopped**

2 **tablespoons finely chopped fresh parsley**

¼ **teaspoon salt**

6 **slices oat bread, crusts removed (reserve crusts to make into bread crumbs for use some other time)**

1 **tablespoon butter, softened**

*1.* Combine the eggs, tomato, parsley, and salt in a small bowl.

*2.* Roll each bread slice lightly with a rolling pin into a 5 × 3-inch rectangle. Spread each slice with ½ teaspoon of the butter. Spread about 2 tablespoons of the egg mixture on top of the butter. Starting from one narrow end, roll up each sandwich tightly, jelly-roll fashion. Wrap each roll in plastic wrap and refrigerate at least 1 hour or up to overnight.

*3.* Cut each roll crosswise into 3 slices, making a total of 18 pinwheel sandwiches.

Per serving (3 pinwheel sandwiches): 99 Cal, 5 g Fat, 2 g Sat Fat, 76 mg Chol, 171 mg Sod, 11 g Carb, 1 g Fib, 4 g Prot, 15 mg Calc. ***POINTS: 2.***

———◆———

*Chef's Tip:* Here's how to get clean-cut, well-shaped pinwheels: Use a soft bread, such as oat-bran or potato bread, which will flatten easily with a rolling pin. Remove the crusts first to help make the rolling out easier and prevent the bread from cracking. Cut the pinwheels with a sharp, serrated knife, using a sawing motion.

*Egg-and-Tomato Pinwheel Sandwiches, Smoked-Salmon-and-Cucumber Canapés,
Cheese Scones, Maids of Honour, and Ginger-Meringue Creams*

# Cheese Scones

**MAKES 16 SERVINGS**

When we think of scones, we often think of the sweet currant variety, but once you try these tangy cheese scones you'll be converted. Extra-sharp cheddar cheese and a touch of mustard make them full-flavored and satisfying.

1½ cups all-purpose flour
½ cup whole-wheat flour
1 tablespoon baking powder
¾ teaspoon dry mustard
¼ teaspoon salt
¼ cup cold butter, cut into small pieces
4 ounces extra-sharp cheddar cheese, shredded (1 cup)
½ cup + 2 tablespoons fat-free milk

*1.* Preheat oven to 425°F. Spray a baking sheet with nonstick spray.

*2.* Combine the all-purpose flour, whole-wheat flour, baking powder, mustard, and salt in a large bowl. With a pastry blender, cut in the butter until the mixture is crumbly.

*3.* Add ¾ cup of the cheese and stir with a fork. Add the milk and stir with a fork until the dry ingredients are just moistened. Gather the mixture into a ball. On a lightly floured surface, roll lightly into a 7–8 inch circle. Cut into 16 circles with a 1¾-inch round cutter, dipped in flour between each cut.

*4.* Place the circles on the baking sheet; sprinkle the remaining ¼ cup cheese on the tops of the circles. Bake until golden brown and a toothpick inserted in the center comes out clean, about 12 minutes. Transfer the scones to a rack to cool 2–3 minutes. Serve warm, or cool completely and serve at room temperature.

Per serving (1 scone): 114 Cal, 5 g Fat, 3 g Sat Fat, 15 mg Chol, 196 mg Sod, 12 g Carb, 1 g Fib, 4 g Prot, 104 mg Calc. ***POINTS: 2.***

*Chef's Tip:* If you don't plan on eating all the scones right away, cool them completely, then freeze in a zip-close plastic bag for up to two months.

# Bran Tea Bread

Surprisingly, this moist and rich tea bread is made with no fat except for the small amount found in the egg and walnuts. Store it, well-wrapped, for up to three days at room temperature, or freeze for up to three months. If you prefer, substitute an extra ½ cup fat-free milk for the brewed tea, and ¾ teaspoon cinnamon and ¼ teaspoon each ground cloves and nutmeg for the apple-pie spice.

| |
|---|
| 1 cup all-bran cereal |
| 1 cup raisins |
| ⅔ cup packed brown sugar |
| ½ cup cold tea |
| ½ cup fat-free milk |
| 1 cup all-purpose flour |
| 2 teaspoons baking powder |
| 1¼ teaspoons apple-pie spice |
| ¼ teaspoon salt |
| 1 large egg, lightly beaten |
| ½ cup chopped walnuts |

1. Combine the cereal, raisins, sugar, tea, and milk in a large bowl; set aside to soak for 30–40 minutes.
2. Preheat the oven to 350°F. Spray an 8-inch loaf pan with nonstick spray, then line with wax paper.
3. Combine the flour, baking powder, apple-pie spice, and salt in a medium bowl; set aside.
4. Stir the egg and walnuts into the cereal mixture. Add the flour mixture and stir until just blended. Scrape the mixture into the loaf pan and spread smooth. Bake until a toothpick inserted in the center comes out clean, about 1 hour. Cool in the pan on a rack about 10 minutes; remove from the pan and cool completely on the rack. Cut into 12 slices.

Per serving (1 slice): 178 Cal, 4 g Fat, 0 g Sat Fat, 18 mg Chol, 175 mg Sod, 35 g Carb, 2 g Fib, 3 g Prot, 86 mg Calc. *POINTS: 3.*

# Chelsea Buns

**MAKES 12 SERVINGS**

Spiced raisin bread is popular, in various forms, throughout the world. Here, the spiced bread dough is turned into Chelsea buns, which were first made in the Chelsea Bun House in Chelsea, London, in the eighteenth century. Store any leftover buns, well-wrapped, in the freezer for up to three months. Bring to room temperature before serving.

¾ cup warm (105–115°F)
   fat-free milk
1 teaspoon granulated sugar
1 package active dry yeast
2½ cups all-purpose flour
⅓ cup whole-wheat flour
1 teaspoon salt
½ teaspoon ground cardamom
¼ teaspoon cinnamon
1 large egg, lightly beaten
¼ cup golden raisins
¼ cup currants
¼ cup packed light brown sugar
1 teaspoon grated lemon rind
1 tablespoon honey

1. Combine the milk and granulated sugar in a medium bowl. Sprinkle in the yeast and let stand until foamy, about 5 minutes.
2. Combine the all-purpose flour, whole-wheat flour, salt, cardamom, and cinnamon in a food processor. With the machine running, scrape the yeast mixture and the egg through the feed tube; pulse about 1 minute, until the dough forms a ball. If necessary, turn the dough out onto a lightly floured surface and knead a few times until smooth.
3. Spray a large bowl with nonstick spray; put the dough in the bowl. Cover lightly with plastic wrap and let the dough rise in a warm spot until it doubles in size, about 1 hour.
4. Meanwhile, combine the raisins, currants, brown sugar, and lemon rind in a small bowl; set aside. Spray a 9-inch square baking pan with nonstick spray.
5. Punch down the dough. Sprinkle a work surface lightly with flour. Turn the dough onto the surface and knead lightly. With a floured rolling pin, roll into a 12-inch square. Sprinkle the raisin mixture over the dough and roll up jelly-roll fashion, moistening one edge to seal. With a sharp knife, using a sawing motion, cut into 12 slices and place, cut-sides down, in the pan. Cover lightly with plastic wrap and let rise in a warm spot until they double in size, about 30 minutes. Preheat the oven to 375°F.
6. Bake the buns until they sound hollow when tapped, about 25 minutes. While the buns are still warm, brush with the honey. Remove the buns from the pan and serve warm, or cool completely on a rack.

Per serving (1 bun): 162 Cal, 1 g Fat, 0 g Sat Fat, 18 mg Chol, 211 mg Sod, 35 g Carb, 2 g Fib, 5 g Prot, 35 mg Calc. ***POINTS: 3.***

# Dundee Cake

**MAKES 24 SERVINGS**

This light fruitcake, hailing from the town of Dundee, Scotland, is a popular afternoon-tea treat. We've left out the typical candied fruits and added freshly grated orange rind and a touch of brandy to give flavor. The top of a Dundee cake is traditionally studded completely with whole almonds but a simple border of almonds does the trick here.

| | |
|---|---|
| 1½ **cups all-purpose flour** | 1. Preheat the oven to 300°F. Spray an 8-inch springform pan with |

1½ **cups all-purpose flour**
1 **teaspoon baking powder**
½ **teaspoon cinnamon**
¼ **teaspoon ground nutmeg**
¼ **teaspoon ground allspice**
¼ **teaspoon salt**
6 **tablespoons butter, softened**
¾ **cup sugar**
3 **large eggs**
½ **cup raisins**
½ **cup golden raisins**
¼ **cup currants**
¼ **cup sliced almonds,**
  **coarsely chopped**
1 **tablespoon grated orange rind**
1 **tablespoon brandy or**
  **vanilla extract**
24 **blanched whole almonds**

1. Preheat the oven to 300°F. Spray an 8-inch springform pan with nonstick spray and line the bottom and sides with wax paper.
2. Combine the flour, baking powder, cinnamon, nutmeg, allspice, and salt in a medium bowl; set aside.
3. With an electric mixer at high speed, beat the butter and sugar until light and fluffy. Add the eggs, one at a time, beating well after each addition. With the mixer at low speed, stir in the flour mixture, raisins, golden raisins, currants, chopped almonds, orange rind, and brandy. Mix, until all of the flour is just moistened. Scrape the batter into the pan and spread smooth. Arrange the whole almonds in a circle around the top outer edge of the cake.
4. Bake until a cake tester inserted in the center comes out clean, about 1½ hours. Cool in the pan on a rack 15 minutes, then remove the cake from the pan and cool completely on the rack. Cut into 24 slices.

Per serving (1 slice): 126 Cal, 5 g Fat, 2 g Sat Fat, 34 mg Chol, 73 mg Sod, 19 g Carb, 1 g Fib, 2 g Prot, 27 mg Calc. **POINTS: 3.**

---

*Chef's Tip:* Store any leftover cake, well-wrapped, at room temperature for up to three days or in the freezer for up to two months. Bring to room temperature before serving.

# Maids of Honour

**MAKES 12 SERVINGS**

These almond tartlets originated in King Henry VIII's palace at Hampton Court, where they were popular with the Queen's Maids of Honour. The recipe was a closely guarded secret and was only made public in the early 1950s on a television program about historic dishes of Britain. Store any leftover tartlets in an airtight container at room temperature for up to two days or in the freezer for up to two months. Bring to room temperature before serving.

¾ cup all-purpose flour
⅛ teaspoon salt
3 tablespoons cold butter
3–4 tablespoons ice water
⅓ cup slivered almonds
3 tablespoons sugar
1 large egg
1 teaspoon brandy or
   vanilla extract
2 tablespoons seedless
   strawberry jam

*1.* Preheat the oven to 400°F. Spray 12 (2¼-inch) tartlet pans or mini-muffin cups with nonstick spray.

*2.* Combine the flour and salt in a medium bowl. With a pastry blender, cut in the butter until the mixture is crumbly. Add the ice water and mix with a knife until the mixture just forms a ball.

*3.* On a lightly floured surface, roll out the pastry to between ¹⁄₁₆- and ⅛-inch thick. With a 2¾-inch cookie cutter, cut out 12 rounds and fit them into the pans.

*4.* Pulse the almonds and sugar in a food processor until finely ground. Add the egg and brandy and process until smooth. Spoon ½ teaspoon of the jam into the bottom of each tart shell. Top with a scant tablespoon of the almond mixture. Bake until golden, about 15 minutes. Cool in the pans on a rack 5 minutes, then transfer to the rack to cool completely. Serve at room temperature.

Per serving (1 tartlet): 99 Cal, 5 g Fat, 2 g Sat Fat, 25 mg Chol, 50 mg Sod, 12 g Carb, 1 g Fib, 2 g Prot, 13 mg Calc. ***POINTS: 2.***

———◆———

*Chef's Tip:* For a pretty presentation, place a tablespoon or two of confectioners' sugar in a sieve and sift it over the tartlets.

# Ginger-Meringue Creams

## MAKES 6 SERVINGS

All sweetness and light, meringues keep well for up to a month if stored in an airtight container in a dry place. Avoid making them on humid days. They need dry air to dry out completely after baking. Assemble them with the topping and ginger just before you're ready to serve. Buy crystallized ginger in bulk from specialty or health-food stores. It is much cheaper than purchasing it from the spice rack in the supermarket. This recipe is easily doubled.

2 **egg whites**
¼ **teaspoon cream of tartar**
6 **tablespoons sugar**
6 **tablespoons light non-dairy whipped topping**
6 **teaspoons chopped crystallized ginger**

1. Preheat the oven to 225°F. Line a large baking sheet with foil.
2. With an electric mixer at medium speed, beat the egg whites and the cream of tartar in a large bowl until just frothy. Gradually beat in the sugar, 2 tablespoons at a time, until the sugar completely dissolves and the whites stand in stiff, glossy peaks, about 6 minutes.
3. Spoon the egg white mixture onto the baking sheet, making 6 (3-inch) rounds. Spread the mixture with the back of a spoon, leaving about ½ inch between each meringue.
4. Bake the meringues until they feel crisp to the touch, about 2 hours. Turn the oven off and leave the meringues in the oven until they are crisp and dry to the touch, about 1 hour longer.
5. Carefully loosen the meringues from the foil, then transfer to a rack to cool completely.
6. Spoon 1 tablespoon whipped topping onto each meringue, then sprinkle with the ginger. Serve at once.

Per serving (1 meringue): 74 Cal, 1 g Fat, 0 g Sat Fat, 0 mg Chol, 32 mg Sod, 16 g Carb, 0 g Fib, 1 g Prot, 7 mg Calc. *POINTS: 2.*

# *winter*

# HANUKKAH DINNER

*Zucchini-and-Potato Latkes*
—
*Roasted Pear and Apple Compote*
—
*Thyme-Roasted Chicken with Sherry Gravy*
—
*Fruited Couscous*
—
*Parsnip Puree*
—
*Wilted Garlic–Flavored Spinach*
—
*Chopped Vegetable Salad*
—
*Almond Mishmishya*

## Zucchini-and-Potato Latkes

### MAKES 16 SERVINGS

Tender inside and browned crisp outside, these latkes are the perfect start for your holiday dinner.

**5 teaspoons olive or vegetable oil**
**3 (8-ounce) russet potatoes, peeled**
**1 medium (6-ounce) zucchini, peeled**
**1 small onion, grated**
**1 large egg**
**1 tablespoon all-purpose flour**
**¾ teaspoon kosher salt**
**⅛ teaspoon freshly ground pepper**

*1.* Preheat the oven to 450°F. Brush 2 large nonstick baking sheets each with 1½ teaspoons of the oil. Cook the potatoes in a saucepan with boiling water to cover, 6 minutes; drain. Cover with cold water to cool.

*2.* Meanwhile, grate the zucchini on a double layer of paper towels; let stand 3 minutes. Combine the zucchini with the onion, egg, flour, salt, and pepper in a large bowl. Drain the potatoes, pat dry, then coarsely grate. Stir into the zucchini mixture.

*3.* Heat the baking sheets in the oven until hot, about 4 minutes. Drop scant ¼ cup measures of the potato mixture onto the baking sheets, forming a total of 16 (3-inch) pancakes; lightly flatten each.

*4.* Bake until browned on the bottom, 8–9 minutes. Brush the tops of the pancakes with the remaining 2 teaspoons oil, then turn and bake until cooked through, 5–7 minutes.

Per serving (1 latke): 55 Cal, 2 g Fat, 0 g Sat Fat, 13 mg Chol, 79 mg Sod, 9 g Carb, 1 g Fib, 1 g Prot, 8 mg Calc. ***POINTS: 1.***

# Roasted Pear and Apple Compote

This sweet and spicy combo makes a great accompaniment to either the latkes or the chicken. Choose a spicy pear such as Bosc or Comice and an apple with complex sweetness such as Braeburn, Gala, or Fuji. You can make the compote up to three days ahead, cool, then refrigerate in an airtight container. Simply allow it to come to room temperature before serving.

1½ **pounds pears, peeled, cored, and quartered**

1½ **pounds apples, peeled, cored, and cut into 8 wedges**

2 **shallots, peeled and cut into quarters**

1 **tablespoon vegetable oil**

1 **cup apple cider**

1 **whole clove**

⅛ **teaspoon cinnamon**

¼ **teaspoon kosher salt**

2 **teaspoons brandy (optional)**

*1.* Adjust the racks to divide the oven in thirds. Preheat the oven to 425°F.

*2.* Toss the pears, apples, and shallots with the oil on a jelly-roll pan. Place the pan in the bottom third of the oven and roast until the fruit is lightly browned and tender, about 30 minutes. Let the mixture cool slightly on the pan, then transfer to a chopping board and chop into large chunks.

*3.* Meanwhile, bring the cider to a boil in a small saucepan. Reduce the heat to medium and cook at a high simmer, with small bubbles breaking the surface, until reduced by half, about 15 minutes. Add the clove and cinnamon and continue simmering until the cider is syrupy and reduced to 2 tablespoons, about 7 minutes. Remove the clove and stir in the pear-apple mixture with the salt and brandy, if using. Serve warm or at room temperature.

Per serving (generous ⅓ cup): 119 Cal, 2 g Fat, 0 g Sat Fat, 0 mg Chol, 50 mg Sod, 27 g Carb, 3 g Fib, 1 g Prot, 19 mg Calc. *POINTS: 2.*

*Roasted Pear and Apple Compote, Thyme-Roasted Chicken with
Sherry Gravy, and Fruited Couscous*

# *Thyme-Roasted Chicken with Sherry Gravy*

**MAKES 8 SERVINGS**

Rubbing the thyme-pesto mixture under the skin of the chicken keeps the flavor where
you want it—on the meat—while leaving the skin on during the roasting keeps the chicken
moist. Remove and discard the skin just before you're ready to carve the chicken. Sherry and roasted
vegetables make a delicious gravy for the thyme-flavored chicken. The gravy is kept light by
skimming off all the fat that rises to the top.

| | |
|---|---|
| 1 | (4½-pound) roasting chicken |
| 1 | (½-ounce) bunch fresh thyme, leaves removed |
| 1 | large garlic clove |
| ½ | teaspoon salt |
| 2 | large carrots, finely chopped |
| ½ | fennel bulb, finely chopped |
| 2 | shallots, finely chopped |
| ⅔–1¼ | cups low-sodium chicken broth |
| ¼ | cup dry sherry |
| 1 | tablespoon all-purpose flour |
| 2 | tablespoons cold water |

1. Preheat oven to 350°F. Spray a roasting pan with nonstick spray.
2. Remove the large fatty flaps from around the neck cavity of the
chicken, being careful not to cut into the skin covering the breast.
Finely chop the thyme, garlic, and salt on a chopping board.
Carefully rub the mixture under the skin of the chicken, over the
breast and legs. Tuck the wings behind the chicken and tie the legs
together with kitchen twine.
3. Combine the carrots, fennel, and shallots in the center of the
roasting pan. Place the chicken, breast-side up, on the vegetables;
roast 20 minutes. Pour ⅓ cup of the broth over the chicken; roast
30 minutes. Pour another ⅓ cup broth over the chicken; roast
until an instant-read thermometer inserted in the thigh registers
180°F, 20–25 minutes more. Transfer the chicken to a board; let
stand 10 minutes. Discard the twine and skin, then transfer the
chicken to a platter and carve.
4. Meanwhile, add the sherry to the juices and vegetables in the
roasting pan; bring to a boil, scraping up the browned bits from
the bottom of the pan. Strain through a fine strainer into a 2-cup
measure, pressing the vegetables to extract their liquid. Add broth
(if necessary) to equal 2 cups. Let the gravy stand 1–2 minutes
until the fat rises to top; spoon off all fat (3–4 tablespoons). Blend
the flour and water in a saucepan; gradually stir in the gravy.
Cook, stirring constantly, until the mixture boils and thickens.
Serve with the chicken.

Per serving (⅛ of chicken with ¼ cup gravy): 176 Cal, 6 g Fat, 2 g Sat Fat,
74 mg Chol, 225 mg Sod, 3 g Carb, 0 g Fib, 26 g Prot, 27 mg Calc. ***POINTS: 4.***

# Fruited Couscous

This sweet fruited couscous can be made ahead and kept, covered, in the refrigerator for up to two days. Bring it to room temperature for about two hours, then fluff with a fork before serving.

¾ cup orange juice

⅔ cup currants

⅔ cup diced dried apricots

1 small onion, chopped

2 tablespoons white-wine vinegar

2 teaspoons olive oil

1 teaspoon kosher salt

2⅓ cups water

2 cups low-sodium chicken broth

2⅓ cups couscous

⅓ cup finely chopped fresh cilantro

2 large scallions, thinly sliced

*1.* Combine the orange juice, currants, apricots, onion, vinegar, oil, and ½ teaspoon of the salt in a small bowl; set aside.

*2.* Bring the water, broth, and remaining ½ teaspoon salt to a boil in a large saucepan. Stir in the couscous; cover and remove from the heat. Let stand until all the liquid has absorbed, about 5 minutes.

*3.* Transfer the couscous to a large bowl; let cool. Add the juice and fruit mixture, the cilantro, and scallions; toss with a fork to coat. Serve at room temperature.

Per serving (1 cup): 296 Cal, 2 g Fat, 0 g Sat Fat, 0 mg Chol, 219 mg Sod, 62 g Carb, 5 g Fib, 9 g Prot, 38 mg Calc. ***POINTS: 5.***

*Chef's Tip:* To get a light and fluffy-textured appearance to the couscous, scrape the soaked couscous from the top with a fork, bit by bit, allowing it to fall into the bowl. Use a large fork to lightly toss the remaining ingredients into the couscous.

# Parsnip Puree

**MAKES 8 SERVINGS**

Creamy smooth, sweet, and garlicky, this parsnip side dish is a cinch to prepare. To make ahead, transfer the pureed mixture to a microwavable dish and refrigerate, covered, for up to 24 hours. To reheat, bring the puree to room temperature, then microwave, partially covered, on High, stirring once or twice, until heated through, 3 to 4 minutes.

8 large garlic cloves, skin on

2 pounds parsnips (about 3 large), peeled and cut into ½-inch slices

2 cups low-sodium chicken broth

1 tablespoon butter, softened

1½ teaspoons white-wine vinegar

½ teaspoon salt

⅛ teaspoon white pepper

*1.* Place the garlic cloves in a medium nonstick skillet over medium heat. Cook, turning the cloves occasionally, until charred and soft to the touch, 30–35 minutes.

*2.* Bring the parsnips and broth to a boil in a large saucepan. Reduce the heat and simmer, covered, until tender, about 15 minutes. Remove from the heat and let stand 15 minutes.

*3.* Place the butter, vinegar, salt, and pepper in a food processor. Add half of the parsnips and cooking liquid. Split the skin on the garlic cloves and squeeze the garlic into the parsnip mixture; puree. Transfer to a microwavable dish. Puree the remaining parsnips and cooking liquid and stir into the parsnip puree in the dish. Microwave, partially covered, on High, stirring once, until heated through, about 2 minutes.

Per serving (generous ⅛ cup): 105 Cal, 2 g Fat, 1 g Sat Fat, 4 mg Chol, 180 mg Sod, 21 g Carb, 4 g Fib, 2 g Prot, 46 mg Calc. ***POINTS: 1.***

# Wilted Garlic–Flavored Spinach

Bagged, triple-washed fresh spinach leaves make recipes such as this a cinch for cooks. Mature spinach leaves may have thick stems, so trim them if necessary. If you see packaged baby spinach leaves, make this your first choice; the stems are very tender and need no trimming. This dish is best made at the last minute.

1 tablespoon olive oil

3 large garlic cloves, minced

3 (9-ounce) bags fresh baby or regular spinach leaves

¼ cup low-sodium chicken broth

1 teaspoon kosher salt

*1.* Heat a deep 12-inch nonstick skillet over medium heat. Swirl in the oil, then add the garlic and cook, stirring constantly, until fragrant, about 1 minute. Add half of the spinach and the broth, then cover; cook just until the spinach begins to wilt, 1–2 minutes.

*2.* Add the remaining spinach, sprinkle with the salt and cook, stirring once or twice, until all the spinach is wilted, about 3 minutes.

Per serving (about ⅓ cup): 38 Cal, 2 g Fat, 0 g Sat Fat, 0 mg Chol, 272 mg Sod, 4 g Carb, 3 g Fib, 3 g Prot, 97 mg Calc. *POINTS: 0.*

# Chopped Vegetable Salad

This wholesome salad, which combines traditional ingredients and flavors of the
Middle East, offers a welcome crunchy texture to this Hanukkah dinner.
It will keep in the refrigerator, covered, for up to three days.

1 pound green cabbage,
   coarsely shredded (about
   4 cups)
1 (15-ounce) can chickpeas
   (garbanzo beans), rinsed
   and drained
5 plum tomatoes, diced
1 large red bell pepper, seeded
   and diced
½ long seedless cucumber, diced
3 scallions, chopped
Freshly grated rind of 1 lemon
¼ cup fresh lemon juice
3 tablespoons chopped
   fresh mint
1 teaspoon kosher salt

Combine the cabbage, chickpeas, tomatoes, bell pepper, cucumber,
scallions, lemon rind, lemon juice, mint, and salt in a large bowl;
toss well to coat. Serve at once or cover and refrigerate until
ready to serve.

Per serving (generous 1 cup): 89 Cal, 1 g Fat, 0 g Sat Fat, 0 mg Chol, 298 mg Sod,
17 g Carb, 4 g Fib, 5 g Prot, 53 mg Calc. *POINTS: 1.*

———◆———

*Chef's Tip:* Spoon each serving of the salad into a small bowl to serve on the side.

# Almond Mishmishya

### MAKES 20 SERVINGS

These Hanukkah favorites get their name from the Arabic *mishmesh*, meaning apricot. To give a lovely light orange hue to the candies, use light-colored apricots (preferably from California) that are still moist and plump. Reserve the orange juice from plumping the apricots—it's delicious in a smoothie. Store the candies in an airtight container in the refrigerator for up to a month.

  1 **cup orange juice**
 12 **ounces dried apricots**
1½ **cups + ⅓ cup sugar**
  2 **tablespoons (from a**
    **7- or 8-ounce tube or can)**
    **almond paste**
 40 **whole blanched almonds,**
    **toasted**

*1.* Bring the juice to a boil in a large saucepan. Remove the pan from the heat and add the apricots, pushing them under the juice. Cover and let stand 30 minutes.

*2.* Drain the apricots. Lightly pat dry with paper towels. Process the apricots with 1½ cups of the sugar and the almond paste in a food processor until smooth. Transfer the apricot paste to a bowl, cover with plastic wrap, and refrigerate until firm, at least 3 hours or up to overnight.

*3.* Line a jelly-roll pan with wax paper. Fill a level measuring tablespoon with the apricot mixture; remove and roll into a ball. Repeat, making a total of 40 balls. Roll the apricot balls in the remaining ⅓ cup sugar. Lightly press 1 almond into each ball, slightly flattening each ball into a disk and making sure the apricot mixture completely surrounds the nut. Let the candies stand uncovered 2–3 days to dry.

Per serving (2 candies): 132 Cal, 2 g Fat, 0 g Sat Fat, 0 mg Chol, 2 mg Sod, 30 g Carb, 2 g Fib, 1 g Prot, 16 mg Calc. **POINTS: 2.**

———◆———

*Chef's Tip:* To toast the almonds, place them in a small dry skillet over medium-low heat. Cook, shaking the pan and stirring constantly, until lightly browned and fragrant, 4 to 5 minutes. Watch them carefully when toasting; almonds can burn quickly. Transfer the nuts to a plate to cool. For a pretty presentation, place each candy in a small foil or paper candy cup.

*Clams Oreganata*

—

*Calamari and Shrimp Tomato Sauce with Linguine*

—

*Pizza with Roasted Tomatoes and Anchovies*

—

*Crab-Stuffed Lobster Tails*

—

*Scungilli Salad*

—

*Mussels Fra Diavolo*

—

*Spiced Oranges in Vin Santo*

—

*Anisette Toasts*

## Clams Oreganata

**MAKES 8 SERVINGS**

This is the real deal, in the authentic style of an Italian family classic.
If you're not comfortable opening clams yourself, have the fishmonger open
them, reserving the juice and shells.

2 slices firm white bread, made into fine crumbs

¾ teaspoon minced fresh oregano

¼ teaspoon grated lemon rind

1 small garlic clove, minced

24 cherrystone clams, scrubbed and shucked (24 half-shells and ¼ cup of clam juice reserved)

1 tablespoon extra-virgin olive oil

8 lemon wedges

*1.* Toast the bread crumbs in a nonstick skillet over medium heat, stirring frequently, until golden, 5–7 minutes; let cool.

*2.* Combine the crumbs, oregano, lemon rind, and garlic in a medium bowl, rubbing with fingertips to infuse the crumbs with flavor. Stir in 2 tablespoons of the clam juice and the oil (mixture should be crumbly).

*3.* Preheat the broiler. Arrange the 24 clam half-shells on a large broiler pan or jelly-roll pan. Place a clam in each shell and top with the crumb mixture. Sprinkle ½ teaspoon clam juice over each. Broil 4 inches from the heat until the crumbs are golden and clams are just cooked, 8–9 minutes. Serve with lemon wedges.

Per serving (3 clams): 88 Cal, 3 g Fat, 0 g Sat Fat, 25 mg Chol, 88 mg Sod, 6 g Carb, 0 g Fib, 10 g Prot, 43 mg Calc. *POINTS: 2.*

# Calamari and Shrimp Tomato Sauce with Linguine

Light up Christmas Eve with this spicy, rich, and sumptuous sauce. Make it ahead (you'll get about 12 cups) and refrigerate in an airtight container for up to 24 hours. For this menu, you'll be using 6 cups of the sauce in this dish, 4 cups in the Mussels Fra Diavolo, and 2 cups in the Crab-Stuffed Lobster Tails.

¾ **pound large shrimp, peeled and deveined**

8 **large garlic cloves, finely chopped**

1 **teaspoon crushed red pepper**

2½ **teaspoons olive oil**

2 **onions, finely chopped**

½ **pound cleaned squid, bodies cut into ½-inch rings**

¾ **cup dry white wine**

2 **(35-ounce) cans whole plum tomatoes in juice, pureed in blender with the juice**

1 **(6-ounce) can tomato paste**

1 **teaspoon dried thyme**

1½ **teaspoons salt**

1 **small carrot, peeled**

1 **pound linguine**

1. Toss the shrimp with 1 teaspoon of the garlic and ½ teaspoon of the crushed red pepper in a bowl. Heat a 5–6 quart saucepan over medium-high heat. Swirl in 1½ teaspoons of the oil, then add the shrimp and cook until golden, about 1 minute on each side. Transfer the shrimp to a zip-close plastic bag and refrigerate.

2. Swirl the remaining 1 teaspoon oil into the same saucepan. Add the onions and cook, stirring occasionally, until translucent, about 4 minutes. Add the squid and the remaining garlic; cook until the squid is just opaque in the center, stirring frequently, about 1 minute. Add the wine and simmer 1 minute. Add the tomatoes, tomato paste, thyme, salt, carrot, and the remaining ½ teaspoon crushed red pepper; bring to a boil, stirring to scrape the browned bits from the bottom of the pan. Reduce the heat and simmer, covered, about 1 hour.

3. Remove and discard the carrot. Add the shrimp and cook until the shrimp are just opaque in the center, about 3 minutes. Cover and refrigerate for up to 24 hours.

4. Cook the linguine according to package directions; drain and return to the pot. Heat 6 cups of the Calamari and Shrimp Tomato Sauce and pour 4 cups onto the drained pasta. Transfer to a large serving bowl. Serve with the extra 2 cups sauce.

Per serving (1½ cups linguine and sauce with extra ¼ cup sauce): 311 Cal, 3 g Fat, 0 g Sat Fat, 79 mg Chol, 787 mg Sod, 55 g Carb, 4 g Fib, 16 g Prot, 68 mg Calc. **POINTS: 6.**

# Pizza with Roasted Tomatoes and Anchovies

**MAKES 12 SERVINGS**

Crisp and light, this pizza is a delightfully different and delicious way to bring fish to the Christmas Eve meal. The dough can be made the day before and kept in a lightly oiled zip-close plastic bag in the refrigerator, where it will rise slowly overnight. Remove the dough from the bag and let it rest on a floured board at least 30 minutes before using. The tomatoes can be roasted and peeled, then chopped with the anchovies the day before and stored in an airtight container in the refrigerator.

- 6 large plum tomatoes, cut lengthwise in half
- 1 teaspoon + 2 tablespoons extra-virgin olive oil
- ¾ teaspoon salt
- ⅔ cup warm (105–115°F) water
- ½ teaspoon sugar
- 1½ teaspoons active dry yeast
- 2 cups all-purpose flour
- 2 tablespoons cornmeal
- 1½ teaspoons minced fresh rosemary
- 1 large garlic clove, minced
- 1 (2-ounce) can flat anchovies in olive oil, drained on paper towels and finely chopped

*1.* Preheat the oven to 275°F. On a shallow broiler pan, toss the tomatoes with 1 teaspoon of the oil and ¼ teaspoon of the salt; arrange cut-side up. Bake until softened and reduced but still very moist, about 1 hour and 35 minutes.

*2.* Meanwhile, to make the dough, combine the water and sugar in a 2-cup measuring cup; sprinkle in the yeast and let stand until foamy, about 5 minutes. Combine the flour and remaining ½ teaspoon salt in a food processor. With the machine running, scrape the yeast mixture through the feed tube; pulse about 1 minute, until the dough forms a ball. Turn the dough onto a lightly floured surface and knead a few times until smooth.

*3.* Spray a large bowl with nonstick spray; put the dough in the bowl. Cover lightly with plastic wrap and let rise in a warm spot until it doubles in size, about 1 hour. Arrange one rack on the bottom rung of the oven. Preheat the oven to 450°F.

*4.* Sprinkle a heavy-duty baking sheet with the cornmeal. Sprinkle a work surface lightly with flour. Turn the dough onto the surface. Roll with a lightly floured rolling pin to a 12 × 14-inch rectangle; transfer to the baking sheet. Combine the remaining 2 tablespoons oil, the rosemary, and garlic in a small bowl; spread with fingertips over the entire surface of the dough.

*5.* Remove and discard the skins from the tomatoes. Coarsely chop the tomatoes with the anchovies; scatter evenly over the dough. Bake on the bottom rack of the oven until the pizza is browned and crisp, 12–14 minutes. Cut into 24 rectangles.

Per serving (2 rectangles): 121 Cal, 3 g Fat, 0 g Sat Fat, 3 mg Chol, 286 mg Sod, 19 g Carb, 1 g Fib, 4 g Prot, 15 mg Calc. ***POINTS: 2.***

# Crab-Stuffed Lobster Tails

**MAKES 8 SERVINGS**

Simplicity itself, the lobster tails are baked with a little of the prepared Calamari and Shrimp Tomato Sauce, topped with a crab dressing, and broiled. This recipe is best prepared last minute.

1 **tablespoon unsalted butter**

1 **garlic clove, minced**

1 **slice firm white bread, made into crumbs**

8 **(3-ounce) rock lobster tails, fresh or frozen, thawed**

2 **cups Calamari and Shrimp Tomato Sauce [page 230]**

1 **tablespoon olive oil**

6 **ounces cooked lump crabmeat, picked over and flaked**

**Freshly grated rind of 1 lemon**

*1.* Melt the butter in a small nonstick skillet over medium heat, then add the garlic and bread crumbs. Cook, stirring frequently, until golden and fragrant, 2–3 minutes; set aside.

*2.* Arrange one oven rack in the center of the oven and one above that. Preheat the oven to 400°F.

*3.* With kitchen shears, remove the soft undercover of the lobster tails; crack through the hard upper shells with a cleaver, press down to lie flat. Place, shell-side down, in a 9 × 13-inch baking dish. Drizzle each tail with 2 tablespoons of the Calamari and Shrimp Tomato Sauce and sprinkle the oil over all. Cover lightly with foil and bake until the lobster is just opaque in the center, 9–11 minutes.

*4.* Meanwhile, combine the buttered bread crumbs with the crab and lemon rind in a small bowl. Lightly press the mixture onto the meat of the lobster tails. Turn the oven to broil. Broil 4 inches from the heat until golden, 1–2 minutes. Heat the remaining 1 cup sauce to serve with the lobster tails.

Per serving (1 stuffed lobster tail with 2 tablespoons sauce): 158 Cal, 5 g Fat, 1 g Sat Fat, 101 mg Chol, 550 mg Sod, 6 g Carb, 1 g Fib, 23 g Prot, 90 mg Calc. ***POINTS: 3.***

◆

*Chef's Tip:* A 6-ounce can of white crabmeat is a bit less expensive than lump crabmeat and can be substituted in this recipe since large chunks of crab are not necessary.

*Crab-Stuffed Lobster Tails with Calamari and Shrimp Tomato Sauce*

# Scungilli Salad

Once you have acquired a taste for this unusual shellfish, you've become a true Italian at heart. Scungilli (really a whelk and a distant cousin to the conch) is sold in Italian markets fresh, frozen, or canned. Fresh scungilli is enjoyed by those familiar with it, but it needs cleaning. To save time use canned, which usually labels the scungilli as conch. This dish is fairly common on menus in Italian seacoast neighborhoods.

1¼ pounds fresh scungilli (conch), or 3/4 pound drained, rinsed canned conch, patted dry

¾ cup very thinly shaved red onion

2 celery stalks, sliced on the diagonal and blanched

2 garlic cloves, finely chopped

2 tablespoons finely chopped fresh parsley

2 tablespoons fresh lemon juice

2 teaspoons red-wine vinegar

4 teaspoons extra-virgin olive oil

⅛–¼ teaspoon crushed red pepper

*1.* To clean the fresh scungilli, trim away the thin membrane and the projecting tube on the side of the knob and remove the tube-like intestines under the membrane; rinse out the area. Trim the black colored flesh away from the white flesh (the black flesh, though tough, is edible and can be left on, if desired). Thinly slice the white flesh. For the canned scungilli, drain and rinse well, then cut up any large pieces.

*2.* Toss the scungilli with the onion, celery, garlic, parsley, lemon juice, vinegar, oil, and crushed red pepper in a large bowl. Serve at once or cover and refrigerate for up to 8 hours.

Per serving (½ cup): 80 Cal, 3 g Fat, 0 g Sat Fat, 151 mg Chol, 35 mg Sod, 4 g Carb, 0 g Fib, 9 g Prot, 27 mg Calc. **POINTS: 2.**

---

*Chef's Tip:* Blanching the celery slightly tenderizes it and sets the color. To blanch it, plunge celery into a pan of boiling water for 30 seconds, then drain and put in ice water to stop the cooking. Consider serving the salad on a Boston lettuce-lined platter.

# Mussels Fra Diavolo

**MAKES 8 SERVINGS**

Using the Calamari and Shrimp Tomato Sauce from this menu makes this dish spicy and easy to prepare. The mussels are best cooked just before you are ready to serve them.

2 pounds (about 60) mussels
1 tablespoon olive oil
1 onion, chopped
2 large garlic cloves, finely chopped
⅓ cup dry white wine
4 cups Calamari and Shrimp Tomato Sauce [page 230]

*1.* To prepare the mussels, soak them in lightly salted cold water 45 minutes. Drain and debeard by pulling off any fuzzy threads on the side of the mussel shell.

*2.* Heat a large Dutch oven over medium heat. Swirl in the oil, then add the onion and garlic; cook until softened, 3–4 minutes. Add the wine and mussels; bring to a boil. Reduce the heat and simmer, covered, until the shells open, 4–6 minutes. Transfer the mussels and juices to a deep platter or large bowl. Heat the sauce and pour over the mussels. Serve at once or keep warm in a just-warm oven until ready to serve.

Per serving (about 8 mussels with generous ½ cup sauce): 97 Cal, 3 g Fat, 0 g Sat Fat, 51 mg Chol, 451 mg Sod, 9 g Carb, 2 g Fib, 9 g Prot, 55 mg Calc. **POINTS: 2.**

——◆——

*Chef's Tip:* When buying mussels, look for tightly closed shells or shells that close when lightly tapped. Scrub them with a stiff brush under cold running water to remove any sand. Discard any mussels with shells that remain open.

# Spiced Oranges in Vin Santo

This light and refreshing sweet is a delicious accompaniment to the Anisette Toasts. You can make the oranges ahead of time and keep them in the refrigerator up to four days.

⅔ cup water
⅓ cup sugar
1 star anise pod
4 whole black peppercorns
¼ cup Vin Santo wine or semisweet sherry
4 large navel oranges, all peel and pith removed

*1.* Combine the water, sugar, star anise, and peppercorns in a saucepan; bring to a boil. Reduce the heat to medium and boil 7 minutes. Remove from the heat; add the wine and let cool.

*2.* Slice the oranges crosswise into ¼-inch rounds. Place in an airtight container. Pour the wine syrup over the oranges; cover and refrigerate at least 3 hours or up to 4 days before serving.

Per serving (generous ½ cup): 80 Cal, 0 g Fat, 0 g Sat Fat, 0 mg Chol, 1 mg Sod, 20 g Carb, 2 g Fib, 1 g Prot, 38 mg Calc. *POINTS: 1.*

———◆———

*Chef's Tip:* To avoid bitterness, make sure to cut away all the white pith from the oranges. Serve the oranges in a glass bowl with the star anise and peppercorns left in the syrup.

236  WEIGHT WATCHERS ENTERTAINS *winter*

# Anisette Toasts

A simple finish to a rich dinner, anisette toasts are perfect for dunking into espresso, cappuccino, or the Italian dessert wine, Vin Santo. You can make them ahead and store in airtight containers at room temperature for up to two weeks or freeze for up to a month.

3 large eggs

1 cup sugar

1 tablespoon walnut or vegetable oil

1 (1-ounce) bottle pure anise extract

2⅓ cups all-purpose flour

1 teaspoon baking soda

½ teaspoon salt

*1.* Beat the eggs, sugar, oil, and anise extract in a large bowl with a wooden spoon until blended.

*2.* Preheat the oven to 350°F.

*3.* Sift the flour, baking soda, and salt over the egg mixture; beat with a wooden spoon until blended. Freeze 10 minutes. Spray a baking sheet with nonstick spray; lightly dust with flour.

*4.* Scrape the dough onto the center of the baking sheet to form a 4 × 15-inch loaf, tapering the ends like a football (this will be flat now and will rise to round as it bakes). Bake until set and golden, 28–30 minutes.

*5.* Cool on the baking sheet 10 minutes. Loosen the edges and under the bottom of the loaf with a sharp knife, then transfer the loaf to a board. With a serrated knife, slice the loaf on a slight angle about ½-inch thick to make 24 slices.

*6.* Adjust the racks to divide the oven in thirds. Reduce the oven temperature to 300°F. Arrange the toast slices cut-side up on 2 large baking sheets. Bake until light golden, about 12 minutes, switching the baking sheets from one shelf to another halfway through. Remove the toasts from the baking sheets and cool completely on racks.

Per serving (1 toast): 94 Cal, 1 g Fat, 0 g Sat Fat, 27 mg Chol, 109 mg Sod, 18 g Carb, 0 g Fib, 2 g Prot, 5 mg Calc. *POINTS: 2.*

———◆———

*Chef's Tip:* Using the whole ounce of anise extract infuses bold and delicious flavor into these traditional cookies. For best results, make sure to use only pure anise extract.

# KWANZAA FEAST

*Roasted Red Pepper and Apricot Relish*
—
*Minted Turkey Meatballs*
—
*Crostini with Spicy Bean Puree*
—
*Seven Vegetable Couscous*
—
*Harissa Sauce*
—
*Tandoori Chicken Skewers*
—
*Sweet Potato–Yogurt Bread*
—
*Orange Chiffon Cake*

## Roasted Red Pepper and Apricot Relish

**MAKES 12 SERVINGS**

This sweet-fiery pepper relish makes a great topping for the Minted Turkey Meatballs. You'll find the leftovers are terrific on whole-wheat crackers or as a spread for roast turkey or chicken sandwiches. Make the relish, without the parsley, up to three days ahead and store it, covered, in the refrigerator. Stir in the parsley just before serving.

1 tablespoon vegetable oil
½ cup minced red onion
½ teaspoon minced garlic
½ cup low-sodium chicken broth
¾ cup minced roasted red
   bell peppers
½ cup minced dried apricots
1–2 tablespoons red-wine vinegar
1 teaspoon honey mustard
2–3 drops hot pepper sauce
   Freshly ground pepper, to taste
1 tablespoon chopped
   fresh parsley

*1.* Heat a large nonstick skillet over medium heat. Swirl in the oil, then add the onion and garlic. Cook, stirring frequently, until softened, about 2 minutes.

*2.* Add the broth, roasted peppers, apricots, vinegar, and mustard; bring to a boil. Reduce the heat and simmer, uncovered, until most of the liquid has evaporated, about 15 minutes. Season to taste with the pepper sauce and ground pepper; let cool to room temperature. Stir in the parsley and serve at room temperature.

Per serving (2 tablespoons): 25 Cal, 2 g Fat, 0 g Sat Fat, 0 mg Chol, 25 mg Sod, 3 g Carb, 0 g Fib, 0 g Prot, 4 mg Calc. ***POINTS: 1.***

# Minted Turkey Meatballs

**MAKES 6 SERVINGS**

Use a gentle touch as you mix and you'll be rewarded with light, melt-in-your-mouth meatballs—with a nugget of tangy, creamy goat cheese in the center. Serve as an appetizer with the Roasted Red Pepper and Apricot Relish.

¾ **pound ground skinless turkey breast**

3 **tablespoons plain dry bread crumbs**

2 **tablespoons minced onion**

1½ **teaspoons chopped fresh mint**

1 **teaspoon minced jalapeño pepper (wear gloves to prevent irritation)**

1 **teaspoon fresh lemon juice**

½ **teaspoon grated lemon rind**

¼ **teaspoon ground coriander**

¼ **teaspoon salt**

**Freshly ground pepper, to taste**

3 **tablespoons crumbled goat cheese**

*1.* Spray a baking sheet with nonstick spray.

*2.* Combine the turkey, bread crumbs, onion, mint, jalapeño, lemon juice, lemon rind, coriander, salt, and pepper in a bowl. Shape about 2 tablespoons of the mixture into a ball. Press about ½ teaspoon of the goat cheese into the center of the ball and roll to completely enclose the cheese. Repeat with the remaining turkey mixture and cheese, making a total of 18 meatballs. Place the meatballs on the baking sheet; cover and refrigerate at least 1 hour or up to 24 hours.

*3.* Preheat the oven to 350°F. Bake the meatballs until cooked through and golden, about 15 minutes.

Per serving (3 meatballs): 120 Cal, 6 g Fat, 2 g Sat Fat, 50 mg Chol, 210 mg Sod, 3 g Carb, 0 g Fib, 12 g Prot, 26 mg Calc. ***POINTS: 3.***

◆

*Chef's Tip:* Setting the Kwanzaa table calls for bright, colorful cloths of red, green, and black. A special mat holds some of the symbols of Kwanzaa: corn to symbolize children; fruits and vegetables to represent the harvest; a cup for unity; seven candles to embody the seven principles; and gifts to show loyalty and support.

*Minted Turkey Meatballs, Roasted Red Pepper and Apricot Relish,*
*and Crostini with Spicy Bean Puree*

# Crostini with Spicy Bean Puree

**MAKES 6 SERVINGS**

This rich, savory spread is perfect to make ahead. You can easily double the recipe and keep the puree, covered and refrigerated, for up to four days. Use it as a spread when you serve peasant bread or make a pita salad sandwich for lunch.

1   **cup canned cannellini (white kidney beans), rinsed and drained**

3   **garlic cloves, thinly sliced**

1   **tablespoon fresh lemon juice**

½   **teaspoon salt**

¼   **teaspoon cumin seeds, toasted**

⅛   **teaspoon cayenne**

2   **tablespoons extra-virgin olive oil**

1   **teaspoon water (optional)**

6   **(¼-inch thick) slices French or Italian bread**

1   **garlic clove, peeled and halved**

**Crushed red pepper, for garnish**

**Flat-leaf parsley leaves, for garnish**

*1.* Puree the beans, the sliced garlic, lemon juice, salt, cumin, and cayenne in a food processor or blender. With the machine running, gradually add 1 tablespoon of the oil through the feed tube until blended. Transfer to a bowl; add the water to thin the puree, if necessary.

*2.* Preheat the broiler. With a pastry brush, lightly brush the bread slices with the remaining 1 tablespoon oil; rub with the cut sides of the halved garlic. Place the bread on a baking sheet and broil until lightly browned, 1–2 minutes. Spread 2 tablespoons of the puree on each bread slice, garnish with the crushed red pepper and parsley.

Per serving (1 crostini): 90 Cal, 3 g Fat, 0 g Sat Fat, 0 mg Chol, 360 mg Sod, 13 g Carb, 2 g Fib, 3 g Prot, 28 mg Calc. **POINTS: 2.**

———◆———

*Chef's Tip:* Toasting cumin seeds brings out their fabulous flavor. To toast, place 2 to 3 tablespoons cumin seeds in a small dry skillet over medium-low heat. Toast, shaking the pan and stirring constantly, until lightly browned and fragrant, 3 to 4 minutes. Store the cooled seeds in a small jar.

# Seven Vegetable Couscous

**MAKES 6 SERVINGS**

The seven vegetables in this glorious dish represent Nguzo Saba (the Seven Principles) of Kwanzaa: Umoja (unity), Kujichagulia (self-determination), Ujima (collective work and responsibility), Ujamaa (cooperative economics), Nia (purpose), Kuumba (creativity), and Imani (Faith). It also stands for the seven symbols of Kwanzaa: Mazao (the crops), Mkeka (the mat), Kinara (the candle holder), Vibunzi (the corn), Mishumaa Saba (the seven candles), Kikombe Cha Umoja (the unity cup), and Zawadi (the gifts). Serve the couscous with the Harissa Sauce [page 244].

4 **cups low-sodium vegetable broth**

3 **garlic cloves, crushed**

1 **teaspoon curry powder**

½ **teaspoon ground turmeric**

½ **teaspoon salt**

⅛ **teaspoon freshly grated nutmeg**

1 **cinnamon stick**

2 **carrots, diagonally sliced ½-inch thick**

½ **cup pearl onions**

3 **canned artichoke hearts, rinsed, drained, and quartered**

½ **cup canned chickpeas (garbanzo beans), rinsed and drained**

3 **tablespoons raisins**

1 **medium zucchini, cubed**

½ **cup peeled, seeded, and cubed tomato**

1 **(10-ounce) bag triple-washed spinach, torn**

1 **cup couscous**

2 **tablespoons chopped toasted peanuts**

1 **tablespoon drained capers**

4 **lemon wedges**

*1.* Bring 2 cups of the broth, the garlic, curry powder, turmeric, salt, nutmeg, and cinnamon stick to a boil in a large saucepan. Reduce the heat; add the carrots and onions and simmer, until the carrots are barely tender, about 12 minutes.

*2.* Add the artichoke hearts, chickpeas, and raisins to the broth mixture. Simmer 5 minutes. Add the zucchini and tomato; simmer until the zucchini is tender, about 5 minutes. Add the spinach and simmer until wilted, about 5 minutes. Discard the cinnamon stick.

*3.* Bring the remaining 2 cups broth to a boil in a medium saucepan; add the couscous. Return to a boil, cover the pan tightly, and remove from the heat. Let the couscous stand 5 minutes. Uncover and gently fluff with a fork.

*4.* To serve, place the couscous in the center of a platter. Arrange the vegetables and spoon a little of the broth around the couscous. Garnish with the peanuts, capers, and lemon wedges.

Per serving (½ cup vegetables with ½ cup couscous): 250 Cal, 3 g Fat, 0 g Sat Fat, 0 mg Chol, 500 mg Sod, 48 g Carb, 8 g Fib, 11 g Prot, 106 mg Calc. *POINTS: 4.*

# Molding Couscous

Couscous, a light, fluffy, grain-like pasta, is perfect for molding and shaping into a variety of interesting presentations.

*1.* A traditional way to serve couscous is to mound it on a big serving platter, with a savory stew spooned on top or at the side. Garnishes such as olives, lemon wedges, capers, toasted almond slices, and currants can be sprinkled over the dish.

*2.* To make individual couscous molds that have a more elegant look, use teacups, small custard or soufflé cups, or specially-made ring molds from a cookware store. Spray the mold with a little nonstick spray. Spoon the couscous into the mold and press it down lightly with the back of the spoon. Put the serving plate on top of the mold, flip the whole thing over, and tap the mold to release the couscous.

*3.* Spoon the stew around and into the center of the ring mold. Add a sprinkling of garnish and a few drops of that Tunisian answer to hot sauce—*harissa* [page 244]. If you prefer, use a large ring mold or other favorite mold.

# Harissa Sauce

MAKES 12 SERVINGS

This brick-red Tunisian condiment adds a jolt of fire to a host of grain-based dishes, such as our Seven Vegetable Couscous. If you have any *harissa* leftover from your Kwanzaa feast, substitute it for hot pepper sauce in another recipe, but dilute it to taste with a bit of water. *Harissa* can be kept in the refrigerator for up to two weeks.

4 **ounces mild dried red chiles, such as New Mexico chiles**
2 **garlic cloves, mashed to a paste**
1 **teaspoon fresh lemon juice**
¾ **teaspoon ground caraway**
½ **teaspoon ground coriander**
1 **tablespoon olive oil**

*1.* Combine the chiles and enough cold water to cover in a bowl; let stand 15 minutes. Drain the chiles, pressing out any excess water, then coarsely chop.

*2.* Process the chiles, garlic, lemon juice, caraway, and coriander to a fine paste in a food processor or blender. With the machine running, gradually add the oil through the feed tube until blended. Transfer sauce to a bowl; cover and refrigerate until ready to serve.

Per serving (1 teaspoon): 35 Cal, 1 g Fat, 0 g Sat Fat, 0 mg Chol, 0 mg Sod, 4 g Carb, 5 g Fib, 1 g Prot, 9 mg Calc. **POINTS: 0.**

———◆———

*Chef's Tip:* If you want to save time, use prepared *harissa*—it's available in cans or jars in Middle Eastern specialty stores or the ethnic section of many supermarkets.

# *Tandoori Chicken Skewers*

**MAKES 6 SERVINGS**

What's the secret of great tandoori? The spices. Selecting and toasting whole spices, instead of relying on ground spices or using a commercial curry blend, makes all the difference. For our spice blend, we choose whole cumin, coriander, and cardamom seeds. To toast the spices, place them in a dry skillet over low heat, and stir occasionally until there is a definite aroma (usually about 3 minutes). Cool, then grind in a spice grinder, coffee grinder, or with a mortar and pestle.

**Juice of 1 lemon**
**½ teaspoon salt**
**1½ pounds skinless boneless**
**  chicken breasts,**
**  cut into chunks**
**½ teaspoon saffron threads,**
**  crushed**
**¼ cup boiling water**
**1 cup plain fat-free yogurt**
**2 tablespoons grated peeled**
**  fresh ginger**
**4 garlic cloves, minced**
**1 teaspoon cumin seeds,**
**  toasted**
**1 teaspoon cardamom seeds,**
**  toasted**
**1 teaspoon coriander seeds,**
**  toasted**
**½ teaspoon cayenne**

*1.* Combine the lemon juice and salt in a large bowl; add the chicken and toss to coat.

*2.* Place the saffron threads in a cup; add the boiling water and let the mixture come to room temperature. Add the saffron mixture to the chicken; toss again to coat. Cover and refrigerate at least 30 minutes or up to 3 hours.

*3.* Combine the yogurt, ginger, garlic, cumin, cardamom, coriander, and cayenne in a large zip-close plastic bag; mix well. Add the chicken, seal the bag, and turn several times to coat. Refrigerate the chicken, turning the bag occasionally, 2 hours or overnight.

*4.* Soak 12 (6-inch) wooden skewers in enough water to cover for 30 minutes.

*5.* Spray a broiler rack with nonstick spray. Preheat the broiler.

*6.* Remove the chicken from the yogurt marinade; discard the marinade. Thread the chicken onto the skewers, leaving about ¼ inch between the pieces. Broil the skewers 5 inches from the heat, turning frequently, until browned and cooked through, 5–7 minutes.

Per serving (2 skewers): 150 Cal, 2 g Fat, 0 g Sat Fat, 65 mg Chol, 290 mg Sod, 6 g Carb, 0 g Fib, 28 g Prot, 92 mg Calc. ***POINTS: 3.***

# Sweet Potato–Yogurt Bread

**MAKES 24 SERVINGS**

We use a white-fleshed sweet potato, called *boniato* or Cuban sweet potato, which can be found in Latin and Caribbean markets. Substitute a regular orange-fleshed sweet potato, if you prefer.

- 1 (9-ounce) white-fleshed sweet potato, peeled and quartered, cooked until tender and pureed
- 1 cup plain low-fat yogurt
- ¾ cup warm (105°-115°F) water
- 1½ tablespoons honey
- 1 package active dry yeast
- 3 cups all-purpose or bread flour
- 1 cup whole-wheat flour
- ¼ cup instant nonfat dry milk
- 2 teaspoons salt

*1.* Combine the sweet potato and yogurt.

*2.* Combine the water and honey in a 2-cup measuring cup; sprinkle in the yeast and let stand until foamy, about 5 minutes.

*3.* Combine the all-purpose flour, whole-wheat flour, dry milk, and salt in a food processor. With the machine running, scrape the yeast mixture and sweet potato mixture through the feed tube; pulse about 1 minute until the dough forms a ball. Turn the dough onto a lightly floured surface; knead briefly until smooth.

*4.* Spray a large bowl with nonstick spray; put the dough in the bowl. Cover lightly with plastic wrap and let the dough rise in a warm spot until it doubles in size, about 35 minutes.

*5.* Spray 2 (4 x 8-inch) nonstick loaf pans with nonstick spray. Punch down the dough. Sprinkle a work surface lightly with flour. Turn out the dough; cut in half. Shape each half into a loaf and transfer to the pans. Cover lightly with plastic wrap and let rise in a warm spot until they double in size, about 45 minutes.

*6.* Preheat the oven to 375°F. Slash the top of each loaf in 2 or 3 places with a sharp paring knife. Bake the loaves until they are golden brown and sound hollow when lightly tapped, about 25 minutes. Remove the loaves from the pans and cool completely on a rack. Cut each loaf into 12 slices.

Per serving (1 slice): 103 Cal, 0 g Fat, 0 g Sat Fat, 0 mg Chol, 292 mg Sod, 22 g Carb, 2 g Fib, 3 g Prot, 7 mg Calc. ***POINTS: 2.***

---

*Chef's Tip:* To make by hand, combine water, honey, and yeast in a large bowl; set aside until foamy. Stir in yogurt and sweet potato puree, then stir in 1 cup of the all-purpose flour, the whole-wheat flour, and salt. Gradually add the remaining 2 cups all-purpose flour until dough starts to gather around the spoon. Knead until dough is smooth, about 10 minutes, adding flour if necessary.

# *Orange Chiffon Cake*

**MAKES 16 SERVINGS**

A chiffon cake is similar to an angel food cake—light and airy. The addition of vegetable oil, however, is what makes chiffon cake especially rich and moist. Juicy, fresh oranges add even more moisture in our version. If you plan to make this cake ahead of time, it will keep, well wrapped, for up to two days at room temperature. Freeze any leftover cake for up to a month.

2¼ cups cake flour
1½ cups granulated sugar
1 tablespoon baking powder
1 teaspoon salt
5 egg yolks
Juice and rind from 2 oranges
½ cup vegetable oil
8 egg whites
1 teaspoon cream of tartar
Confectioners' sugar

*1.* Preheat the oven to 350°F. Spray a 10-inch tube pan with nonstick spray and dust with flour.

*2.* Sift together the flour, 1 cup of the granulated sugar, the baking powder, and salt in a bowl; make a well in the center. Whisk the egg yolks, orange juice and rind, and the oil in a medium bowl. Pour the orange mixture into the flour mixture, and stir until all the flour is just moistened and the mixture is smooth.

*3.* With an electric mixer on low speed, beat the egg whites in a large bowl until frothy. Add the cream of tartar; increase the speed to medium and add the remaining ½ cup granulated sugar, 1 tablespoon at a time, until medium peaks form. Using a large rubber spatula or a balloon whip, gently fold the beaten whites into the flour mixture until just combined. Pour into the pan.

*4.* Bake immediately until golden brown and the top springs back when pressed, about 1 hour.

*5.* Immediately invert the pan onto a rack; cool completely. When cool, release the cake from the sides of the pan with a spatula. Invert to unmold. Turn the cake right side up and dust the top lightly with confectioners' sugar.

Per serving (1⁄16 of cake): 150 Cal, 5 g Fat, 1 g Sat Fat, 35 mg Chol, 130 mg Sod, 23 g Carb, 0 g Fib, 2 g Prot, 64 mg Calc. ***POINTS: 3.***

———◆———

*Chef's Tip:* For a distinctive twist, substitute olive oil for the vegetable oil in this recipe. But use light or regular olive oil versus extra-virgin, which is too assertive tasting and will overwhelm the orange flavor.

*Raspberry Mimosas*
—
*Scrambled Eggs with Caramelized Onions and Peppers*
—
*Baked Turkey Hash*
—
*Pecan-Pear Scones*
—
*French-Toast Casserole with Fresh Strawberries*
—
*Breakfast Colada Parfaits*
—
*Baked Apple and Pear Compote*
—
*Blueberry-Almond-Crunch Coffeecake*

## Raspberry Mimosas

**MAKES 12 SERVINGS**

A twist on classic champagne and orange juice, here we add fresh raspberries, sliced oranges, and mint. Non-alcoholic sparkling white wine makes a good, kid-friendly substitute for the champagne.

2 **cups orange juice**

1 **cup reduced-calorie cranberry juice**

1½ **cups fresh raspberries**

1 **orange, thinly sliced**

1 **tablespoon chopped fresh mint**

1 **(750-ml) bottle champagne or sparkling white wine, chilled**

1 **liter lemon-lime seltzer, chilled**

2 **trays ice cubes**

Combine the orange juice, cranberry juice, raspberries, orange slices, and mint in a 3-quart punch bowl. Gently stir in the champagne, seltzer, and ice cubes.

Per serving (1 cup): 78 Cal, 0 g Fat, 0 g Sat Fat, 0 mg Chol, 7 mg Sod, 9 g Carb, 1 g Fib, 1 g Prot, 23 mg Calc. *POINTS: 1.*

◆

*Chef's Tip:* For a colorful accent, freeze a single berry in each ice cube.

# Scrambled Eggs with
# Caramelized Onions and Peppers

**MAKES 12 SERVINGS**

Colorful bell peppers, sweet caramelized onions, cherry tomatoes, and Canadian bacon, spooned alongside a mound of herbed scrambled eggs, make a comforting and easy-to-serve buffet dish. If the pepper mixture gets a little dry while cooking, just add 3 to 4 tablespoons of water. This will not only hasten the cooking time, it will also prevent the need to add more oil. The onion and pepper mixture can be prepared up to a day ahead and refrigerated. When ready to serve, reheat the pepper mixture, then stir in the cherry tomatoes and bacon and cook for 5 minutes.

1 tablespoon olive oil

2 large onions, cut into
¼-inch slices

2 green bell peppers, seeded
and cut into ¼-inch strips

2 red bell peppers, seeded and
cut into ¼-inch strips

2 yellow bell peppers, seeded
and cut into ¼-inch strips

3 garlic cloves, minced

1 teaspoon salt

1 pint cherry tomatoes, halved

1 (6-ounce) package Canadian
bacon, diced

3 (4-ounce) containers fat-free
egg substitute

1 tablespoon chopped
fresh parsley

1 tablespoon chopped
fresh chives

1 tablespoon chopped
fresh tarragon

*1.* Heat an extra-large nonstick skillet over medium-high heat. Swirl in the oil, then add the onions, green, red, and yellow bell peppers, garlic, and ½ teaspoon of the salt. Cook, stirring occasionally, until softened, about 15 minutes. Stir in the tomatoes and bacon and cook until the bacon is cooked through, about 5 minutes longer. Place to one side of a large platter. Cover with foil and keep warm. Wipe the skillet clean.

*2.* Spray the same skillet with nonstick spray and set over medium heat. Add the egg substitute, parsley, chives, tarragon, and the remaining ½ teaspoon salt. Cook, stirring often, until the mixture is just set, about 5 minutes. Spoon the egg mixture alongside the onions and peppers. Serve at once.

Per serving (½ cup vegetables and bacon with ⅓ cup scrambled eggs): 76 Cal, 3 g Fat, 1 g Sat Fat, 8 mg Chol, 459 mg Sod, 7 g Carb, 2 g Fib, 7 g Prot, 25 mg Calc. **POINTS: 1.**

———◆———

*Chef's Tip:* For a pretty presentation, place the pepper mixture diagonally across both sides of a large oval platter and spoon the scrambled eggs down the center. Garnish the eggs with sprigs of fresh parsley, chives, and tarragon.

# Baked Turkey Hash

**MAKES 12 SERVINGS**

One-dish recipes, such as this hearty hash, keep a buffet menu simple. To make ahead, assemble the casserole, without the crumb topping, and refrigerate, covered, for up to 24 hours. To reheat, sprinkle with the topping, then bake as directed, until heated through to the center, about 55 minutes.

5 large baking potatoes, peeled and cut into ¼-inch cubes

1 tablespoon + 1 teaspoon olive oil

2 large onions, sliced

1 (8-ounce) package fresh white mushrooms, sliced

2 cups cubed cooked skinless turkey breast

1 (12-ounce) can fat-free evaporated milk

½ cup low-sodium chicken broth

2 tablespoons chopped fresh parsley

½ teaspoon salt

¼ cup plain dry bread crumbs

*1.* Preheat the oven to 375°F. Spray a 9 × 13-inch baking dish with nonstick spray.

*2.* Place the potatoes and enough water to cover in a large saucepan; bring to a boil. Reduce the heat and simmer, uncovered, until the potatoes are almost tender, about 10 minutes. Drain and set aside.

*3.* Meanwhile, heat an extra-large nonstick skillet over medium-high heat. Swirl in 1 tablespoon of the oil, then add the onions and mushrooms. Cook, stirring occasionally, until softened, about 8 minutes. Stir in the potatoes, turkey, milk, broth, parsley, and salt. Spoon the mixture into the baking dish.

*4.* Combine the bread crumbs with the remaining 1 teaspoon oil in a small bowl. Sprinkle the crumb mixture over the casserole. Bake, uncovered, until the topping is browned and the filling is hot and bubbly, about 45 minutes.

Per serving (¾ cup): 163 Cal, 3 g Fat, 1 g Sat Fat, 18 mg Chol, 173 mg Sod, 23 g Carb, 2 g Fib, 11 g Prot, 104 mg Calc. *POINTS: 3.*

*Chef's Tip:* Use any pretty casserole dish that has a 3½ quart capacity for baking and serving this hash.

# *Pecan-Pear Scones*

**MAKES 12 SERVINGS**

The combination of molasses, nuts, and cinnamon give these wonderful scones a gingerbread-like flavor. To make fresh the morning of the buffet, measure out the dry ingredients the night before and store in a zip-close plastic bag. Measure the wet ingredients into a large measuring cup; cover and refrigerate. Scones also freeze beautifully, so you may want to bake them ahead of time, store them in your freezer, then warm them in the oven when ready to serve.

1½ **cups reduced-fat all-purpose baking mix**
2 **tablespoons chopped pecans**
1 **tablespoon sugar**
½ **teaspoon cinnamon**
⅔ **cup low-fat (1%) milk**
2 **tablespoons molasses**
1 **tablespoon butter, melted**
1 **small ripe pear, peeled, cored, and chopped (about ½ cup)**

*1.* Preheat the oven to 425°F.

*2.* Combine the baking mix, pecans, sugar, and cinnamon in a large bowl. Whisk together the milk and molasses in a small bowl until blended. Add the milk mixture and the butter to the dry ingredients; stir until just blended. Fold in the pear.

*3.* Turn the dough out onto a lightly floured surface. With floured hands, knead the dough about 10 times, until it just holds together; do not overmix. Divide the dough in half. On a lightly floured surface, shape each half into a 6-inch round; with a floured knife, cut each round into 6 wedges. Using a wide spatula, place the wedges, 1 inch apart, on a large, ungreased baking sheet.

*4.* Bake until the scones are golden brown and just cooked through, about 15 minutes. Serve warm, or transfer to a rack to cool.

Per serving (1 scone): 96 Cal, 3 g Fat, 1 g Sat Fat, 3 mg Chol, 178 mg Sod, 15 g Carb, 1 g Fib, 2 g Prot, 39 mg Calc. *POINTS: 2.*

# French-Toast Casserole with Fresh Strawberries

**MAKES 12 SERVINGS**

A cross between French toast and bread pudding, this dish is perfect for a crowd. To save precious last-minute-preparation time, assemble the casserole, without baking it, the night before your buffet, then refrigerate it, covered, until cooking time. Soaking the bread in the milk mixture for 24 hours makes for a moister dish. The strawberries can be prepared up to an hour ahead.

12 slices low-fat raisin bread, cut diagonally in half
3 cups low-fat (1%) milk
2 (4-ounce) containers fat-free egg substitute
2 tablespoons sugar
1 teaspoon vanilla extract
½ teaspoon cinnamon
1 pint strawberries
3 tablespoons maple syrup
2 tablespoons orange juice
1 tablespoon chopped fresh mint

*1.* Preheat the oven to 350°F. Spray a 9 × 13-inch baking dish with nonstick spray.

*2.* Arrange the bread slices in the baking dish. Whisk together the milk, egg substitute, sugar, vanilla, and cinnamon in a large bowl; pour the milk mixture over the bread slices. Refrigerate, covered, at least 30 minutes or up to 24 hours.

*3.* Bake until a knife inserted in the center comes out clean and the top is lightly browned, about 50 minutes.

*4.* Meanwhile, to prepare the strawberries, rinse and hull them. Coarsely chop half of the strawberries and quarter the remaining berries lengthwise. Combine the chopped and the quartered berries with the maple syrup, orange juice, and mint in a small bowl. Refrigerate, covered, until ready to serve. Serve with the casserole.

Per serving (¹⁄₁₂ of casserole and 2 tablespoons strawberries): 136 Cal, 2 g Fat, 1 g Sat Fat, 2 mg Chol, 160 mg Sod, 24 g Carb, 2 g Fib, 6 g Prot, 108 mg Calc. *POINTS: 2.*

*Raspberry Mimosas and French-Toast Casserole with Fresh Strawberries*

# Breakfast Colada Parfaits

### MAKES 12 SERVINGS

Bring a touch of the tropics to your New Year's brunch with these refreshing piña colada–flavored parfaits. For a different twist, whip this into a luscious smoothie by whirling all the ingredients (except the granola) in a blender with a little orange juice.

6 cups fat-free vanilla yogurt
1 teaspoon coconut extract
1 teaspoon rum extract
1½ cups low-fat granola cereal
1½ cups canned crushed
    pineapple, drained
2 medium bananas, sliced
¼ cup flaked coconut

Combine the yogurt, coconut extract, and rum extract in a medium bowl. Alternately layer the granola, yogurt mixture, pineapple, bananas, and coconut into 12 (6-ounce) parfait glasses.

Per serving (1 parfait): 175 Cal, 3 g Fat, 2 g Sat Fat, 2 mg Chol, 64 mg Sod, 34 g Carb, 2 g Fib, 6 g Prot, 178 mg Calc. *POINTS: 3.*

———◆———

*Chef's Tip:* If you like—and to save time assembling these—present the yogurt in a pretty glass serving bowl with smaller bowls of the granola, fruit, and coconut alongside, letting guests serve themselves.

# Baked Apple and Pear Compote

**MAKES 12 SERVINGS**

This cinnamon-laced fruit compote is delicious on its own or spooned over hot oatmeal or farina. The compote can be made ahead, transferred to a 2-quart microwavable dish and stored, covered with plastic wrap, in the refrigerator for up to three days. To reheat, turn back one corner of the plastic wrap to vent and microwave, on High, until hot, about 3 minutes.

3  **Red Delicious apples, peeled and cut into 1½-inch chunks**
3  **Granny Smith apples, peeled and cut into 1½-inch chunks**
3  **firm-ripe Bartlett pears, peeled and cut into 1½-inch chunks**
¼  **cup sugar**
1  **tablespoon grated lemon rind**
1  **tablespoon fresh lemon juice**
1  **teaspoon cinnamon**
¼  **teaspoon ground allspice**

*1.* Place one of the oven racks on the lowest rung. Preheat the oven to 450°F. Spray a 12 × 17-inch shallow baking pan with nonstick spray.

*2.* Combine the apples, pears, sugar, lemon rind, lemon juice, cinnamon, and allspice in a large bowl until well coated. Transfer the apple mixture to the baking pan, spreading the fruit out into one even layer. Bake on the lowest rack until the fruit is tender and the top is browned, about 30 minutes. Serve warm.

Per serving (½ cup): 88 Cal, 0 g Fat, 0 g Sat Fat, 0 mg Chol, 1 mg Sod, 23 g Carb, 3 g Fib, 0 g Prot, 11 mg Calc. ***POINTS: 1.***

*Chef's Tip:* When baking the fruit, use a large shallow baking pan or two smaller pans, making sure to spread the fruit out in one layer to achieve even browning and prevent steaming.

# Blueberry-Almond-Crunch Coffee Cake

**MAKES 12 SERVINGS**

This delicious blueberry-filled coffee cake with a crunchy nut topping can easily be doubled and baked in a 9 × 13-inch baking dish. If fresh blueberries aren't available, frozen are fine—there's no need to thaw before adding them to the batter. The coffee cake can be made up to three months ahead and frozen. To store, simply wrap in heavy-duty foil and freeze. Bring to room temperature before serving or warm slightly in the oven.

2 tablespoons sliced almonds, chopped

2 tablespoons + ½ cup sugar

¼ teaspoon cinnamon

2 cups reduced-fat all-purpose baking mix

½ cup fat-free milk

½ cup fat-free sour cream

1 large egg

3 tablespoons butter, melted

1½ cups fresh or frozen blueberries

*1.* Preheat the oven to 400°F. Spray a 10-inch springform pan with nonstick spray.

*2.* To prepare the topping, combine the almonds, 2 tablespoons of the sugar, and the cinnamon in a small bowl; set aside.

*3.* Combine the baking mix and the remaining ½ cup sugar in a large bowl. Whisk together the milk, sour cream, egg, and butter in a small bowl. Add the milk mixture to the dry ingredients; stir until just blended. Fold in the blueberries. Pour the batter into the pan; top with the nut mixture.

*4.* Bake until a toothpick inserted in the center comes out clean and the topping is golden, about 45 minutes. Cool, in the pan, on a rack, about 15 minutes. Remove the outer ring from the springform pan, then cut the cake into 12 wedges and serve warm. Or cool completely and serve at room temperature.

Per serving (½ of cake): 173 Cal, 5 g Fat, 2 g Sat Fat, 26 mg Chol, 260 mg Sod, 28 g Carb, 1 g Fib, 4 g Prot, 59 mg Calc. ***POINTS: 4.***

# CHINESE NEW YEAR'S CELEBRATION

*Stir-Fried Clams in Black-Bean Sauce*
–
*Steamed Pork Dumplings*
–
*Golden Turnip Cake*
–
*Sweet-and-Sour Chicken*
–
*Pearl Balls*
–
*Roasted Red Snapper with Ginger-Garlic Sauce*
–
*Vegetable Longevity Noodles*
–
*Orange Segments in Ginger Syrup*

## Stir-Fried Clams in Black-Bean Sauce

**MAKES 8 SERVINGS**

Because clams have a similar shape to coins, they are served at New Year as a symbol of prosperity. Clams can be gritty and sandy, so you'll need to rinse them several times in cold water. Discard any opened raw clams that don't close when tapped gently.

1 tablespoon peanut oil

2 tablespoons minced peeled fresh ginger

6 garlic cloves, minced

40 littleneck clams, washed in several changes of cold water and scrubbed

¾ cup clam juice

3 tablespoons Chinese cooking wine

3 tablespoons black-bean sauce

3 scallions, chopped

*1.* Heat a nonstick wok or large, deep skillet over medium-high heat until a drop of water sizzles. Swirl in the oil, then add the ginger and garlic. Stir-fry until fragrant, about 30 seconds.

*2.* Add the clams and clam juice; cook, stirring occasionally, until the clams just begin to open, 3–4 minutes. Add the wine and black-bean sauce; cover and cook until the clams open fully, about 3 minutes. Discard any clams that don't open. Sprinkle with the scallions and serve.

Per serving (5 clams with ⅛ of sauce): 75 Cal, 2 g Fat, 0 g Sat Fat, 22 mg Chol, 173 mg Sod, 4 g Carb, 0 g Fib, 9 g Prot, 43 mg Calc. ***POINTS: 2.***

# Steamed Pork Dumplings

These little purse-like dumplings, known as *shu mai*, are a popular item in dim sum restaurants. You can find wonton wrappers in the refrigerator case of most supermarkets and Asian grocery stores. To save time, the filling can be made up to two days ahead and kept, covered, in the refrigerator. The dumplings can be formed, wrapped in damp paper towels in a covered container, and refrigerated for up to four hours before steaming.

¾ **pound pork tenderloin, trimmed of all visible fat**

4 **scallions, finely chopped**

1 **tablespoon minced peeled fresh ginger**

1 **tablespoon Chinese cooking wine or rice wine**

1 **tablespoon reduced-sodium soy sauce**

1 **tablespoon cornstarch**

1 **teaspoon Asian (dark) sesame oil**

¼ **teaspoon salt**

32 **(3-inch round) wonton wrappers**

*1.* Finely chop the pork and place in a large bowl. Add the scallions, ginger, wine, soy sauce, cornstarch, oil, and salt; mix well.

*2.* Using a 2¼-inch round cutter, cut out circles from the wonton wrappers. Place 8 wonton circles on a work surface and place 2 level teaspoons of filling in the center of each. Gather the wonton wrapper up around the filling leaving the top open slightly, like a purse. Place the filled dumpling on a baking sheet, then repeat with the remaining wrappers and filling, making a total of 32 dumplings.

*3.* Spray the bottom of a bamboo steamer or steamer basket with nonstick spray. Place 16 of the dumplings in the steamer; set over a large pot, with 4 inches of boiling water. Cover and steam, until the pork is cooked through, 3–5 minutes. Carefully transfer the dumplings to a serving platter and keep warm. Repeat with the remaining dumplings. Serve with additional soy sauce for dipping.

Per serving (4 dumplings): 158 Cal, 3 g Fat, 1 g Sat Fat, 43 mg Chol, 199 mg Sod, 19 g Carb, 1 g Fib, 13 g Prot, 14 mg Calc. ***POINTS: 3.***

*Chef's Tip:* Serve the dumplings on a platter with some reduced-sodium soy sauce in an Asian tea cup alongside. Mix some finely chopped scallions with the soy sauce for color.

## Making Chinese Dumplings

Chinese dumplings, one variety of small, tasty dishes called dim sum, are little packages filled with intensely-flavored meat, poultry, fish, or vegetable fillings. According to custom, finding a coin in your dumpling on New Year's Day foretells good fortune in the coming year. When making dumplings, arrange your work area so that your work flows in a single direction, with the wrappers and filling at one end of the assembly line, a work area in the center, and a baking sheet or steamer insert on which to place finished dumplings at the other end. The dumplings pictured below are a bite-size version called *shu mai*.

*1.* Place the wonton wrapper on a clean work surface. Spoon 2 teaspoons of filling in the center of the wrapper. Use a teaspoon dipped in cold water to portion the filling, and use only the amount of filling called for in the recipe (overfilling may cause spillage from the wrapper during steaming).

*2.* Using your fingertips, gather and crimp the wrapper around the filling, leaving the top open slightly, like a purse.

*3.* Spray the bottom of the steamer with nonstick spray. Carefully arrange the dumplings in a steamer, leaving room between each for steam to circulate. Set over a large pot with 4 inches of boiling water. Cover and steam until cooked through, 3–5 minutes.

# Golden Turnip Cake

**MAKES 16 SERVINGS**

Turnip cakes, a staple on dim sum menus, are served as a symbol of prosperity on New Year's Day.

**2 pounds daikon radish, peeled and shredded**

**4 cups cold water**

**12 dried shiitake mushrooms**

**1¼ cups hot water**

**2 ounces thin-sliced bacon, finely chopped**

**2 tablespoons reduced-sodium soy sauce**

**2 teaspoons sugar**

**2 cups rice flour**

**½ teaspoon salt**

*1.* Bring the radish and cold water to a boil in a large saucepan. Reduce the heat and simmer, covered, until tender, 20–25 minutes. Drain, reserving 1 cup of the cooking liquid. Lightly squeeze the excess liquid from the radish; set aside.

*2.* Combine the mushrooms with the hot water in a bowl; soak until softened, 12–15 minutes. Drain the mushrooms, reserving ¾ cup soaking liquid. Squeeze excess liquid from the mushrooms. Remove and discard the stems, then finely chop the mushrooms.

*3.* Heat a nonstick skillet over medium heat; add the bacon. Cook until crisp, 4–5 minutes. Add the mushrooms, 1 tablespoon of the soy sauce, and the sugar; cook about 2 minutes.

*4.* Combine the rice flour, salt, 1 cup radish cooking liquid, ¾ cup mushroom soaking liquid and remaining 1 tablespoon soy sauce in a large bowl. Stir in the radish and the mushroom mixture; mix well. Pour into a 9-inch round cake pan.

*5.* Place the cake pan in a bamboo steamer over a large pan with 4 inches of simmering water. Cover and steam until firm, about 1 hour. Place the cake pan on a rack; cool 1 hour. Cover and refrigerate 3 hours.

*6.* Invert cake onto a board; cut into quarters. Cut the quarters into 2-inch wide strips. Cut each strip crosswise into ½-inch slices, making a total of 48 slices.

*7.* Spray a large nonstick skillet with nonstick spray; set over medium heat. Add 8 turnip cake slices; cook until golden brown, 2–3 minutes on each side; keep warm. Repeat with remaining slices.

Per serving (3 pieces): 116 Cal, 4 g Fat, 1 g Sat Fat, 3 mg Chol, 175 mg Sod, 19 g Carb, 1 g Fib, 2 g Prot, 13 mg Calc. ***POINTS: 2.***

# Sweet-and-Sour Chicken

It is a Chinese belief that something both sweet and sour should be eaten on Chinese New Year. Here's an all-time sweet-and-sour favorite. Substitute lean pork tenderloin pieces for the chicken, if you prefer.

1½ **pounds skinless boneless chicken thighs, trimmed of all visible fat and cut into ½-inch chunks**

7 **tablespoons honey**

3 **tablespoons + 1 teaspoon cornstarch**

3 **tablespoons reduced-sodium soy sauce**

2 **tablespoons Chinese cooking wine or rice wine**

½ **cup ketchup**

⅓ **cup white vinegar**

1 **(20-ounce) can pineapple chunks in juice, drained, ⅔ cup juice reserved**

1 **teaspoon peanut oil**

1½ **tablespoons minced peeled fresh ginger**

2 **red bell peppers, seeded and cut into ½-inch pieces**

1. Combine the chicken, 1 tablespoon of the honey, 2 tablespoons of the cornstarch, 1 tablespoon of the soy sauce, and the wine in a medium bowl; toss well to coat and set aside.

2. Combine the remaining 6 tablespoons honey, 4 teaspoons cornstarch, 2 tablespoons soy sauce, the ketchup, vinegar, and the reserved pineapple juice in a bowl; set aside.

3. Remove the chicken from the marinade, reserving any marinade in the bottom of the bowl. Heat a nonstick wok or large, deep skillet over medium-high heat until a drop of water sizzles. Swirl in the oil, then add the chicken. Stir-fry until almost cooked through, 2–3 minutes. Add the ginger and stir-fry until fragrant, about 30 seconds. Add the bell peppers; stir-fry until crisp-tender, about 3 minutes. Stir in the pineapple chunks, ketchup mixture, and the reserved marinade; cook, stirring constantly, until the mixture boils and thickens, and the chicken is just cooked through, 1–2 minutes.

Per serving (¾ cup): 269 Cal, 6 g Fat, 2 g Sat Fat, 58 mg Chol, 483 mg Sod, 36 g Carb, 1 g Fib, 19 g Prot, 34 mg Calc. *POINTS: 6.*

# Pearl Balls

**MAKES 8 SERVINGS**

A classic Chinese rice dish, Pearl Balls are made with short-grain rice (such as pearl, glutinous, or Arborio rice), pork or chicken, and seasonings, then steamed. They are traditionally served to the gods during Chinese New Year. To make ahead, prepare and steam them as directed, then cool to room temperature. Store them in a zip-close plastic bag in the refrigerator for up to two days. To reheat, set up a steamer basket as directed in the recipe and steam, covered, until heated through, 5 to 8 minutes.

- 1 **cup short-grain rice**
- 1 **pound ground skinless chicken breasts**
- ¼ **cup chopped fresh cilantro**
- 2 **tablespoons reduced-sodium soy sauce**
- 1 **tablespoon minced peeled fresh ginger**
- 1 **tablespoon Asian (dark) sesame oil**
- 1 **tablespoon cornstarch**
- 1 **scallion, finely chopped**
- 1 **egg, lightly beaten**
- ½ **teaspoon salt**

*1.* Rinse the rice in a strainer under cold running water until the water runs clear. Drain the rice and transfer to a bowl. Cover the rice with cold water and let soak 1 hour. Drain the rice and spread it out in an even layer on a baking sheet.

*2.* Combine the chicken, cilantro, soy sauce, ginger, oil, cornstarch, scallion, egg, and salt in a medium bowl; mix well. With damp hands, shape the mixture into 24 balls. Gently roll each ball in the rice so that the outside is completely coated.

*3.* Line a bamboo steamer or steamer basket with wax paper. Place the rice balls in the steamer; set over a large saucepan with 4 inches of boiling water. Cover and steam until the rice is translucent and the pearl balls are cooked through, 20–25 minutes. Arrange the pearl balls on a platter and serve.

Per serving (3 pearl balls): 188 Cal, 4 g Fat, 1 g Sat Fat, 58 mg Chol, 483 mg Sod, 21 g Carb, 0 g Fib, 15 g Prot, 20 mg Calc. ***POINTS: 4.***

◆

*Chef's Tip:* If you can find one, serve the pearl balls on an eight-sided plate or tray, a symbol of prosperity. Put a little reduced-sodium soy sauce in a small ramekin for dipping.

# Roasted Red Snapper with Ginger-Garlic Sauce

**MAKES 8 SERVINGS**

Whole fish is served as part of the New Year's celebration to signify togetherness and abundance. This recipe needs to be baked last minute, but you can sprinkle the fish with the seasonings up to an hour ahead and keep it covered, in the refrigerator. Prepare the Ginger-Garlic Sauce up to an hour ahead and store in a small bowl at room temperature. Remove and discard the skin on the fish before eating.

2 (3-pound) whole red snapper or 1 (5-pound) grouper, cleaned, tails and heads on

4 tablespoons reduced-sodium soy sauce

2 tablespoons minced peeled fresh ginger

1 tablespoon Asian (dark) sesame oil

6 garlic cloves, minced

8 scallions, chopped (about 1½ cups)

*1.* Preheat the oven to 500°F. Line a baking sheet with foil and spray lightly with nonstick spray; set aside.

*2.* With a sharp knife make 4 deep cuts (down to the bone) crosswise on each side of the fish; place on the baking sheet. Sprinkle the fish with 1 tablespoon of the soy sauce, 1 tablespoon of the ginger, 1 teaspoon of the oil, and 3 of the garlic cloves. Sprinkle with ½ cup of the scallions. Roast until the fish is just opaque in the center, 30–35 minutes for the snapper or 45–55 minutes for the grouper. Remove from the oven and transfer to a serving platter.

*3.* To prepare the Ginger-Garlic Sauce, heat a small nonstick skillet over medium-high heat. Swirl in the remaining 2 teaspoons oil, then add the remaining 1 tablespoon ginger and 3 garlic cloves. Cook, stirring constantly, until fragrant, about 30 seconds. Add the remaining 1 cup scallions and cook 1 minute. Stir in the remaining 3 tablespoons soy sauce. Pour some of the sauce over the fish and serve the remaining sauce alongside.

Per serving (⅛ of fish): 302 Cal, 5 g Fat, 1 g Sat Fat, 157 mg Chol, 546 mg Sod, 3 g Carb, 1 g Fib, 57 g Prot, 59 mg Calc. ***POINTS: 6.***

*Chef's Tip:* Place the fish on an oval platter and garnish with pickled ginger slices and sprigs of flat-leaf parsley.

*Pearl Balls, Roasted Red Snapper with Ginger-Garlic Sauce,*
*and Vegetable Longevity Noodles*

# Vegetable Longevity Noodles

**MAKES 8 SERVINGS**

Long, uncut noodles are eaten to signify long life in the Chinese culture. Since fresh tofu is considered unlucky because of its white color—which signifies death and misfortune—we use dried tofu.

12 ounces lo mein noodles
   or fettuccine

6 dried shiitake mushrooms

½ cup low-sodium chicken or
   vegetable broth

2 tablespoons reduced-sodium
   soy sauce

2 tablespoons bottled
   oyster sauce

1 tablespoon sugar

2 teaspoons Asian (dark)
   sesame oil

3 garlic cloves, minced

2 carrots, peeled and thinly
   sliced on an angle

3 ounces dried tofu, cut into
   small cubes

½ small head napa cabbage,
   shredded (about 4 cups)

6 ounces fresh snow peas,
   trimmed and halved crosswise

3 scallions, cut into
   ¼-inch pieces

*1.* Bring a large pot of lightly salted water to a boil. Add the noodles and cook according to package directions; drain and rinse under cold water.

*2.* Meanwhile, combine the mushrooms with enough hot water to cover; soak 15 minutes. Drain; remove and discard the stems, then squeeze the excess liquid from the mushrooms. Thinly slice the mushrooms and set aside.

*3.* Combine the broth, soy sauce, oyster sauce, and sugar in a small bowl; set aside.

*4.* Heat a nonstick wok or large, deep skillet over medium-high heat until a drop of water sizzles. Swirl in the oil, then add the garlic. Stir-fry until fragrant, about 15 seconds. Add the carrots and tofu; stir-fry 1 minute. Add the sliced mushrooms, cabbage, snow peas, and scallions; stir-fry until the cabbage wilts, about 3 minutes. Add the noodles and broth mixture; cook, stirring frequently until hot and bubbling, about 2 minutes. Spoon into a large serving bowl.

Per serving (1 cup): 208 Cal, 4 g Fat, 1 g Sat Fat, 37 mg Chol, 539 mg Sod, 36 g Carb, 3 g Fib, 9 g Prot, 84 mg Calc. **POINTS: 4.**

*Chef's Tip:* Adorn the bowl of noodles with one or two decorative scallion fans. Here's how to make one: Cut away all but 2 to 3 inches of the green part attached to the bulb of the scallion; trim the roots from the bulb. With a sharp pointed knife, make ½-inch long, thin slits into the bulb and into the green end. Place in iced water until the ends fan open, about 10 minutes.

# Orange Segments in Ginger Syrup

**MAKES 8 SERVINGS**

Oranges and tangerines are eaten at Chinese New Year because it is believed that they represent wealth, good fortune, and happiness. The syrup can be made up to three days in advance and stored in an airtight container in the refrigerator. The almonds can be toasted and stored in a zip-close plastic bag for up to a week at room temperature, a month in the refrigerator or three months in the freezer.

¾ **cup sugar**

½ **cup water**

12 **quarter-size slices fresh ginger, unpeeled**

3 **tablespoons slivered blanched almonds**

6 **navel oranges, sectioned**

*1.* Combine the sugar, water, and ginger in a small saucepan; bring to a boil. Reduce the heat to medium and simmer 5 minutes. Remove from the heat and cool 30 minutes. Transfer to a bowl and refrigerate 1 hour.

*2.* Place the almonds in a small skillet over medium heat. Cook, shaking the pan and stirring constantly, until lightly toasted and fragrant, 4–5 minutes. Watch them carefully when toasting; almonds can burn quickly. Transfer to a bowl to cool.

*3.* Divide the orange sections among 8 bowls. Pour 2 tablespoons of the ginger syrup over each and sprinkle with the toasted almonds.

Per serving (¾ cup orange sections with 2 tablespoons syrup): 138 Cal, 2 g Fat, 0 g Sat Fat, 0 mg Chol, 1 mg Sod, 31 g Carb, 3 g Fib, 2 g Prot, 48 mg Calc. ***POINTS: 2.***

———◆———

*Chef's Tip:* To section an orange, use a sharp paring knife and slice away the top and bottom ends of the orange. Put the orange on end on a chopping board and slice away the rind, removing all of the pith. Working over a large bowl to catch the juices, cut the orange sections out from between the membranes, letting each one fall into the bowl, as you cut it free. Discard any seeds.

# DINNER FOR LOVERS

*Cupid's Cocktail*
—
*Forest Mushroom Turnovers*
—
*Oyster Stew*
—
*Poached Cornish Game Hen with Tarragon*
—
*Asparagus Spears with Lemon Sauce*
—
*Orzo and Rice Pilaf*
—
*Caramel and Pear Polenta Soufflés*

## Cupid's Cocktail

### MAKES 2 SERVINGS

It's the ice cubes (a frozen concoction of orange juice, cranberry juice, white wine, and orange liqueur) that work Cupid's magic in this sparkling cocktail. As the cubes melt, the drinks turn a gorgeous blush and the flavor becomes wonderfully intense.

⅓ cup orange juice
⅓ cup cranberry juice
2 tablespoons dry white wine
1 teaspoon Grand Marnier
    liqueur
2 teaspoons sugar
Seltzer
Sliced or whole strawberries,
    for garnish

*1.* Combine the orange juice, cranberry juice, wine, Grand Marnier, and sugar in a bowl; stir until the sugar dissolves. Pour the mixture into ice cube trays and freeze.

*2.* To serve, fill 2 tall glasses with the frozen juice cubes. Slowly fill each glass with seltzer. Garnish each serving with strawberries.

Per serving (1 drink): 80 Cal, 0 g Fat, 0 g Sat Fat, 0 mg Chol, 55 mg Sod, 14 g Carb, 0 g Fib, 0 g Prot, 21 mg Calc. **POINTS: 2.**

◆

*Chef's Tip:* To make a frozen version of the cocktail, fill a blender with the ice cubes and a splash of seltzer. Blend at medium-low speed just until the mixture is smooth. Pour into 2 martini or margarita glasses, then garnish with the strawberries.

*Cupid's Cocktail and Forest Mushroom Turnovers*

# Forest Mushroom Turnovers

**MAKES 4 SERVINGS**

These tempting bites are sure to whet the appetite for the romantic feast ahead. An assortment of exotic mushrooms gives the filling its wonderful woodsy flavor. Our choice includes white, shiitake, and cremini mushrooms, but use whatever looks best at the market.

1 cup water

1 ounce dried cèpes (porcini mushrooms)

2 tablespoons low-sodium chicken broth

2 tablespoons minced shallots

1 garlic clove, minced

¼ pound assorted fresh mushrooms (such as white, shiitake, and cremini), coarsely chopped

3 tablespoons dry white wine

¼ cup light sour cream

1 tablespoon chopped flat-leaf parsley

¼ teaspoon salt

Freshly ground pepper, to taste

4 (12 x 17-inch) sheets phyllo dough, at room temperature

2 tablespoons butter, melted

4 teaspoons plain dry bread crumbs

*1.* To make the filling, bring the water to a simmer in a saucepan. Remove from the heat and add the cèpes; let soak 30 minutes. Lift the cèpes out of the water using a slotted spoon; coarsely chop.

*2.* Heat a large nonstick skillet over medium heat. Add the broth, shallots, and garlic. Cook until softened, about 3 minutes. Add the assorted mushrooms, cèpes, and wine. Cook until the mushrooms are tender and the liquid has almost completely evaporated, 8-10 minutes. Transfer the mushroom mixture to a bowl and cool completely. Fold in the sour cream, parsley, salt, and pepper.

*3.* Place 1 sheet of phyllo with the long side facing you on a work surface. As you work, cover the remaining phyllo with plastic wrap to keep them from drying out. Lightly brush the phyllo sheet with melted butter; sprinkle with 2 teaspoons of the bread crumbs. Repeat with 2 more phyllo sheets, brushing each with a little more butter and 1 teaspoon bread crumbs. Top with the remaining sheet and brush lightly with butter. With a sharp knife, cut the layered sheets lengthwise into 4 equal strips.

*4.* Spray a large baking sheet with nonstick spray; set aside.

*5.* Place one-quarter of the filling in the center of the bottom end of one strip. Fold up one corner around filling to form a triangle. Continue folding all the way up to the top of the strip (flag-style). Place the triangle, seam-side down, on the baking sheet and lightly brush with butter. Repeat with the remaining 3 strips, filling, and butter. Refrigerate the turnovers 20 minutes.

*6.* Meanwhile, preheat the oven to 400°F. Bake the turnovers until golden brown and very hot inside, 8–10 minutes. Serve at once.

Per serving (1 turnover): 135 Cal, 3 g Fat, 1 g Sat Fat, 30 mg Chol, 286 mg Sod, 18 g Carb, 2 g Fib, 7 g Prot, 24 mg Calc. *POINTS: 3.*

# Oyster Stew

They say oysters are for lovers, so what better way to show your love than to share
this ultra-creamy stew with someone special? Since the stew serves four, enjoy the leftovers
as a romantic prelude to dinner the next day. The crumbled bacon and whipped butter topping
add a hint of smoke and richness to the dish.

1 tablespoon vegetable oil

1 slice bacon, minced

1 small onion, minced

2 tablespoons all-purpose flour

½ cup fat-free milk

½ cup fat-free evaporated milk

6 raw oysters, shucked, juices
   drained and reserved

½ cup clam juice

½ cup finely diced
   yellow potatoes

1 small bay leaf

⅛ teaspoon salt

Freshly ground pepper, to taste

2 teaspoons whipped
   unsalted butter

*1.* Heat a medium saucepan over medium heat. Swirl in the oil,
then add the bacon. Cook until crisp, about 3 minutes. With a
slotted spoon, transfer the bacon to a small bowl; set aside.

*2.* Add the onion to the saucepan; cook, stirring frequently, until
softened, about 5 minutes. Stir in the flour; cook over low heat,
stirring constantly, until the mixture is pale gold and fragrant,
about 1 minute.

*3.* Meanwhile, bring the milk and evaporated milk just to a
simmer in a small saucepan. Whisking constantly, slowly add the
hot milk mixture, reserved oyster juice, and the clam juice to the
flour mixture until blended. Add the potatoes and bay leaf; bring
to a boil, stirring constantly. Reduce the heat and simmer, covered,
stirring occasionally, until the potatoes are tender, 6-8 minutes.
Discard the bay leaf.

*4.* Add the whole oysters; simmer until barely cooked and their
edges begin to curl, 3–4 minutes. Add the salt and pepper. Ladle
the soup into 4 heated bowls. Top each serving with ½ teaspoon
butter and sprinkle with the crumbled bacon.

Per serving (¾ cup): 123 Cal, 4 g Fat, 2 g Sat Fat, 20 mg Chol, 237 mg Sod,
15 g Carb, 1 g Fib, 8 g Prot, 198 mg Calc. ***POINTS: 3.***

# Poached Cornish Game Hen with Tarragon

**MAKES 2 SERVINGS**

Cornish game hen is the perfect size to serve two, but sometimes it's a bit tough and dry when roasted. Our solution for a moist bird is to cook it in chicken broth with tarragon, orange rind, and vegetables. Since Cornish game hens are often sold in packages of two, try poaching both hens at the same time. Refrigerate the extra hen for up to three days to top a luncheon salad.

1 (1½-pound) Cornish game hen
¼ teaspoon salt
Freshly ground pepper, to taste
2 stems fresh tarragon, or
   ½ teaspoon dried
1 (2-inch) piece orange rind
4 cups low-sodium
   chicken broth
1 leek, cleaned and thinly sliced
1 parsnip, peeled and
   thinly sliced
1 onion, halved and thinly sliced
1 celery stalk, thinly sliced
Minced fresh tarragon, parsley,
   or chives
Grated orange rind

*1.* Season the game hen with the salt and pepper; put the tarragon stems and orange rind in the cavity. Tie the legs together with kitchen string.

*2.* Bring the broth, leek, parsnip, onion, and celery to a boil in a large saucepan. Carefully lower the hen into the broth to allow the cavity to fill completely. Reduce the heat to low, then simmer until an instant-read thermometer inserted in the thigh registers 180°F, 25–30 minutes.

*3.* Transfer the hen to a cutting board; reserve the broth. Cut the hen in half; remove the rib cage, cartilage, and skin, leaving the wings, thighs, and drumsticks intact. Discard the tarragon and orange rind.

*4.* Place each hen half, cut-side down, in a large shallow soup bowl. Ladle the broth and vegetables over each serving; sprinkle with minced tarragon and grated orange rind. Serve at once.

Per serving (½ Cornish game hen with ⅓ cup broth and ½ cup vegetables): 200 Cal, 4 g Fat, 1 g Sat Fat, 91 mg Chol, 222 mg Sod, 17 g Carb, 3 g Fib, 23 g Prot, 74 mg Calc. *POINTS: 4.*

———◆———

*Chef's Tip:* To make this dish a day ahead, prepare the recipe as directed through Step *3*. Transfer the meat to a small baking dish; moisten with ½ cup broth, cover tightly and refrigerate. Refrigerate the remaining broth and vegetables in a separate container. To reheat, bake the hen in the covered dish in a 400°F oven, about 20 minutes. Bring the broth and vegetables to a boil in a saucepan.

# Asparagus Spears with Lemon Sauce

### MAKES 2 SERVINGS

Asparagus is one of the few foods you can acceptably eat with your fingers. So grab a spear, get closer to your Valentine, and enjoy! For a fragrant and thoughtful touch, put a finger bowl near each plate and float a perfect rose petal or paper-thin slice of lemon on top.

½ cup low-sodium chicken broth
2 tablespoons fresh lemon juice
1 teaspoon grated peeled
   fresh ginger
½ teaspoon grated lemon rind
⅛ teaspoon salt
Freshly ground pepper, to taste
8 asparagus spears, trimmed
   and peeled

*1.* To make the lemon sauce, bring the broth, lemon juice, ginger, and lemon rind to a boil in a small saucepan. Reduce the heat and simmer, until the mixture is reduced to about ¼ cup. Strain the sauce through a fine sieve into a bowl; add the salt and pepper. Cover and keep warm.

*2.* Put the asparagus in a steamer basket; set in a saucepan over 1 inch of boiling water. Cover tightly and steam until very tender, about 6 minutes. Transfer the asparagus to a platter; drizzle with the lemon sauce.

Per serving (4 spears with 2 tablespoons sauce): 25 Cal, 0 g Fat, 0 g Sat Fat, 1 mg Chol, 32 mg Sod, 4 g Carb, 1 g Fib, 2 g Prot, 15 mg Calc. ***POINTS: 0.***

———◆———

*Chef's Tip:* Double the lemon sauce and save half for another use. Spoon over vegetables for a glossy sheen and piquant, refreshing flavor; brush on chicken or fish while baking for a golden glaze; or add to vegetable or shellfish stir-fries for extra zip. Refrigerate the sauce for up to three days or freeze for up to three months. Reheat in a bowl set over simmering water.

# Orzo and Rice Pilaf

**MAKES 4 SERVINGS**

Replacing half the rice with orzo (tiny, rice-shaped pasta from Italy) gives otherwise ordinary pilaf a delicious twist. For lunch the next day, combine any leftover pilaf with chopped fresh tomatoes, cucumbers, bell peppers, or celery, add a few drops of vinegar or fresh lemon juice, and serve on a bed of lettuce. You can also add the pilaf to chicken or vegetable broth for a quick but soul-sustaining soup.

2 teaspoons vegetable oil
½ small red onion, finely chopped
¼ cup long-grain white rice
¼ cup orzo
1½ cups low-sodium chicken or vegetable broth
¼ teaspoon salt
Freshly ground pepper, to taste
1 tablespoon chopped flat-leaf parsley

*1.* Heat a nonstick saucepan over medium heat. Swirl in the oil, then add the onion. Cook, stirring frequently, until softened, about 4 minutes. Add the rice and orzo; cook, stirring constantly, until lightly toasted, 2–3 minutes.

*2.* Add the broth, salt, and pepper; bring to a boil. Reduce the heat and simmer, covered, until tender, 18–20 minutes. Fluff the pilaf with a fork; stir in the parsley. Serve at once.

Per serving (1½ cups): 138 Cal, 3 g Fat, 1 g Sat Fat, 1 mg Chol, 188 mg Sod, 23 g Carb, 1 g Fib, 4 g Prot, 16 mg Calc. *POINTS: 3.*

———◆———

*Chef's Tip:* To boost the pilaf's nutritional value and fiber content, use a long-grain brown rice. Since brown rice takes about 40 minutes to cook, prepare the recipe as directed except do not toast the rice and cook the rice in the broth about 20 minutes before adding the orzo. This will allow the rice and the orzo to finish cooking at the same time.

*Caramel and Pear Polenta Soufflés*

# Caramel and Pear Polenta Soufflés

**MAKES 4 SERVINGS**

Think all soufflés are full of egg yolks, butter, and flour? Not these! But thanks to a rich, creamy polenta, sweetened with caramelized sugar and pear puree, these mini soufflés taste equally indulgent. Keep the sweetness of Valentine's Day alive by saving two of these soufflés to serve another day. Though not quite as light and puffy, they are delicious chilled.

½ cup sugar
1 tablespoon cold water
2 ripe pears, peeled, quartered, and cored
¼ cup pear or apple juice
1 small piece cinnamon stick
1 whole clove
1¼ cups fat-free milk
1 (2-inch) piece orange rind
5 tablespoons yellow cornmeal
3 egg whites

1. Combine 3 tablespoons of the sugar and the water in a medium saucepan. Cook over medium heat until the sugar melts and turns a deep caramel brown, 2–3 minutes.

2. Add the pears, pear juice, cinnamon, and clove; bring to a boil. Reduce the heat and simmer until the pears are very tender, about 10 minutes. Discard the cinnamon and clove. Transfer the pears and the cooking liquid to a blender and puree. Set aside.

3. Bring the milk, 3 tablespoons of the sugar, and the orange rind to a boil in a medium saucepan. Reduce the heat and simmer, until fragrant, about 2 minutes. Discard the orange rind. Add the cornmeal in a thin stream, stirring constantly until blended. Stir in the pear puree. Cook, stirring frequently, until the mixture pulls away from the sides of the pan, about 20 minutes.

4. Meanwhile, preheat the oven to 400°F. Spray 4 (4-ounce) soufflé or custard cups with nonstick spray; arrange on a baking sheet.

5. With an electric mixer at high speed, beat the egg whites until foamy. Gradually add the remaining 2 tablespoons sugar; beat until medium peaks form. Using a large rubber spatula, gently fold half the beaten whites into the polenta mixture, until almost combined. Repeat with the remaining beaten whites. Pour the batter into the soufflé cups. Bake the soufflés until puffed and the tops are golden, about 25 minutes. Serve at once.

Per serving (1 soufflé): 140 Cal, 2 g Fat, 1 g Sat Fat, 5 mg Chol, 80 mg Sod, 27 g Carb, 1 g Fib, 5 g Prot, 85 mg Calc. **POINTS: 3.**

*Cajun-Style Crab Cakes*
—
*Pan-Seared Red Snapper*
—
*Gumbo*
—
*Southern-Style Green Bean Salad*
—
*Red Beans and Rice*
—
*Collard Greens with Hot Bacon Vinaigrette*
—
*Orange Ambrosia*
—
*Fresh Berry Napoleons*

## Cajun-Style Crab Cakes

**MAKES 8 SERVINGS**

Whether you use fresh, frozen, or canned crabmeat, be sure to carefully pick through the crab to remove every last trace of shell and cartilage.

**3 slices firm white bread, crusts removed, made into crumbs**
**1 large egg, lightly beaten**
**¼ cup low-fat buttermilk**
**1 teaspoon fresh lemon juice**
**½ pound cooked fresh or frozen crabmeat, picked over**
**2 scallions, chopped**
**½ teaspoon minced garlic**
**½ teaspoon Cajun spice blend, or to taste**
**½ teaspoon salt**
**¼ teaspoon mustard powder**
**Freshly ground pepper, to taste**
**1 cup plain dry bread crumbs**

*1.* Spray a nonstick baking sheet with nonstick spray.
*2.* Combine the fresh bread crumbs, egg, buttermilk, and lemon juice in a bowl; let stand until the crumbs absorb the liquid.
*3.* Combine the crab, scallions, garlic, Cajun spice, salt, mustard, and pepper in another bowl. Gently fold the crumb mixture into crab mixture until blended. Shape into 16 small or 8 large patties.
*4.* Place the dry bread crumbs on a plate; add the patties, gently turning to coat evenly. Transfer to the baking sheet, cover, and refrigerate until firm, at least 1 hour or up to overnight.
*5.* Preheat the oven to 425°F. Bake the crab cakes until heated through and crispy, 10–15 minutes. (Broil the cakes 5 inches from the heat, 1–2 minutes until crisp, if necessary.) Serve at once.

Per serving (2 small or 1 large crab cake): 170 Cal, 3 g Fat, 1 g Sat Fat, 65 mg Chol, 600 mg Sod, 22 g Carb, 1 g Fib, 13 g Prot, 92 mg Calc. ***POINTS: 3.***

# Pan-Seared Red Snapper

**MAKES 8 SERVINGS**

Everyone will enjoy this slightly less fiery version of a pan-blackened fish. The pungent buttermilk marinade is great for snapper, but you can try it with chicken or pork cutlets, too.

¼ cup low-fat buttermilk

2 teaspoons dried oregano

2 teaspoons chili powder

1 teaspoon salt

½ teaspoon mustard powder

¼ teaspoon cayenne

Freshly ground pepper, to taste

8 (4-ounce) red snapper fillets, with skin

½ cup all-purpose flour

2 tablespoons vegetable oil

Lemon wedges, for garnish

*1.* To make the marinade, combine the buttermilk, oregano, chili powder, ½ teaspoon of the salt, the mustard, cayenne, and pepper in a large zip-close plastic bag. Add the snapper fillets and seal the bag; turn several times to coat. Refrigerate, turning the bag occasionally, 2–3 hours.

*2.* Transfer the fillets to a colander and drain briefly. Place the flour in a shallow bowl or pie plate, dip the fillets in the flour to coat very lightly on both sides. Shake off any excess flour.

*3.* Meanwhile, heat a large cast-iron or nonstick skillet over high heat. Swirl in 1 tablespoon of the oil, then add 4 of the fillets, skin-side down. Cook, turning once, until the fish is deep brown and just opaque in the center, 2–3 minutes on each side. Repeat with the remaining 1 tablespoon oil and 4 fillets. Garnish with the lemon wedges and serve.

Per serving (1 fillet): 160 Cal, 4 g Fat, 0 g Sat Fat, 40 mg Chol, 480 mg Sod, 5 g Carb, 0 g Fib, 24 g Prot, 63 mg Calc. *POINTS: 4.*

---

*Chef's Tip:* To season your cast-iron skillet before using: Place the clean, dry skillet over medium-high heat. Swirl in enough oil to coat the bottom by about ¼ inch. When the oil just begins to smoke, remove the pan from the heat and carefully pour off the hot oil. Cool the pan slightly, then sprinkle it with a thin layer of salt. Rub the salt into the pan with paper towels to remove the excess oil.

*Gumbo*

# Gumbo

**MAKES 8 SERVINGS**

There are many styles of gumbo, the thick stew-like Creole specialty renowned throughout Louisiana. But one thing all gumbos have in common is a dark roux, a thickener made with flour and butter. Instead of browning the flour in butter, we toast it in the oven, with equally satisfying results.

⅓ cup all-purpose flour

2½ ounces skinless boneless chicken breast

¼ cup chopped Andouille or other spicy sausage

1 green bell pepper, seeded and chopped

1 celery stalk, chopped

1 small onion, chopped

¾ cup thickly sliced okra

1 tablespoon minced garlic

½ small jalapeño pepper, seeded and minced (wear gloves to prevent irritation)

2 teaspoons dried oregano

2 teaspoons dried basil

½ teaspoon dried thyme

1 bay leaf

½ teaspoon salt

Freshly ground pepper, to taste

6 cups low-sodium chicken broth

¼ pound shrimp, peeled, deveined, and chopped

½ cup peeled, seeded, and chopped tomato

1 cup cooked long-grain white rice

3 scallions, thinly sliced

1. Preheat the oven to 350°F. Bake the flour in a small cast-iron skillet or baking pan, stirring occasionally, until dark brown, 10–12 minutes. Set aside.

2. Heat a large pot or Dutch oven over medium heat. Then add the chicken and sausage. Cook, stirring frequently, until browned, about 5 minutes. Drain off any fat.

3. Add the bell pepper, celery, and onion. Cook until the vegetables are tender, about 8 minutes. Add the okra, garlic, jalapeño, oregano, basil, thyme, bay leaf, salt, and pepper. Cook, stirring, until fragrant, about 2 minutes. Add 5½ cups of the broth and bring to a boil. Reduce the heat and simmer, uncovered, until the okra is barely tender, about 10 minutes.

4. Combine the browned flour with the remaining ½ cup broth in a bowl. Gradually add the flour mixture to the stew, whisking vigorously. Bring the stew to a boil. Reduce the heat and simmer, uncovered, until thickened and the flavors are blended, about 45 minutes.

5. Add the shrimp, tomato, and cooked rice; simmer until the shrimp is just cooked through, about 5 minutes. Sprinkle with the scallions and serve at once.

Per serving (1 cup): 103 Cal, 2 g Fat, 1 g Sat Fat, 14 mg Chol, 210 mg Sod, 14 g Carb, 1 g Fib, 7 g Prot, 49 mg Calc. *POINTS: 2.*

# Southern-Style Green Bean Salad

**MAKES 8 SERVINGS**

We include savory—an herb related to the mint family—in this dressing. Savory has a strong taste, so if you've never tried it before, you may want to cut back the amount we suggest here. The beans and the dressing can be made a day ahead, but refrigerate them separately so the beans will remain bright green.

1½ cups low-sodium chicken or vegetable broth

1 tablespoon cornstarch

1 tablespoon water

¼ cup minced flat-leaf parsley

3 tablespoons tarragon vinegar

2 tablespoons minced onion

1 tablespoon olive oil

1 tablespoon minced fresh thyme

1 tablespoon minced fresh savory, or 1 teaspoon dried

½ teaspoon mustard powder

½ teaspoon salt

Freshly ground pepper, to taste

1 pound green beans, trimmed and cut diagonally into 2-inch pieces

1 strip thick-slice bacon, cut into 4 pieces

2 heads Boston lettuce, torn

4 scallions, thinly sliced

*1.* Bring the broth to simmer over medium heat in a saucepan. Meanwhile, combine the cornstarch and water in a cup. Stir the cornstarch mixture into the broth, return the broth to a simmer and cook, stirring constantly, until thickened, about 2 minutes. Transfer the broth mixture to a bowl; cool to room temperature. Stir in the parsley, vinegar, onion, oil, thyme, savory, mustard, salt, and pepper; set aside.

*2.* Bring a large saucepan of water to a boil. Add the beans and the bacon. Cook until the beans are tender, 6–8 minutes. Drain, then discard the bacon. Transfer the beans to a large bowl of ice water. Cool 1 minute, then drain on paper towels.

*3.* To assemble the salad, combine the green beans, lettuce, and scallions in a large bowl. Add the dressing; toss to coat.

Per serving (½ cup): 80 Cal, 3 g Fat, 1 g Sat Fat, 0 mg Chol, 70 mg Sod, 9 g Carb, 4 g Fib, 2 g Prot, 57 mg Calc. ***POINTS: 1.***

# *Red Beans and Rice*

**MAKES 8 SERVINGS**

The combination of red beans and rice is a staple among Creole cooks. Traditionally, a big pot of this nourishing fare was put on to simmer every Monday, while women were busy with the laundry. Whatever its history, this hearty mix of beans, rice, ham, and Andouille— a spicy, smoked sausage—is positively addictive.

1 cup dried red beans, picked over, rinsed, and drained

¼ pound smoked ham or smoked sausage (such as Andouille), cut into 1-inch cubes

¼ pound Andouille or other smoked sausage, cut into 1-inch cubes

2 stalks celery, diced

1 yellow onion, diced

1 green bell pepper, seeded and diced

3 garlic cloves, crushed

¼ cup chopped fresh parsley

1 teaspoon chopped fresh thyme

1 bay leaf

½ teaspoon salt

Freshly ground pepper, to taste

2 teaspoons Worcestershire sauce

Dash hot pepper sauce

4 cups hot cooked long-grain white rice

*1.* Soak the beans in a bowl, in enough cool water to cover by 2 inches, overnight.

*2.* Drain the beans. Transfer to a large pot or Dutch oven; add enough cold water to cover the beans by 2 inches and bring to a boil. Reduce the heat and simmer (adding more water to keep the beans covered, if necessary) until the beans are tender to the bite, about 1½ hours.

*3.* Add the ham, sausage, celery, onion, bell pepper, garlic, parsley, thyme, bay leaf, salt, and pepper. Simmer, until the cooking liquid is thickened, about 45 minutes. Discard the bay leaf.

*4.* Stir in the Worcestershire and hot sauce. Serve with the rice.

Per serving (½ cup beans plus ½ cup rice): 180 Cal, 6 g Fat, 2 g Sat Fat, 15 mg Chol, 250 mg Sod, 87 g Carb, 13 g Fib, 23 g Prot, 90 mg Calc. *POINTS: 3.*

—◆—

*Chef's Tip:* The flavor of these beans definitely improves with time, so make them three days ahead of the party, but prepare the rice shortly before dinner. Traditions differ when it comes to serving red beans and rice. Some families combine the beans and rice, and others top the rice with the beans.

# Collard Greens with Hot Bacon Vinaigrette

**MAKES 8 SERVINGS**

Collard greens don't normally enjoy great popularity outside the South. Maybe that's because they're traditionally stewed with bacon for hours until very tender and almost pulpy. We've updated the dish by adding delicate-tasting champagne vinegar to the bacon vinaigrette and by shortening the cooking time so the greens have more texture and crunch.

2 **pounds collard greens**

2 **slices bacon, minced**

1 **tablespoon minced shallots**

2 **tablespoons champagne vinegar**

1 **tablespoon olive oil**

½ **teaspoon salt**

¼ **teaspoon freshly ground pepper, or to taste**

*1.* Bring a large pot of water to a boil. Meanwhile, remove the tough stems from the collard greens. Rinse in several changes of cool water until there are no traces of sand or dirt. Drain. Add the greens to the boiling water and cook until tender, 2–3 minutes. Drain again.

*2.* To make the vinaigrette, heat a large nonstick skillet over medium-high heat. Add the bacon and cook until crisp. Add the shallots and cook, stirring constantly, 2 minutes. Whisk in the vinegar and oil. Add the drained collard greens and toss to coat. Season with the salt and pepper. Serve warm.

Per serving (½ cup): 60 Cal, 2 g Fat, 0 g Sat Fat, 0 mg Chol, 200 mg Sod, 7 g Carb, 4 g Fib, 3 g Prot, 165 mg Calc. ***POINTS: 1.***

# Orange Ambrosia

**MAKES 8 SERVINGS**

Ambrosia is a chilled fruit dessert that usually consists of oranges, bananas, and coconut. Serve this cool, refreshing course to your guests after dinner while you assemble the Napoleons and prepare steaming café au lait.

4 navel oranges, peeled and sliced ¼-inch thick

2 tablespoons light sour cream

1 tablespoon molasses

¼ cup shredded unsweetened coconut

1 tablespoon chopped fresh mint

*1.* Arrange the orange slices on a platter or on individual salad plates.

*2.* Combine the sour cream and molasses in a bowl; drizzle over the oranges. Sprinkle the salad with the coconut and mint. Serve at once.

Per serving (2–3 orange slices with 1 teaspoon drizzle): 80 Cal, 3 g Fat, 2 g Sat Fat, 5 mg Chol, 5 mg Sod, 12 g Carb, 2 g Fib, 1 g Prot, 42 mg Calc. *POINTS: 1.*

*Fresh Berry Napoleons*

# *Fresh Berry Napoleons*

**MAKES 8 SERVINGS**

We lightly spray melted butter between the phyllo layers with a small mister bottle, using only a fraction of fat. (You can find misters or small spray bottles at most drugstores.)

8 **(12 × 17-inch) sheets phyllo dough, thawed according to package directions**

2 **tablespoons melted unsalted butter**

5 **tablespoons plain dry bread crumbs**

4 **tablespoons granulated sugar**

1 **egg white**

¼ **cup heavy cream**

½ **cup light sour cream**

1 **tablespoon packed light brown sugar**

½ **teaspoon vanilla extract**

2 **cups assorted fresh berries (sliced strawberries, blueberries, raspberries, or currants)**

**Confectioners' sugar**

*1.* Preheat the oven to 350°F. Spray a nonstick baking sheet with nonstick spray.

*2.* Place 1 sheet of phyllo with the long side facing you on a work surface (cover remaining phyllo with plastic wrap to keep moist). Lightly spray the phyllo sheet with melted butter and sprinkle with 2 teaspoons of the bread crumbs. Repeat with the remaining phyllo sheets, melted butter, and bread crumbs to form a stack. With a sharp knife or pizza wheel, cut the stack into 24 rectangles.

*3.* Transfer the rectangles to the baking sheet, sprinkle with 1 tablespoon of the granulated sugar. Bake until crisp and golden brown, 6–8 minutes. Transfer to a rack and cool completely.

*4.* To make the filling, whisk the egg white and the remaining 3 tablespoons granulated sugar in a mixing bowl, over a pan of simmering water, until the egg white reaches 160°F. Remove the bowl from the simmering water and, with an electric mixer on medium speed, beat the mixture until stiff glossy peaks form. In a small bowl, with the mixer on medium-high speed, whip the heavy cream until thick.

*5.* Combine the sour cream, brown sugar, and vanilla in a bowl. Using a rubber spatula, gently fold in the whipped cream until just blended, then fold in the beaten egg white.

*6.* To assemble, place about 1 teaspoon of the filling on a plate, top with a phyllo rectangle. Gently spread with 2 tablespoons of the filling, then sprinkle 2 tablespoons of the fruit on top. Stack another rectangle, 2 tablespoons filling, and 2 tablespoons fruit on top. Add a third rectangle and dust lightly with confectioners' sugar. Repeat with remaining rectangles, filling, fruit, and confectioners' sugar to make 8 napoleons.

Per serving (1 napoleon): 170 Cal, 6 g Fat, 3 g Sat Fat, 15 mg Chol, 135 mg Sod, 27 g Carb, 3 g Fib, 4 g Prot, 38 mg Calc. *POINTS: 3.*

# ST. PATRICK'S DAY SUPPER

*Smoked Salmon Canapés*

—

*Carrot and Turnip Toss*

—

*Champs*

—

*Brown Soda Bread*

—

*Corned Beef with Cabbage and Boiled Vegetables*

—

*Honey-Almond Oat Pudding*

—

*Custard Sauce*

—

*Irish Coffee*

---

## Smoked Salmon Canapés

**MAKES 6 SERVINGS**

Irish smoked salmon is highly regarded among connoisseurs. It's a wonderful treat, so be sure to use any leftovers to add to a hot or cold pasta dish, or to savor on top of some leftover brown bread the next morning. Cocktail rye bread comes in 8-ounce packages, each slice about a 2-inch square.

2 ounces light cream cheese
  or Neufchâtel

1 tablespoon minced fresh dill

1 teaspoon minced shallots

¼ teaspoon salt

6 slices cocktail rye or
  pumpernickel bread, cut in
  half on the diagonal

3 thin slices (about 3 ounces)
  smoked salmon, cut in fourths

1 tablespoon salmon caviar

12 fresh dill sprigs

12 capers

Combine the cream cheese, dill, shallots, and salt. Spread 1 teaspoon of the cream cheese mixture on each piece of rye or pumpernickel. Drape a piece of salmon on top. Garnish each canapé with ¼ teaspoon caviar, a fresh dill sprig, and a caper.

Per serving (2 canapés): 70 Cal, 2 g Fat, 1g Sat Fat, 20 mg Chol, 570 mg Sod, 8 g Carb, 1 g Fib, 6 g Prot, 30 mg Calc. *POINTS: 1.*

# Carrot and Turnip Toss

The most labor-intensive part to this otherwise simple dish is dicing the vegetables. So dice the carrots and turnip ahead of time and keep them covered in the refrigerator for up to two days. You'll need to chop the onion just before you use it to keep the flavor fresh. Alternatively, prepare the whole dish ahead of time and store it, covered, in the refrigerator for up to three days. Reheat in a covered microwavable dish on High until well heated through, about 4 minutes.

2 teaspoons canola oil

2 teaspoons butter

1 large onion, chopped

4 carrots, diced (about 2 cups)

1 yellow turnip, peeled and
   diced (about 4 cups)

⅓ cup water

½ teaspoon salt

¼ teaspoon freshly ground
   pepper

⅛ teaspoon ground nutmeg

*1.* Heat a large nonstick saucepan over medium-high heat. Swirl in the oil and butter, then add the onion. Cook, stirring occasionally, until golden, 7–10 minutes.

*2.* Add the carrots, turnip, water, salt, pepper, and nutmeg; bring to a boil. Reduce the heat and simmer, covered, stirring occasionally, until the vegetables are tender, about 20 minutes.

Per serving (scant 1 cup): 68 Cal, 3 g Fat, 1 g Sat Fat, 3 mg Chol, 453 mg Sod, 11 g Carb, 3 g Fib, 1 g Prot, 36 mg Calc. *POINTS: 1.*

# Champs

**MAKES 6 SERVINGS**

Champs, and its counterpart, colcannon, are made from whipped potatoes. To make champs, stir in plenty of minced scallions. For colcannon, replace the scallions with cooked, shredded green cabbage. You can make this dish in the morning, keeping it refrigerated. Then reheat, covered, in a 350°F oven until very hot, about 15 minutes. Remove the cover during the last 5 minutes for a crisp, golden crust.

**3** medium russet or Yukon Gold
  potatoes, peeled
  and quartered
**¾** teaspoon salt
**¾** cup fat-free buttermilk
**4** scallions, white and light
  green portion only, minced
**2** teaspoons minced fresh
  chives (optional)
Freshly ground pepper, to taste

*1.* Preheat the oven to 350°F. Spray a nonstick 8-inch square baking pan with nonstick spray.

*2.* Place the potatoes, ½ teaspoon of the salt, and enough water to cover in a large saucepan; bring to a boil. Reduce the heat and simmer, covered, until tender, 15–20 minutes; drain. With a ricer or potato masher, puree the potatoes.

*3.* Add the buttermilk, scallions, chives (if using), the remaining ¼ teaspoon salt, and the pepper. Beat well with a wooden spoon until light and fluffy.

*4.* Scrape the potato mixture into the baking pan and spread smooth. Bake until the top is crisp and golden, about 10 minutes.

Per serving (⅙ cup): 70 Cal, 0 g Fat, 0 g Sat Fat, 0 mg Chol, 230 mg Sod, 15 g Carb, 2 g Fib, 3 g Prot, 46 Calc. *POINTS: 1.*

———◆———

*Chef's Tip:* For the fluffiest whipped potatoes, take this tip from professional chefs: After you drain the potatoes, and before you mash them, dry them by returning them to the pot set over low heat. Shake the pot from time to time and heat the potatoes until steam stops rising from them, 2–3 minutes.

# Brown Soda Bread

**MAKES 12 SERVINGS**

This sturdy peasant bread is so easy to blend and bake, you may want to include it as a staple for weekend breakfasts. If you like, add up to ¼ cup of dried currants or raisins and ½ teaspoon caraway seeds to the bread along with the buttermilk, for extra flavor and moisture.

3 cups all-purpose flour
1 cup whole-wheat flour
½ teaspoon baking soda
½ teaspoon salt
1½ cups fat-free buttermilk

*1.* Preheat oven to 350°F. Spray a baking sheet with nonstick spray.
*2.* Combine the all-purpose flour, whole-wheat flour, baking soda, and salt in a large bowl. Add the buttermilk and stir with a wooden spoon until just moistened. Gather the mixture into a ball. On a lightly floured surface, knead the dough 2–3 times. Divide the dough in half, and press into 2 (1½-inch thick) disks. Transfer to the baking sheet. With a sharp knife, cut an ✕ over the surface of each loaf.
*3.* Bake until golden brown and a toothpick inserted in the center comes out clean, about 45 minutes. Transfer the loaves to a rack to cool completely. Cut each loaf into 12 slices.

Per serving (2 slices): 110 Cal, 0 g Fat, 0 g Sat Fat, 0 mg Chol, 12 mg Sod, 22 g Carb, 1 g Fib, 4 g Prot, 29 mg Calc. ***POINTS: 2.***

*Chef's Tip:* The traditional method of storing an Irish soda bread is still the best. Wrap the completely cooled loaf in a clean tea towel and keep at room temperature. Soda breads can be kept this way for up to two days.

# Corned Beef with Cabbage and Boiled Vegetables

**MAKES 6 SERVINGS**

Two classic companions for corned beef and cabbage are sharp mustard and a biting horseradish. One small dish of each, served alongside, will add a wollop of flavor, but not a single **POINT** to this honest, home-style entrée. This dish reheats beautifully, so go ahead and make it the day before your celebration. Let the covered pot come to a very slow boil, then simmer until the corned beef is completely heated through.

1¼ **pounds corned beef, trimmed of all visible fat**

1 **small head green cabbage, cored and cut into 6 wedges**

18 **baby carrots**

6 **small purple-top turnips, peeled and halved**

1 **cup pearl onions or small pickling onions**

6 **small red potatoes, scrubbed and left whole**

*1.* Bring the corned beef and enough water to cover to a boil in a large saucepan or Dutch oven. Reduce the heat and simmer, partially covered, until almost tender, about 1½ hours.

*2.* Add the cabbage, carrots, turnips, onions, and potatoes to the pan; return to a boil. Reduce the heat and simmer, partially covered, until the vegetables and corned beef are fork tender, about 45 minutes.

*3.* Transfer the corned beef to a platter and carve into slices. Lift the vegetables from the broth with a slotted spoon and serve with the corned beef.

Per serving (⅙ of dinner): 320 Cal, 12 g Fat, 5 g Sat Fat, 60 mg Chol, 790 mg Sod, 36 g Carb, 7 g Fib, 16 g Prot, 117 mg Calc. **POINTS: 7.**

*Corned Beef with Cabbage and Boiled Vegetables*

# Honey-Almond Oat Pudding

**MAKES 6 SERVINGS**

The Irish have devised numerous recipes to show off oats, their staple grain. This wonderful steamed pudding includes almonds and honey. Pair it with the Custard Sauce for a sumptuous dessert. If you want to save time on St Patrick's Day, make the pudding the day before and refrigerate it, covered. Reheat it, uncovered, in a 350°F oven until very hot, about 15 minutes.

- 1 cup fat-free milk
- 1 cup quick-cooking oats
- 2 tablespoons ground blanched almonds
- ¼ cup honey
- 2 tablespoons dried currants or raisins
- 1 large egg, lightly beaten
- 1 teaspoon grated orange rind
- ½ teaspoon salt
- ¼ teaspoon cinnamon
- 3 egg whites

*1.* Preheat the oven to 350°F. Lightly spray a 1-quart baking dish or 6 (4-ounce) custard or soufflé cups with nonstick spray.

*2.* Bring the milk to a boil. Add the oatmeal gradually, stirring constantly. Reduce the heat and simmer, stirring frequently, until creamy and fully cooked, 3–4 minutes. Transfer to a mixing bowl and allow the oatmeal to cool slightly.

*3.* Stir the almonds, honey, currants, egg, orange rind, salt, and cinnamon into the oatmeal.

*4.* With an electric mixer on medium speed, beat the egg whites to medium peaks. Fold them into the oatmeal mixture then spoon into the baking dish or custard cups. Cover loosely with foil. Stand the baking dish or custard cups on a baking sheet and bake until puffed and set, about 1½ hours for a single large pudding or 45 minutes for individual puddings.

Per serving (⅙ of pudding or 1 individual pudding): 130 Cal, 3 g Fat, 0 g Sat Fat, 35 mg Chol, 135 mg Sod, 20 g Carb, 2 g Fib, 6 g Prot, 74 mg Calc. **POINTS: 2.**

———◆———

*Chef's Tip:* For a lighter textured and moister pudding, make a water bath as follows: Put the filled casserole or cups in a baking dish with sides at least 2 inches high. Set the pan on the oven rack, then pour in enough boiling water to come at least 1 inch up the sides of the casserole or cups. Cover loosely with foil and bake as directed above.

# *Custard Sauce*

This suave sauce is lighter both in texture and calories than a traditional custard sauce, and it's easier to make, too. Make it up to two days ahead and keep it refrigerated. Serve it cold or reheat it gently over a hot water bath. Enjoy any leftovers drizzled over fresh fruit.

**1 cup milk**
**¼ cup sugar**
**½ teaspoon vanilla extract**
**1 large egg**

*1.* Combine the milk, 2 tablespoons of the sugar, and the vanilla in a medium saucepan; bring to a simmer over medium heat.

*2.* While the milk is heating, combine the remaining 2 tablespoons sugar with the egg in a medium bowl; whisk until combined. Slowly pour the hot milk mixture into the egg mixture, whisking constantly. Return the mixture to the saucepan and cook over low heat, stirring constantly, until the mixture coats a spoon, about 3 minutes. (Do not let the mixture boil.)

*3.* Strain the sauce through a fine-meshed sieve into a pitcher. Serve at once, or pour into a container and refrigerate.

Per serving (scant 2 tablespoons): 35 Cal, 1 g Fat, 0 Sat Fat, 20 mg Chol, 15 mg Sod, 5 g Carb, 0 g Fib, 1 g Prot, 26 mg Calc. *POINTS: 1.*

---

*Chef's Tip:* Cook light colored, delicate sauces such as this in a stainless steel, nonstick, or enamel-lined pot to keep the color creamy and light. Aluminum pots can turn light sauces a grayish color. You may have been warned never to let a custard sauce return to a boil once the egg is added, and we agree.

For greater control, cook the sauce over a hot water bath once the milk and eggs are combined.

# *Irish Coffee*

What could be more bolstering on a blustery March night than a cup of rich dark coffee, fortified with a "wee drop" of Irish whiskey. We substitute a high-quality creamy frozen yogurt for the higher fat whipped cream. Sample the yogurt before selecting a brand to serve to your guests. It should be rich and smooth, virtually indistinguishable from premium brand ice cream. Increase the amount of coffee you normally use to brew a pot by about one-fourth for a potent brew. Warm the cups before making the Irish coffee by rinsing them in hot water to chase the chill.

3 tablespoons sugar
6 (1-ounce) shots Irish whiskey
3 cups strong brewed coffee
1½ cups premium vanilla
    low-fat frozen yogurt
Cinnamon or cocoa powder,
    for dusting

Divide the sugar evenly between 6 coffee cups or mugs. Pour one shot of whiskey into each cup, then the coffee, pouring to within 2 inches of the rim. Stir to dissolve the sugar. Top each cup with ¼ cup of the frozen yogurt. Dust with cinnamon or cocoa powder, if desired, and serve at once.

Per serving (1 drink): 170 Cal, 2 g Fat, 0 g Sat Fat, 0 mg Chol, 25 mg Sod, 21 g Carb, 0 g Fib, 3 g Prot, 102 mg Calc. *POINTS: 4.*

———◆———

*Chef's Tip:* If you prefer, let your guests add sugar to their own taste. Set out a bowl of sugar cubes or raw sugar, or serve swizzle sticks coated with coarse sugar. You can find these sticks at gourmet or confectionary shops.

# CARIBBEAN DREAMS DINNER

*Carrot Salad*
–
*Jamaican Meat Patties*
–
*Cuban Black-Bean Soup*
–
*Beef Pilau*
–
*Goat Curry*
–
*Green Papaya Salsa*
–
*Glazed Pineapple with Green Peppercorns*
–
*Ricotta Ice Cream*

## *Carrot Salad*

**MAKES 4 SERVINGS**

Hardly your typical carrot-raisin salad, this unusual dish gets its mysteriously rich flavor
from cooked dates, scallions, lemon juice, cilantro, cumin, and cayenne.

1 **pound carrots, thinly sliced**

1 **garlic clove, peeled**

**Juice of ½ lemon**

1 **teaspoon chopped
fresh cilantro**

1 **teaspoon chopped
flat-leaf parsley**

½ **teaspoon ground cumin**

**Pinch cayenne**

2 **teaspoons olive oil**

½ **cup thinly sliced scallions
(white and light green
portion only)**

½ **cup chopped dates**

*1.* Simmer the carrots, garlic, and enough water to cover in a
saucepan until tender, 5–6 minutes. Transfer the carrots to a bowl
with a slotted spoon.

*2.* Simmer the cooking liquid until it reduces to ½ cup, about
10 minutes. Remove from the heat; discard the garlic. Add the
lemon juice, cilantro, parsley, cumin, and cayenne. Pour the
mixture over the carrots.

*3.* Heat a medium nonstick skillet over medium heat. Swirl in the
oil, then add the scallions. Cook until tender, about 2 minutes.
Add the dates; reduce the heat to low and cook, stirring frequently,
until the dates disintegrate, about 5 minutes. Add to the carrots,
tossing gently to coat. Transfer the mixture to a serving bowl,
cover, and refrigerate until chilled, about 1 hour.

Per serving (¾ cup): 70 Cal, 2 g Fat, 0 g Sat Fat, 0 mg Chol, 30 mg Sod, 12 g Carb,
3 g Fib, 1 g Prot, 35 mg Calc. ***POINTS: 1.***

# Jamaican Meat Patties

**MAKES 8 SERVINGS**

The brilliant gold of these spicy turnovers comes from curry powder and turmeric.
Using a food processor makes short work of getting perfect pastry.

**PASTRY:**
- 1 cup all-purpose flour, sifted
- 1½ teaspoons baking powder
- ½ teaspoon curry powder
- ¼ teaspoon ground turmeric
- ⅛ teaspoon salt
- ¼ cup part-skim ricotta, chilled
- 2 tablespoons fat-free milk, chilled
- 1 egg white, chilled
- 2 tablespoons unsalted butter, diced and chilled

**FILLING:**
- 1 teaspoon vegetable oil
- 1 onion, chopped
- 2 garlic cloves, minced
- 2 teaspoons curry powder
- ¼ teaspoon dried thyme
- ¼ teaspoon salt
- Freshly ground pepper, to taste
- Pinch cayenne
- ¼ pound lean ground beef (10% or less fat)
- ⅓ cup water
- ¼ cup plain dry bread crumbs

*1.* To make the pastry, process the flour, baking powder, curry powder, turmeric, and salt in a food processor until just blended, about 15 seconds. Add the ricotta cheese, milk, egg white, and butter; pulse just long enough for the pastry to form a ball. Wrap the pastry in plastic wrap and refrigerate until firm, about 1 hour.

*2.* To make the filling, heat a large nonstick skillet over medium heat. Swirl in the oil, then add the onion, garlic, curry powder, thyme, salt, pepper, and cayenne. Cook until the onion is tender, about 6 minutes. Add the beef and cook, breaking it up with a wooden spoon, until browned. Drain off any fat. Add the water and bring to a boil. Reduce the heat and simmer, uncovered, until the liquid has reduced by half, 5–10 minutes. Stir in the bread crumbs, then refrigerate until cool.

*3.* On a lightly floured surface, roll the pastry ¼-inch thick. Cut with a 3-inch round cookie cutter. Reroll the scraps to make a total of 8 circles. Spoon 1 rounded tablespoon of the filling onto one-half of each circle of pastry. Fold the pastry over into a half-moon shape. Press the edges of the pastry and crimp to seal. Place on a nonstick baking sheet and refrigerate at least 20 minutes or up to 2 days.

*4.* Preheat the oven to 350°F. Bake the meat patties until golden brown, 15–18 minutes.

Per serving (1 meat patty): 140 Cal, 6 g Fat, 3 g Sat Fat, 15 mg Chol, 210 mg Sod, 16 g Carb, 1 g Fib, 6 g Prot, 40 mg Calc. **POINTS: 3.**

———◆———

*Chef's Tip:* To mix the pastry by hand, whisk the dry ingredients together in a bowl. With a pastry blender or two knives, cut the butter into the flour mixture until the pastry resembles fine crumbs. Stir in the cheese, milk, and egg white until the pastry forms a ball. Leftover patties can be refrigerated for up to two days and reheated in a 350°F oven until heated through, about 5 minutes.

# Cuban Black-Bean Soup

**MAKES 8 SERVINGS**

This black-bean soup may use more spices than you're accustomed to, but unlike the Mexican version, these seasonings are warm and mellow rather than fiery-hot. Whole allspice, which tastes like a combination of cinnamon, nutmeg, and cloves, helps give this soup its unique flavor. Callaloo, the edible leafy green from the taro root, is popular in the Caribbean. If it's available at your market, use instead of spinach but increase the cooking time to 4 or 5 minutes.

1½ cups dried black beans, picked over, rinsed, and drained

5 cups low-sodium chicken or beef broth

4–5 whole black peppercorns

2–3 whole allspice

1 whole clove

⅛ teaspoon cumin seeds

¼ teaspoon dried oregano

¼ teaspoon salt

1 cup water

1 onion, diced

1 green bell pepper, seeded and diced

1 garlic clove, minced

1 tablespoon dry sherry

1 tablespoon fresh lemon juice

1 cup finely shredded fresh spinach leaves

*1.* Bring the beans and broth to a boil in a large heavy saucepan or Dutch oven. Combine the peppercorns, allspice, clove, and cumin in a small piece of cheesecloth; gather into a bundle and tie with kitchen string. Add to the beans with the oregano and salt. Reduce the heat and simmer, uncovered, until the beans are almost tender, about 40 minutes.

*2.* Meanwhile, bring the water to a simmer in a medium saucepan. Add the onion, bell pepper, and garlic. Simmer, stirring often, until the vegetables are tender, 6–8 minutes.

*3.* Add the vegetables and their cooking liquid to the beans. Simmer the soup until the beans are tender enough to mash easily, 10-12 minutes.

*4.* Discard the bag of spices from the soup. Puree one-third of the soup in a blender or food processor, then stir the puree into the remaining soup. Add the sherry, lemon juice, and spinach; simmer 1 minute.

Per serving (¾ cup): 160 Cal, 1 g Fat, 0 g Sat Fat, 0 mg Chol, 80 mg Sod, 26 g Carb, 6 g Fib, 12 g Prot, 190 mg Calc. **POINTS: 2.**

*Chef's Tip:* For a dramatic presentation, serve this soup swirled with the Butternut Squash Soup [page 179] in the Harvest Dinner menu. Prepare the bean soup as directed, except use vegetable broth, puree the entire batch of soup, and omit the spinach. Leftover soup can be refrigerated for up to three days, then thoroughly reheated in a saucepan.

# Beef Pilau

**MAKES 4 SERVINGS**

Many Caribbean recipes, such as this exceptionally tasty beef dish with rice and beans, begin by caramelizing sugar in a pot before adding the remaining ingredients. This lends a mild sweetness to the dish, which is a lovely counterpoint to the heat generated by the hot chiles and fresh ginger.

¾ pound stewing beef, trimmed of all visible fat and cut into 1½-inch chunks
1 tablespoon chopped flat-leaf parsley
¼ teaspoon salt
Freshly ground pepper, to taste
1 tablespoon chopped fresh thyme
1½ tablespoons vegetable oil
1 tablespoon sugar
1 small onion, chopped
2 small garlic cloves, minced
½ teaspoon minced fresh ginger
⅓ cup diced tomato
1 carrot, chopped
1 red bell pepper, seeded and chopped
2 cups water
1 cup long-grain white rice
¾ cup rinsed and drained canned red kidney beans
1 small hot chile pepper, split lengthwise, seeds and ribs removed (wear gloves to prevent irritation)

*1.* Place the beef in a bowl; sprinkle with the parsley, salt, ground pepper, and thyme; toss to coat. Cover and refrigerate 1 hour.

*2.* Heat a large heavy saucepan or Dutch oven over high heat. Swirl in the oil, then add the sugar. Cook, stirring occasionally, until the sugar is browned and has a fragrant aroma, about 4 minutes. Add the beef and cook, stirring occasionally, until the beef is browned, about 8 minutes. Add the onion, garlic, and ginger; cook, stirring frequently, until tender, about 5 minutes. Add the tomato, carrot, and bell pepper; cook 3 minutes. Add the water and bring to a boil. Reduce the heat and simmer, uncovered, until the meat is almost tender, about 40 minutes.

*3.* Add the rice, beans, and chile; bring to a boil. Reduce the heat and simmer, covered, until the rice is tender, about 20 minutes. Discard the chile and serve at once.

Per serving (¾ cup): 290 Cal, 6 g Fat, 1 g Sat Fat, 55 mg Chol, 240 mg Sod, 35 g Carb, 5 g Fib, 23 g Prot, 26 mg Calc. ***POINTS: 6.***

*Chef's Tip:* To add a hint of the Caribbean to other meals, try starting other chicken, lamb, or pork recipes by caramelizing a touch of sugar.

# Goat Curry

Goat is richly flavored meat that's well worth searching out in Caribbean and specialty-meat markets. The majority of goat available comes from the kid or baby goat. Kid meat is as tender and delicate as that of young lamb. Substitute ¾ pound bottom round beef, if you prefer. Be warned, this curry gets its heat from the fiery habanero chile—a small lantern-shaped variety, native to the Caribbean, which ranges in color from light green to bright orange when ripe. Use only a quarter habanero if you prefer curry on the milder side. Serve this curry with the Green Papaya Salsa [page 300].

¾ **pound boneless goat, trimmed of all visible fat**

2 **cups low-sodium beef broth**

1 **teaspoon vegetable oil**

½ **habanero chile, seeded and chopped (wear gloves to prevent irritation)**

1 **teaspoon curry powder**

1 **sprig fresh thyme**

¼ **teaspoon salt**

**Freshly ground pepper, to taste**

½ **cup diced tomato**

2 **scallions, sliced into ½-inch pieces**

**Juice of ½ lime**

*1.* Bring the goat and broth to a boil in a heavy pot or Dutch oven. Reduce the heat and simmer, covered, until the meat is tender enough to shred easily with a fork, about 2 hours. (If necessary, add extra water so that the liquid barely covers the meat.) Transfer the meat to a bowl. When cool enough to handle, shred. Strain the broth and reserve (you should have about 1½ cups).

*2.* Heat a large nonstick skillet over medium heat. Swirl in the oil, then add the habanero. Cook until tender, about 2 minutes. Stir in the shredded meat, curry powder, thyme, salt, and ground pepper. Add the reserved broth and bring to a boil. Reduce the heat and simmer, uncovered, until the flavors are blended and the mixture is slightly thickened, about 45 minutes.

*3.* Add the tomato and scallions; simmer about 10 minutes. Stir in the lime juice.

Per serving (1 cup): 220 Cal, 9 g Fat, 3 g Sat Fat, 145 mg Chol, 460 mg Sod, 3 g Carb, 1 g Fib, 31 g Prot, 50 mg Calc. ***POINTS: 5.***

*Chef's Tip:* This dish reheats beautifully—actually, the flavors improve when made ahead. Prepare the recipe as directed, then cool. Transfer to an airtight container and refrigerate for up to three days.

# Green Papaya Salsa

Here's a fun fact: In Caribbean cooking, there's no need to wait for papaya to ripen before using it. Unripe green papayas are often cooked as a vegetable or made into pickles or salads. This refreshing salsa has a surprisingly rich flavor and makes the perfect cooling counterpart to the Goat Curry [page 299]. Leftover salsa keeps well in the refrigerator for up to two days and is great with most grilled meats.

1 green papaya, peeled
  and seeded
1 carrot
Juice of 1 lime
2 tablespoons chopped
  fresh cilantro
2 teaspoons red-wine vinegar
2 teaspoons molasses
1 teaspoon grated peeled
  fresh ginger
1 garlic clove, minced
¼ teaspoon salt
Freshly ground pepper, to taste

With the largest opening on a 4-sided grater, shred the papaya and carrot into a large bowl. Add the lime juice, cilantro, vinegar, molasses, ginger, garlic, salt, and pepper; toss to coat. Let the salsa stand at room temperature for 30 minutes before serving.

Per serving (2 tablespoons): 20 Cal, 0 g Fat, 0 g Sat Fat, 0 mg Chol, 54 mg Sod, 5 g Carb, 1 g Fib, 0 g Prot, 20 mg Calc. *POINTS: 0.*

———◆———

*Chef's Tip:* If papayas are not readily available at your market, prepare the salsa with diced firm-ripe mango or fresh pineapple instead.

# *Glazed Pineapple with Green Peppercorns*

**MAKES 4 SERVINGS**

Pineapple is a symbol of welcome in the Caribbean—and you'll be glad to welcome this quick, elegant dessert with honey and rum to your repertoire. Green peppercorns add a special flavor and a hint of "pine" to the pineapple, but if you prefer, replace the green peppercorns with cracked black peppercorns. You also have the option of omitting the peppercorns entirely, to enjoy the pure taste of fresh pineapple. This makes a great accompaniment to the Ricotta Ice Cream [page 302].

¼ teaspoon green peppercorns,
   drained, rinsed, and mashed
4 (½-inch thick) slices
   fresh pineapple
2 tablespoons sugar
¼ cup fresh orange juice
1 tablespoon light rum
1½ teaspoons honey

*1.* Rub the mashed peppercorns evenly over both sides of the pineapple, then sprinkle one side with the sugar. Combine the orange juice, rum, and honey in a small bowl.

*2.* Heat a medium skillet over high heat. Add the pineapple slices, sugar-side down; cook until the sugar is browned and there is a distinct caramel aroma, 1–2 minutes. Flip and cook the second side until browned, about 1 minute. Transfer the slices to dessert plates; cover and keep warm.

*3.* Add the orange juice mixture to the skillet. Increase the heat to high and cook until the sauce is reduced and syrupy, about 2 minutes. Pour the sauce over the pineapple and serve at once.

Per serving (1 pineapple slice): 60 Cal, 0 g Fat, 0 g Sat Fat, 0 mg Chol, 15 mg Sod, 15 g Carb, 1 g Fib, 1 g Prot, 12 mg Calc. ***POINTS: 1.***

*Chef's Tip:* We think fresh pineapple tastes best, but if canned pineapple is more convenient, select sliced pineapple packed in natural juices. Prepare the recipe as directed, blotting the canned pineapple with paper towels to remove the excess moisture. This will help the sugar coating to caramelize.

# Ricotta Ice Cream

**MAKES 8 SERVINGS**

Here's an easy four-ingredient alternative to commercially prepared frozen yogurt. Allow the ice cream to soften in the refrigerator one hour before serving to boost the maple syrup and vanilla flavor and keep the texture more creamy than icy. This recipe can be frozen for up to three days.

1 **cup part-skim ricotta cheese**
¾ **cup plain fat-free yogurt**
½ **cup maple syrup**
1½ **teaspoons vanilla extract**

*1.* Puree the ricotta in a food processor. Add the yogurt, maple syrup, and vanilla; process until smooth.
*2.* Transfer the ricotta mixture to an ice cream maker and freeze according to the manufacturer's directions. Spoon the ice cream into a plastic freezer container, cover tightly and freeze until firm, at least 2 hours.

Per serving (1/4 cup): 96 Cal, 2 g Fat, 1 g Sat Fat, 10 mg Chol, 40 mg Sod, 14 g Carb, 0 g Fib, 4 g Prot, 100 mg Calc. **POINTS: 2.**

———◆———

*Chef's Tip:* To make this recipe without an ice cream maker, process the ricotta mixture as directed, then pour it into a shallow baking dish. Cover tightly and freeze until firm, at least 8 hours. Let the mixture soften at room temperature, 5 minutes. Transfer to a food processor and pulse until smooth and creamy. Then transfer to a freezer container and freeze until firm.

*Glazed Pineapple with Green Peppercorns and Ricotta Ice Cream*

# A SWEDISH SMORGASBORD

*Herring and Beet Salad*
—
*Open-Face Shrimp-and-Egg Sandwiches*
—
*Cucumber Salad*
—
*Swedish Meatballs*
—
*Potato Cakes*
—
*Sweet-and-Sour Red Cabbage*
—
*Rice Pudding with Lingonberry Sauce*
—
*Ginger-Almond Cookies*

## Herring and Beet Salad

**MAKES 8 SERVINGS**

Herring appears in all smorgasbords and is usually served as a first course. Top the salad with a teaspoonful of crème fraîche (for an extra ½ **POINT** per serving) and garnish with fresh dill.

3  **medium fresh beets, trimmed (about 1¼ pounds)**
½  **cup white-wine vinegar**
¼  **cup sugar**
2  **tablespoons chopped fresh dill**
1  **teaspoon dry mustard**
¾  **cup pickled herring pieces, rinsed, drained, and patted dry**
1  **red apple, unpeeled and diced**
1  **medium red onion, diced**
1  **cup diced, unpeeled, seedless cucumber**

*1.* Place the beets in a medium saucepan with enough water to cover; bring to a boil. Reduce the heat and simmer, covered, until tender, about 35 minutes. Drain and let the beets cool to room temperature. Peel and cut into ½-inch chunks; set aside.

*2.* Combine the vinegar, sugar, dill, and mustard in a large bowl; stir to dissolve the sugar. Add the beets, herring, apple, onion, and cucumber; toss well to coat. Refrigerate, covered, for at least 2 hours or up to 3 days.

Per serving (¾ cup): 104 Cal, 3 g Fat, 0 g Sat Fat, 2 mg Chol, 127 mg Sod, 19 g Carb, 2 g Fib, 3 g Prot, 26 mg Calc. **POINTS: 2.**

# Open-Face Shrimp-and-Egg Sandwiches

**MAKES 8 SERVINGS**

Heavy, dark rye bread, sometimes called German-style rye, is good and sturdy for open-face sandwiches. It comes in packages weighing about a pound, containing eight (4 × 5-inch) slices. The shrimp and cucumber topping is enlivened with a sprinkling of white-wine vinegar. Try aged white-wine vinegar for best flavor.

2 hard-cooked eggs,
  finely chopped
1 tablespoon reduced-fat
  mayonnaise
1 tablespoon finely minced
  red onion
1 tablespoon chopped fresh dill
4 (2-ounce) slices heavy, dark
  rye bread, cut in half
¼ large seedless cucumber,
  very thinly sliced
3 ounces cooked shrimp,
  chopped
White-wine vinegar,
  for sprinkling
8 sprigs fresh dill

Combine the eggs, mayonnaise, onion, and dill in a small bowl. Spread the egg mixture on the bread slices. Top each with a few slices of the cucumber, then the shrimp. Sprinkle lightly with the vinegar and garnish with the dill sprigs.

Per serving (1 open-face sandwich): 112 Cal, 3 g Fat, 1 g Sat Fat, 74 mg Chol, 242 mg Sod, 15 g Carb, 2 g Fib, 6 g Prot, 35 mg Calc. **POINTS: 2.**

—◆—

*Chef's Tip:* To make partially ahead, combine the eggs, mayonnaise, onion, and dill; store, covered, in the refrigerator for up to two days. Assemble the sandwiches just before you're ready to serve them.

# Cucumber Salad

**MAKES 8 SERVINGS**

Originally a Scandinavian favorite, this crunchy, sweet salad has become a popular treat all across America. If you own a mandolin (slicing machine), this is a perfect time to use it. Otherwise slice the cucumbers as thinly as possible using a sharp knife. This salad lends itself well to making ahead. The vinegar and sugar act as natural preservatives and the cucumbers stay crisp in the marinade for up to a week in the refrigerator.

½ cup white-wine vinegar
¼ cup sugar
¼ cup water
½ teaspoon salt
¼ teaspoon ground white pepper
2 large seedless cucumbers,
  very thinly sliced
  (about 8 cups)
¼ cup chopped fresh dill

Combine the vinegar, sugar, water, salt, and pepper in a large bowl; stir to dissolve the sugar. Add the cucumbers and dill; toss well. Cover and refrigerate for at least 1 hour or up to 1 week.

Per serving (¾ cup): 27 Cal, 0 g Fat, 0 g Sat Fat, 0 mg Chol, 75 mg Sod, 6 g Carb, 1 g Fib, 1 g Prot, 16 mg Calc. *POINTS: 0.*

# Swedish Meatballs

**MAKES 8 SERVINGS**

Often, Swedish meatballs are made into tiny ½-inch balls and served as an appetizer. Here, they are made larger and served as an entrée, as they might be at a typical Swedish smorgasbord. Make them ahead and refrigerate for up to two days, or freeze for up to three months. Reheat thoroughly, in a covered skillet, with a little extra broth or water.

2 teaspoons butter

1 large onion, chopped

4 slices whole-wheat bread, made into crumbs (about 2 cups)

½ cup fat-free milk

1 large egg

1 teaspoon salt

½ teaspoon coarsely ground pepper

½ pound ground lean beef (10% or less fat)

½ pound ground skinless turkey breast

½ pound ground lean pork (10% or less fat)

1 cup low-sodium beef broth

2 tablespoons all-purpose flour

2 tablespoons cold water

1 cup fat-free half-and-half or fat-free sour cream

¼ cup chopped fresh parsley

*1.* Melt the butter in a large nonstick skillet over medium heat, then add the onion. Cook, stirring occasionally, until golden, 7–10 minutes; set aside.

*2.* Preheat the oven to 400°F. Spray a nonstick jelly-roll pan with nonstick spray.

*3.* Combine the bread crumbs and milk in a large bowl; stir in the egg, salt, and pepper. Add the beef, turkey, pork, and cooked onions; mix well with a large fork. Shape into 32 (1½-inch) balls. Place on jelly-roll pan and bake until browned, about 20 minutes.

*4.* Scrape the meatballs and the brown bits from the bottom of the jelly-roll pan into an extra-large skillet. If necessary, pour some of the broth onto the jelly-roll pan to loosen up the brown bits. Add the broth to the skillet and bring to a boil. Reduce the heat and simmer, covered, until meatballs are cooked through, 6–8 minutes.

*5.* Combine the flour and water in a small bowl; stir in the half-and-half. Pour into the skillet and cook, stirring constantly, until the mixture just simmers and thickens slightly. Sprinkle with the parsley just before serving.

Per serving (4 meatballs): 224 Cal, 7 g Fat, 3 g Sat Fat, 81 mg Chol, 462 mg Sod, 14 g Carb, 1 g Fib, 24 g Prot, 88 mg Calc. ***POINTS: 5.***

———◆———

*Chef's Tip:* Meatballs are well-suited to being kept warm in a chafing dish or a casserole dish on a warming tray.

# Potato Cakes

**MAKES 8 SERVINGS**

Here, ordinary mashed potatoes become tasty, golden potato cakes accented with the Scandinavian flavors of dill and nutmeg. Make them ahead of time and store the cooked potato cakes on a baking sheet, covered, in the refrigerator for up to two days. Reheat, on the baking sheet, uncovered, in a 350°F oven until hot, about 10 minutes.

2 **large baking potatoes, scrubbed and cut in eighths**
¼ **cup fat-free milk**
¾ **teaspoon salt**
¼ **teaspoon freshly ground pepper**
**Dash ground nutmeg**
¼ **cup finely chopped onion**
2 **tablespoons chopped fresh dill**
1 **large egg**
4 **teaspoons butter**

*1.* Bring the potatoes, and enough water to cover, to a boil in a saucepan. Reduce the heat and simmer, covered, until tender, about 15 minutes; drain and return the potatoes to the pan.
*2.* Add the milk, salt, pepper, and nutmeg. With a hand-held mixer, beat until the potatoes are mashed. Add the onion, dill, and egg; beat until just blended.
*3.* Melt 2 teaspoons of the butter in an extra-large nonstick skillet over medium-high heat. Drop the potato mixture by scant ¼-cup measures, fitting 8 cakes into the skillet. Cook until crisp and golden, 3–4 minutes on each side. Repeat with the remaining 2 teaspoons butter and the remaining potato mixture, making a total of 16 potato cakes. Keep the potato cakes warm in a warm oven until you're ready to serve them.

Per serving (2 potato cakes): 78 Cal, 3 g Fat, 1 g Sat Fat, 32 mg Chol, 246 mg Sod, 12 g Carb, 1 g Fib, 2 g Prot, 19 mg Calc. ***POINTS: 2.***

◆

*Chef's Tip:* Use a regular saucepan, not a nonstick saucepan, to boil the potatoes. Then when you come to mash the potatoes with the hand-held mixer, you won't damage the nonstick finish.

*Sweet-and-Sour Red Cabbage, Herring and Beet Salad, Cucumber Salad, and Potato Cakes*

# Sweet-and-Sour Red Cabbage

**MAKES 8 SERVINGS**

This recipe shows the skillful use of contrasting sweet, sour, and savory flavors in Scandinavian cooking. Make the cabbage up to three or four days ahead and store it, covered, in the refrigerator. You'll find it tastes even better after the flavors have had a chance to develop. Reheat thoroughly with a little extra broth, if needed.

2 teaspoons sunflower oil
¼ pound sliced Canadian bacon, chopped
4 whole allspice
3 whole cloves
2 tablespoons sugar
1 large onion, chopped
2 McIntosh apples, unpeeled and diced
1 (2½-pound) red cabbage, core removed, shredded
1 cup low-sodium chicken broth
¼ cup red-wine vinegar
¼ cup dry red wine
½ teaspoon salt
2 tablespoons all-purpose flour
3 tablespoons water
3 tablespoons red currant jelly

*1.* Heat a nonstick Dutch oven over medium-high heat. Swirl in the oil, then add the bacon. Cook, stirring occasionally, until browned, 3–5 minutes. Tie the allspice and cloves in a small piece of cheesecloth; set aside.

*2.* Add the sugar to the Dutch oven and cook, stirring constantly, until just golden, about 1 minute. Add the onion, apples, and the cheesecloth bag. Cook, stirring frequently, until softened and fragrant, 3–5 minutes.

*3.* Add the cabbage, broth, vinegar, and salt; bring to a boil. Reduce the heat and simmer, covered, until the cabbage is tender, about 40 minutes.

*4.* Combine the flour and water in a small bowl. Stir in about ¼ cup of the hot liquid from the Dutch oven, then return all to the Dutch oven. Cook, stirring constantly, until the mixture boils and thickens. Stir in the currant jelly. Remove the bag of spices.

Per serving (scant 1 cup): 129 Cal, 3 g Fat, 1 g Sat Fat, 7 mg Chol, 357 mg Sod, 23 g Carb, 4 g Fib, 5 g Prot, 65 mg Calc. **POINTS: 2.**

# *Rice Pudding with Lingonberry Sauce*

Traditionally a whole almond is hidden in the rice pudding. According to Scandinavian folklore, the almond recipient, if single, will be married soon and, if married, will have good luck. You can make the pudding and the sauce ahead of time and keep them, covered, in the refrigerator for up to three days. Either serve them chilled, bring them to room temperature, or reheat and serve warm.

**3 cups low-fat (1%) milk**
**3 cups cooked brown rice**
**½ cup packed light brown sugar**
**¼ teaspoon ground cardamom**
**⅛ teaspoon salt**
**1 teaspoon vanilla extract**
**1 whole almond**
**2 tablespoons cornstarch**
**2 cups cranberry juice**
**½ cup lingonberry preserves or whole-berry cranberry sauce**

*1.* To make the pudding, combine the milk, rice, sugar, cardamom, and salt in a large nonstick saucepan; bring to a boil, stirring occasionally. Reduce the heat and simmer, uncovered, stirring occasionally, until slightly thickened, about 25 minutes. Remove from the heat and stir in the vanilla. Transfer to a serving dish and poke the almond into the center.

*2.* To make the sauce, combine the cornstarch with 3 tablespoons of the cranberry juice in a medium nonstick saucepan; stir in the remaining juice. Cook, stirring constantly, until the mixture boils and thickens; stir in the preserves. Transfer the sauce to a sauce boat and serve with the rice pudding.

Per serving (½ cup rice pudding with ½ cup sauce): 244 Cal, 2 g Fat, 1 g Sat Fat, 4 mg Chol, 96 mg Sod, 52 g Carb, 2 g Fib, 5 g Prot, 135 mg Calc. *POINTS: 5.*

# Ginger-Almond Cookies

**MAKES 60 SERVINGS**

Tender and distinctly gingery, these cookies make a perfect sweet finish to any meal.
Store them in an airtight container at room temperature for up to a week, or in the freezer for
up to three months. Or freeze the unbaked logs, well-wrapped, for up to three months, then
slice off fresh cookies to bake when you want them.

1½  cups all-purpose flour
¼   cup whole-wheat flour
1   teaspoon baking soda
2   teaspoons ground ginger
½   teaspoon ground nutmeg
¼   teaspoon salt
½   cup butter, softened
¾   cup packed dark brown sugar
1   large egg
¾   cup sliced almonds,
    finely chopped

*1.* Combine the all-purpose flour, whole-wheat flour, baking soda, ginger, nutmeg, and salt in a medium bowl; set aside.

*2.* With an electric mixer at high speed, beat the butter and sugar until light and fluffy. Add the egg and beat well. With the mixer at low speed, stir in the flour mixture and the almonds, until all the flour is just moistened and the mixture forms a ball.

*3.* Cut the dough in half and roll each half into an 8-inch log, about 1½ inches in diameter. Wrap each log in wax paper and refrigerate until firm, at least 2 hours.

*4.* Preheat the oven to 350°F. Cut each log into 30 (¼-inch) slices, making a total of 60 cookies. Place, 1 inch apart, on ungreased baking sheets. Bake until golden, 10–12 minutes. Transfer the cookies to a rack to cool completely.

Per serving (1 cookie): 46 Cal, 2 g Fat, 1 g Sat Fat, 8 mg Chol, 43 mg Sod, 6 g Carb, 0 g Fib, 1 g Prot, 7 mg Calc. ***POINTS: 1.***

◆

*Chef's Tip:* If you really love ginger, sprinkle these cookies with a little
ginger sugar right after the cookies come out of the oven. To make ginger sugar,
mix 1 tablespoon granulated sugar with ½ teaspoon ground ginger.

# ABOUT OUR RECIPES

We make every effort to ensure that you will have success with our recipes. For best results and for nutritional accuracy, please keep the following guidelines in mind:

— All recipes feature approximate nutritional information; our recipes are analyzed for Calories (Cal), Total Fat (Fat), Saturated Fat (Sat Fat), Cholesterol (Chol), Sodium (Sod), Carbohydrates (Carb), Dietary Fiber (Fib), Protein (Prot), and Calcium (Calc).

— All recipes include *POINTS* values based on the Weight Watchers **Winning Points** food plan. *POINTS* are calculated from a proprietary formula that takes into account calories, total fat, and dietary fiber.

— Before serving, divide foods—including any vegetables, sauce, or accompaniments—into portions of equal size according to the designated number of servings per recipe.

— Any substitutions made to the ingredients will alter the "Per serving" nutritional information and may affect the *POINTS* value.

— Additionally, substituting fat-free foods for any low-fat ingredients specified in a recipe may affect the consistency, texture, or flavor of the finished dish.

— If you prefer to avoid using alcohol in any recipe, you may substitute an equal amount of water, broth, or juice.

— Nutritional information for recipes that include meat, fish, and poultry are based on cooked skinless boneless portions, with the fat trimmed as specified in the recipe.

# DRY AND LIQUID MEASUREMENT EQUIVALENTS

If you are converting the recipes in this book to metric measurements, use the following chart as a guide.

| TEASPOONS | TABLESPOONS | CUPS | FLUID OUNCES |
|---|---|---|---|
| 3 teaspoons | 1 tablespoon | | ½ fluid ounce |
| 6 teaspoons | 2 tablespoons | ⅛ cup | 1 fluid ounce |
| 8 teaspoons | 2 tablespoons plus 2 teaspoons | ⅙ cup | |
| 12 teaspoons | 4 tablespoons | ¼ cup | 2 fluid ounces |
| 15 teaspoons | 5 tablespoons | ⅓ cup minus 1 teaspoon | |
| 16 teaspoons | 5 tablespoons plus 1 teaspoon | ⅓ cup | |
| 18 teaspoons | 6 tablespoons | ¼ cup plus 2 tablespoons | 3 fluid ounces |
| 24 teaspoons | 8 tablespoons | ½ cup | 4 fluid ounces |
| 30 teaspoons | 10 tablespoons | ½ cup plus 2 tablespoons | 5 fluid ounces |
| 32 teaspoons | 10 tablespoons plus 2 teaspoons | ⅔ cup | |
| 36 teaspoons | 12 tablespoons | ¾ cup | 6 fluid ounces |
| 42 teaspoons | 14 tablespoons | 1 cup minus 2 tablespoons | 7 fluid ounces |
| 45 teaspoons | 15 tablespoons | 1 cup minus 1 tablespoon | |
| 48 teaspoons | 16 tablespoons | 1 cup | 8 fluid ounces |

Note: Measurement of less than ⅛ teaspoon is considered a dash or a pinch.

| VOLUME | |
|---|---|
| ¼ teaspoon | 1 milliliter |
| ½ teaspoon | 2 milliliters |
| 1 teaspoon | 5 milliliters |
| 1 tablespoon | 15 milliliters |
| 2 tablespoons | 30 milliliters |
| 3 tablespoons | 45 milliliters |
| ¼ cup | 60 milliliters |
| ⅓ cup | 75 milliliters |
| ½ cup | 125 milliliters |
| ⅔ cup | 150 milliliters |
| ¾ cup | 175 milliliters |
| 1 cup | 225 milliliters |
| 1 quart | 1 liter |

| OVEN TEMPERATURE | |
|---|---|
| 250°F | 120°C |
| 275°F | 140°C |
| 300°F | 150°C |
| 325°F | 160°C |
| 350°F | 180°C |
| 375°F | 190°C |
| 400°F | 200°C |
| 425°F | 220°C |
| 450°F | 230°C |
| 475°F | 250°C |
| 500°F | 260°C |
| 525°F | 270°C |

| WEIGHT | |
|---|---|
| 1 ounce | 30 grams |
| ¼ pound | 120 grams |
| ½ pound | 240 grams |
| ¾ pound | 360 grams |
| 1 pound | 480 grams |

| LENGTH | |
|---|---|
| 1 inch | 25 millimeters |
| 1 inch | 2.5 centimeters |

# NOTES

# NOTES

# NOTES

# INDEX

## A

accompaniments:

Apple and Pear Compote, Baked, 255

Cucumber-Chive Raita, 82, 83

Green Papaya Salsa, 300

Mango-Blueberry Salsa, 100

Mango Salsa, 9, 10

Pear and Apple Compote, Roasted, 221, 222

Red Pepper and Apricot Relish, 238

*see also* sauces; side dishes

acidulated water, 126

almond(s):

-Blueberry-Crunch Coffeecake, 256

Couscous and White Beans with Apricots and, 102, 103

Dove Cookies, 86

Dundee Cake, 215

Ginger Cookies, 312

-Honey Oat Pudding, 292

Macaroons, 23

Maids of Honour, 211, 216

Mishmishya, 228

roasting, 228

toasting, 102

White Gazpacho with Green Grapes, 152

Ambrosia, Orange, 283

American Bounty Cobbler, 157

Anchovies, Pizza with Roasted Tomatoes and, 231

Andouille sausage, in Gumbo, 278, 279

Angel Food Cake, Coconut, 117

Anisette Toasts, 237

appetizers and hors d'oeuvres:

Artichokes in Herb Sauce, 188

Carpaccio-Wrapped Watercress with Blue Cheese Dip, 88

Caviar on New Potatoes with Chive Cream, 12

Cheese Straws, 98

Chicken and Red Chile Tamales, 40

Chicken Kebabs, Jerk, with Pineapple Dipping Sauce, 79

Chicken with Chipotle Cream on Tortilla Chips, 10, 11

Clams, Stir-Fried, in Black-Bean Sauce, 257

Clams Oreganata, 229

Crab Cakes, Cajun-Style, 276

Crab Cakes, Thyme-Flavored Mini, 78

Crostini, Caponata, 67

Crostini, Roast Beef, with Apple-Horseradish Cream, 14

Crostini with Spicy Bean Puree, 240, 241

An Evening at the Oscars (menu), 8

Flatbread Spirals, Savory, 80

Forest Mushroom Turnovers, 268, 269

Ham and Artichoke Nibbles, 26

Herring and Beet Salad, 304, 309

Meat Patties, Jamaican, 296

Pancetta and Shiitake-Stuffed Mushrooms, 15

Pepper-and-Black-Bean Quesadillas, Grilled, 37

Phyllo Cups, Petite, with Yogurt and Rose Petal Jam, 16

Pissaladière, 120, 121

Pizzas, Vegetable, Grilled, 111

Pork Dumplings, Steamed, 258

Portobellos with Tuscan Bean Salad, 150, 151

Potatoes, Barbecued Sliced, with Parmesan, 139

Radicchio, Broiled, Salad with Shaved Fennel and Oranges, 125

Radish Salad with Pears, 119

Red Pepper Mousse in Endive, 189

Red Snapper Seviche, 13

Ricotta-Stuffed Cherry Tomatoes or Mushroom Caps, 136

Rosemary Breadsticks, 201

Shrimp and Egg Sandwiches, Open-Face, 305

Shrimp Cocktail, Cajun-Spiced, with Mango Salsa, 9, 10

Smoked-Salmon-and-Cucumber Canapés, 209, 211

Smoked Salmon Canapés, 286

Spinach and Ricotta Tart, 48

Turkey Meatballs, Minted, 239, 240

Turnip Cake, Golden, 260

Vegetable Sticks with Ranch Dip, 170

Zucchini-and-Potato Latkes, 220

*see also* soups

apple(s):

Chicken-Waldorf Salad, 202, 203

cider, sparkling, in Bellini, 8, 10

Cider, Spiced Eyeball, 171

Clafouti, 127

Horseradish Cream, Roast Beef Crostini with, 14

and Pear Compote, Baked, 255

and Pear Compote, Roasted, 221, 222

Potato, Carrot, and Pea Salad, 186

preventing discoloration of, 126

Pumpkin Bisque, 161

Sage Dressing, 192, 193

Tart, and Celeriac Salad, 126

Applesauce-Poppy Seed Cake, 187

apricot(s):

Almond Mishmishya, 228

Couscous and White Beans with Almonds and, 102, 103

Fruited Couscous, 222, 224

and Roasted Red Pepper Relish, 238

artichoke(s):

and Ham Nibbles, 26

hearts, in Seven Vegetable Couscous, 242

in Herb Sauce, 188